The Experts
"A VAST AND FIEI

"The fascinating, exhaustively researched saga ranges from battlefields to backrooms as Johnson recounts the tale of an intrepid band of Confederate agents. In prose that travels at breakneck speed, we meet a colorful cast of swashbucklers, knaves, and conspirators. A rousing good read."
—**Fergus M. Bordewich,** author of *Bound for Canaan: The Underground Railroad and the War for the Soul of America*

"The history of the Confederate attempt to take the war to New York City with a behind-the-lines attack is a remarkable story overlooked by many students of the Civil War. . . . *'A Vast and Fiendish Plot'* is sure to keep the reader's interest."
—**Rod Gragg,** author of *Confederate Goliath: The Battle of Fort Fisher*

"Fresh, insightful analysis of an amazing turn of events that nearly set New York City ablaze during the Civil War. Readers will be enthralled by the fast-paced narrative and clear writing that transport them into a dangerous and murky world."
—**David J. Eicher,** author of *The Longest Night*

"A fresh and intriguing addition to Civil War literature. Johnson shows how Southerners sought to take revenge on a 'sister city' they felt betrayed them after the outbreak of hostilities in 1861."
—**Brion McClanahan,** author of *The Politically Incorrect Guide to the Founding Fathers*

"Johnson opens up a new chapter in the annals of Civil War history, as he shines much-needed light on a serious Confederate threat that played out in New York in November of 1864. A must-have for everyone's Civil War bookshelf."
—**Marc Leepson,** author of *Saving Monticello, Flag* and *Desperate Engagement*

"Clint Johnson meticulously details a long-neglected chapter of Civil War history. His well-researched volume yields a vivid, fast-paced account of the intruging Confederate attempt to cause mayhem, confusion, and destruction. Johnson weaves a fascinating story that is sure to captivate readers."
—**Daniel W. Barefoot,** author of *Spirits of '76: Ghost Stories of the American Revolution*

"The attack of the Confederate secret service on New York City in November 1864 has never received this detailed a treatment. The book covers the planning, attack and aftermath in a very readable, informative manner."
—**James Durney,** reviewer for The Order of Civil War Obsessively Compulsed blog

New York Herald on November 26, 1864

"A vast and fiendish plot to burn down our Empire City gave rise to the most profound excitement among all classes of our citizens."

"A VAST AND FIENDISH PLOT"

THE CONFEDERATE ATTACK
ON NEW YORK CITY

CLINT JOHNSON

CITADEL PRESS
Kensington Publishing Corp.
www.kensingtonbooks.com

CITADEL PRESS BOOKS are published by

Kensington Publishing Corp.
119 West 40th Street
New York, NY 10018

All Kensington titles, imprints, and distributed lines are available at special quantity discounts for bulk purchases for sales promotions, premiums, fund-raising, educational, or institutional use. Special book excerpts or customized printings can also be created to fit specific needs. For details, write or phone the office of the Kensington special sales manager: Kensington Publishing Corp., 119 West 40th Street, New York, NY 10018, attn: Special Sales Department; phone 1-800-221-2647.

CITADEL PRESS and the Citadel logo are Reg. U.S. Pat. & TM Off.

First printing: March 2010

10 9 8 7 6 5 4 3 2 1

Printed in the United States of America

Library of Congress Control Number: 2009937071

ISBN-13: 978-0-8065-3131-1
ISBN-10: 0-8065-3131-2

The schoolteachers in Arcadia, Florida, taught and inspired me to love and write history. Some are gone. Some are still here. All helped me get to where I am. That's what teachers are supposed to do.

I apologize to them for still dangling my participles, not knowing what a gerund is, and never figuring out how to diagram a sentence.

Contents

Introduction

Researching history is great fun for the writer when he puts down on paper facts that may surprise readers. That is the way it was writing *"A Vast and Fiendish Plot": The Confederate Attack on New York City*.

To understand why the city became a target of eight Confederate officers in November 1864, one must understand that New York City was not always the socially liberal place we know in the twenty-first century.

In the seventeenth century New York City was one of the first colonies to accept Africans as slaves at the same time that Jamestown, Virginia, was treating Africans as indentured servants who would one day be free.

In the early eighteenth century, New York City's government had savagely put down a slave revolt years before they staged any revolt in any Southern slave-holding colony.

In the mid-nineteenth century, New York City was the center of the slave-ship-outfitting industry. Slave ships owned by city residents openly operated out of New York harbor until the American Civil War was halfway over.

The Emerald City, the city's nickname long before the Big Apple, became an economic powerhouse in the first half of the nineteenth century because Southern cotton literally and figuratively flowed through its port. The city's merchants believed what was good for the South was good for New York. That included the preservation of slavery in the South.

President Abraham Lincoln, praised by so many as the best president the nation has ever had, did not win over the city's voters in either 1860 or 1864. In fact, he lost the city by more than two to one both times.

With all that historical background, one would think Southerners would love Manhattan. But Southerners just could not get past the fact that forty cents of every dollar of cotton sold went into the pockets of New Yorkers. Southerners did not like the fancy-pants New York bankers coming south to loan money at exorbitant rates. They did not like four hundred thousand young men in uniform from New York State invading the South.

New York City and the South had made each other prosperous for the first half of the nineteenth century. But by 1864 that did not matter. New York was the largest city in the Union. Since the South was suffering at the hands of that Union, it was only natural that the South picked on the largest target to be found when it came time for a retaliatory strike.

This is the story of how two best friends, the slave-holding South and slave-trading New York City, fell out of love with each other. It the story of how and why the Confederacy targeted Manhattan because of the devastation the South had suffered at the hands of the Union between 1861 and 1864.

Prologue

"A Born Gentleman to the Tips of His Fingers"

In the early morning of September 4, 1864, just days after the conclusion of the Democratic National Convention in Chicago, Confederate general John Hunt Morgan lay dead in a gooseberry bush in the garden of a house in Greeneville, Tennessee.

The boldest of the Confederacy's cavalry leaders did not die on a battlefield with a saber in one hand, a pistol in the other, and his horse's reins in his teeth. He died facedown in a bush clad in a nightshirt, trousers, and boots. He was unarmed, shot down by several Union cavalrymen who never called to him to surrender. They then hoisted his body facedown across a saddle and paraded him around to show what they had done to one of the most famous Confederates of the war.

Morgan the man had nothing to do with the Confederate Secret Service, Copperheads (Northern Democrats who opposed the Civil War), Canadian commissioners, planned attacks on Northern prison camps, or the burning of the nation's largest cities.

Morgan the legend had everything to do with such things.

Morgan the man trained the Confederate officers who would carry out the attacks on Union cities behind their lines. Morgan the legend inspired the men to undertake such dangerous, seemingly impossible missions.

John Hunt Morgan was born the eldest of ten children in 1825 in Huntsville, Alabama, to a pharmacist whose shop failed while John was still a small child. The family moved to Lexington, Kentucky, so that the senior Morgan could find work managing the farm of a wealthy relative.

Life in Kentucky was good for the growing Morgan. He had fine, strong, thoroughbred horses to ride, wide expanses of neighbors' property on which to ride them, and fences to jump. As he grew out of his teenage years, his family was finally restored to a measure of wealth so that Morgan could go to college.

Just being accepted into prestigious Transylvania College, founded in 1780 in his adopted hometown of Lexington, proved that the 17-year-old Morgan was an intelligent youth. The college at the time was considered on the educational par with Harvard and Yale with luminaries such as Senator Henry Clay serving as a law professor and a member of the board of trustees.

It was at Transylvania that the young Morgan first established the reputation he would retain for the rest of his life for rebelling against authority. To the disappointment of his family, Morgan often skipped classes and fell in with the wrong kind of crowd with whom he practiced the unsavory habit of swearing at passersby on campus. On at least one occasion, he fought a duel with one other member of his college fraternity. That was enough misbehavior for the college dean. The dean suspended him for the rest of the term, and he never returned to college.

In 1846, the 21-year-old got his first taste of military life when he and one brother volunteered for a cavalry regiment forming to join the regular U.S. Army fighting the Mexican War. He fought in only one battle, Buena Vista, where he and his brother acquitted themselves well, according to their commanding officers.

By 1849, Morgan, having found that a nation at peace had little use for self-trained army officers, was growing and processing hemp for the manufacture of rope, paper, and other goods. So in 1854, bored with keeping track of the weather and sales, Morgan founded his own company of militia called the Lexington Rifles.

Morgan's wife, Becky, was continually sick after delivering a stillborn child and developed a blood clot that resulted in the amputation of one of her legs. Rather than watch as his once young, vivacious wife wasted away, Morgan spent much of his free time drilling his men.

Morgan's seemingly insatiable need for adventure and military life was finally fulfilled in July 1861 when his wife of thirteen years died. The 36-year-old businessman who had always wanted a military career was now free to become the adventurer he had always wanted to be. He started his career with the Confederacy, showing the guile that would be his trademark. On the night of September 20, 1861, Morgan and fifty men absconded with the rifles that the Union governor of Kentucky had ordered turned over to federal authorities.

Morgan had seemingly complied with the governor's order by loading the rifles onto wagons. But instead of sending the wagons north toward the capital, Morgan sent them south. He diverted attention from the wagons by noisily drilling his men inside the armory to give the impression that the Lexington Rifles would cast their lot with the Union. Late at night, after the drill had been finished, he and the Lexington Rifles rode south and caught up with the wagons. The rifles from the Lexington arsenal were delivered to the Confederacy.

Over the next several months while awaiting orders or a fight, Morgan amused himself by dressing in Union uniforms and regularly crossing into Union-held territory to spy on his new enemy. He was developing tactics and techniques that would come in handy both for military operations and for the spy network he was unintentionally creating.

Morgan seemed born to be a Confederate cavalier, an adventurer who could attract other adventurers to his side. One contemporary described him as standing six feet tall and 185 pounds. Balding at 36, Morgan made up for the lack of hair on his head by growing a luxuriant goatee and mustache that he always kept closely trimmed. On his head, he wore an elegant hat that he pinned up on one side.

In trying to describe him in print, some contemporaries sounded like Sir Walter Scott, the writer of *Ivanhoe*, which was a book Southerners relished as a description of how heroes should act and look. One man who knew Morgan described him as "a born gentleman to the tips of his fingers and to the ends of his eyelashes. He was blue-blooded, romantic and chivalry incarnate." Another described him with:

> His personal appearance and carriage were striking and graceful. His features were eminently handsome and he wore a pleasing expression. His eyes were small, of a grayish blue color, and their glances keen and thoughtful. . . . His constitution seemed impervious to the effects of privation and exposure, and it was scarcely possible to conceive that he suffered from fatigue or lack of sleep.

Morgan was also loquacious. He composed a broadside in July 1862 when he was looking for recruits: I come to liberate you from the despotism of a tyrannical faction and to rescue my native State from the hand of your oppressors. Everywhere the cowardly foe has fled from my avenging arms. My brave army is stigmatized as a band of guerrillas and marauders. Believe it not. I point with pride to their deeds as a refutation to this foul aspersion. We ask only to meet the hireling legions of Lincoln. The eyes of your brethren of the South are upon you. Your gallant fellow citizens are flocking to our standard. Our armies are rapidly advancing to your protection. Then greet them with the willing hands of fifty thousand of Kentucky's brave. Their advance is already with you. Then "Strike for the green graves of your sires!" "Strike for your altars and your fires!" GOD, and your NATIVE LAND.

Kentuckians, Tennesseans, Alabamans, Texans, and some Virginians flocked to Morgan's side, swelling his original fifty men to several thousand. His core command, however, remained fifteen regiments of Kentucky cavalry, including the Second Kentucky Cavalry, which grew out of his original fifty-man Kentucky Rifles.

There were character traits that Morgan and his men shared. Bennett Young, one of Morgan's officers who would later lead a raid into Vermont from Canada, said that the young men who joined Morgan's command "shared the full chivalry and flower of the states of

Kentucky and Tennessee. . . . They were proud and that made them brave." Another of Morgan's men claimed that they were such good horsemen they were like centaurs.

Thomas Hines, a top Morgan aide, wrote of his fellows "[The] rank and file was of the mettle which finds its natural element in active and audacious enterprise, and was yet thrilled with the fire of youth; for there were few men in the division over 25 years of age."

Morgan and his men loved and knew horses. The most prized were Denmarks, a type of high-tailed, long-necked horse first bred in Kentucky in 1850. Morgan himself sometimes rode Gaines Denmark, a dark brown horse that was son to Denmark, the namesake of the breed. Morgan's men could recognize other Kentuckians at a distance by the breed they were riding. They could even recognize Union cavalry at a distance too far away to distinguish their uniforms because the Yankees did not ride as well as they did.

Morgan and his cavalrymen were too restless to be cooped up in camp where other, lesser men such as the infantry were forced to drill and drill again. These young men and boys of Kentucky and Tennessee were eager to be doing something worthwhile for the war effort against the Union. They wanted to have fun accomplishing their missions. They had been brought up knowing how to judge a fast horse, sit still in the saddle without bouncing around like a city slicker, ride for hours without getting saddle sore, and shoot and hit at what they were aiming. All that was part of being a Southern horseman. To do all that and shoot at Yankees was the entertainment of war.

Morgan and his partisan ranger contemporaries Nathan Bedford Forrest (operating in Tennessee and Mississippi) and John Singleton Mosby (operating in northern Virginia) did not have formal military training. Unrestrained from learning the tactics of war from a West Point textbook, all three men developed remarkably similar techniques of fighting. The textbook cavalry command before the war carried carbines, single pistols, and heavy sabers and fought usually from horseback in grand charges on any enemy, whether or not it was infantry or other cavalry. When they were not banging sabers with an opponent, the cavalry's primary job was to scout out the location of the enemy's army and report back.

Morgan, Forrest, and Mosby all started the war leading small numbers of men on raids behind enemy lines where their goal was to disrupt communications, gather intelligence, and steal supplies. Instead of always fighting from horseback, if confronted with an enemy, they usually dismounted so they could better aim their rifles. Many of the men discarded their sabers as unpractical during a time when a rifle could hit a man at three hundred yards. Instead, they carried multiple pistols or pistol cylinders that they could change out if they got involved in lengthy close-in fighting.

Throughout the winter of 1861–62, Morgan and his men honed to a fine art their type of swift raiding around Tennessee and Kentucky. They learned how to spread turpentine and pine knots in order to fire wooden bridges and railroad trestles quickly. They learned how to look like and talk like Union soldiers so that they could don captured uniforms and walk around a military camp listening for details on future military movements and rumors as to what they, Morgan's men, were doing. They put on their civilian clothes and mingled among townsfolk to gather information on when trains would be leaving town so that they could set up ambushes.

Had they been caught wearing Union uniforms or civilian clothes, Morgan's men would have been shot as spies. The men came to accept those risks as part of war. Their ease at playing someone they were not would come in handy when walking the streets of New York City.

Morgan liked surrounding himself with characters, particularly when those men were also hard fighters who could inspire other men. To name an instance, when British soldier of fortune George St. Ledger Grenfell had come calling with a letter of introduction from Robert E. Lee, Morgan took an instant liking to the 62-year-old man with the huge chin whiskers. When Morgan asked why he was fighting for the Confederacy, Grenfell replied, "If England is not fighting a war, I will go find one." Grenfell would help train Morgan's men, turning them from undisciplined boys into fighting men.

Morgan needed men like George "Lightning" Ellsworth, a Canadian by birth, who was living in Texas when he received a note from his old friend Morgan to rush to Kentucky. Ellsworth was a wizard at telegraphy, learning how to listen to the rapid stream of dots and dashes that was Morse code and read out the words without even needing to put the letters down on paper to form messages. Within days of starting on the job with Morgan, Ellsworth learned how to imitate the telegraph keying style of civilian and Union telegraphers.

Whenever Morgan was leading a raid, Ellsworth would tap into a telegraph line running between towns, listen for news, and then spread his own version of the news to throw off Union garrisons looking for Morgan. Ellsworth acquired the nickname Lightning when amused troopers watched him sitting in a river calmly tapping out his messages as a lightning storm raged overhead.

Basil Duke, thirteen years younger than Morgan, was a lawyer and Morgan's brother-in-law, having married one of his commander's sisters just before the war began. Dark skinned compared to Morgan's light complexion and cool and collected compared to Morgan's impulsiveness, Duke proved to be the perfect second in command to Morgan. He also seemed to attract Yankee gunfire. Wounded at Shiloh in April 1862 by a musket ball through his shoulder that came close to his spine, Duke recovered only to be wounded again in December 1862 when an artillery shell fragment crashed into his body. He recovered from that, too, but would spend nearly a year in a prison after being captured in July 1863.

Thomas Hines was a 23-year-old schoolteacher when he joined Morgan's Ninth Kentucky Cavalry as a private reporting to Captain John Breckinridge Castleman, an officer who he would later recruit to free the Confederate prisoners in Illinois. Hines and Morgan both realized that Hines's best skill was acting as an independent scout for the cavalry, slipping in and out of enemy territory to gather information that could be passed on to the officers who would lead the raids. Hines had great powers of observation, a skill that would come in handy when he, Morgan, and others would be locked up in a seemingly unescapable prison.

All through 1862 and into the summer of 1863, Morgan's men struck terror in the hearts of Unionists in Kentucky and Tennessee. In June, Morgan decided that it was time to act on a long-held personal goal—to invade the North. Morgan obtained permission from his commanding officer, General Braxton Bragg, to lead a 1,500-man raid into Kentucky from his base in Sparta, Tennessee. Bragg readily agreed. Once he had permission for the raid, Morgan took 2,500 cavalrymen, 1,000 more than he had permission to take, and started north.

What Bragg did not know, besides the fact that Morgan had taken far more men than had been ordered, was that Morgan did not intend to stay in Kentucky on the southern side of the Ohio River. On July 8, 1863, just days after two different Confederate armies had surrendered at Vicksburg, Mississippi, and retreated from Gettysburg, Pennsylvania, Morgan crossed the Ohio River into Indiana at the head of 1,800 men, having lost about 700 to skirmishes in Kentucky.

For the next two weeks, Morgan and his men, including brother-in-law Duke, his spy protégé Hines, his telegrapher Ellsworth, and future Canada-based agents Captain Robert Martin and Lieutenant John Headley, fought a skirmish nearly every day as the militias of Indiana and Ohio turned out to fight Confederates on Union soil.

Morgan had not made the raid rashly—or so he thought. The general had been told by Confederate sympathizers that the Copperheads in southern Indiana and Ohio would welcome his approach and would even join his ranks. None did. Irritated that these supposed Confederates in waiting did not flock to his side, Morgan did not offer them any protection when his men swapped out their tired horses for the fresh ones found on farms.

Morgan's raid panicked lower Indiana and Ohio. The July 25, 1863, edition of *Harper's Weekly* reported:

> The raid of the rebel Morgan into Indiana, which he seems to be pursuing with great boldness, has thoroughly aroused the people of that State and of Ohio to a sense of their danger. On July 13th General Burnside declared martial law in Cincinnati and in Covington and Newport on the Kentucky side. All business is suspended until further orders, and all citizens are required to organize in accordance with the direction of the State and municipal authorities. There is nothing definite as to Morgan's whereabouts; but it is supposed that he will endeavor to move

around the city of Cincinnati and cross the river between there and Maysville.

Finally, on July 19, 1863, the raid came to an effective end at the Battle of Buffington Island, Ohio, when large numbers of Union soldiers started to press Morgan's men down to the Ohio River. Morgan himself was escaping halfway across the river, holding onto the tail of his swimming horse, when he saw a Union gunboat come around the bend. Looking back to the Ohio side, Morgan saw that hundreds of his men would be unable to follow because the gunboat would soon be in range to shell them both in the water and on the river's banks. Instead of escaping himself, Morgan swung his horse back toward Ohio and returned to the remnants of his command. Those men escaped capture for just another few days until Morgan surrendered the rest of his command on July 26.

The greatest and longest cavalry raid in the war's history was over. Though they had been captured, Morgan and his men considered it a rousing success as they had inflicted more than 600 casualties on the Federals, and captured and paroled more than 6,000 Union soldiers and militiamen, nearly four times their own size force. More than 10 million dollars' worth of Union war material was destroyed before it could be deployed against the Confederacy. The Union army had been thrown into disarray, forced to deal with enemy soldiers in its rear rather than countering the movements of Confederate general Bragg to its front.

Morgan and his officers expected to be sent to the Confederate officer's prison camp on Johnson's Island, Ohio, in Lake Erie, opposite the town of Sandusky. To their angry surprise, they were sent to Ohio State Penitentiary in Columbus. Treated like common criminals instead of Confederate officers, Morgan and his officers were shorn of their beards and hair and dressed in prisoners' civilian clothes.

Morgan's men were targeted for punishment for any infraction. They were put in a dungeon for doing virtually anything such as making comments that were considered anti-Union or for talking after lights out. Escape from the block walls that were twenty-five feet high seemed impossible.

The wily Hines was the one who discovered that escape was possible. He noticed that the floor of his prison cell was always dry, instead of damp as it would have been had it been resting on earth. A few questions of an elderly prison guard confirmed that an air chamber did indeed run under the floors of the cells.

Over the course of several weeks in October 1863, Hines and the other prisoners dug through the concrete floor using knives pilfered from the dining hall. Using a spade they had sneaked into their cellblock, they dug into the earth on the other side of the air shaft. They fashioned a thirty-foot rope made from shredded bedding and a grappling hook from a fireplace poker. On the night of November 27, seven members of Morgan's cavalry, including Morgan and Hines, broke through the floors of their cells, dropped into the air chamber, and then dug their way into the prison yard where they successfully climbed the outer wall.

Hines and Morgan made their way to the train station and bought tickets to Cincinnati, the city Morgan's men had bypassed rather than attack back in July. Morgan sat next to a Federal major on the train south. As the train passed the prison, the major pointed it out and commented that that was where they were keeping the rebel Morgan. Morgan replied, "I hope they will always keep him as safe as he is now." Before dawn, Morgan and Hines had found a young boy to row them across the Ohio River to freedom in Kentucky.

Once word got out that the infamous General Morgan was on the loose, a Southerner in Canada got a bright idea. To throw off what he anticipated to be a pursuit by Union soldiers of the real General Morgan, the man started moving around that country registering at hotels using his real initials of J. H. Morgan. Once word got back to the United States, Union agents began scouring Canada looking for the elusive Confederate general.

Almost immediately, embarrassed Ohio officials charged that Copperheads had somehow sneaked into the prison and helped Morgan break out when the truth was much simpler. Just as he and his men had always done, Morgan had exploited the enemy's weaknesses to their advantage.

Morgan would make his way to Richmond, Virginia, in January

1864, expecting a hero's welcome for the strike he had made against the North. Instead, Confederate officials gave Morgan the cold shoulder, angry that he had ignored his commander's direct orders not to cross the Ohio River. Happily, Morgan was reunited in Richmond with Hines, who had been recaptured in Tennessee on his way south after the Ohio penitentiary escape. Hines had escaped yet again from Union hands.

Morgan expected Hines to rejoin his command so that the two of them could start rebuilding the cavalry force that had been literally broken apart by the raid. Hines sadly told his mentor that he could not put on his gray uniform and strap on his pistols. From this point in the war forward, he would be wearing civilian clothes. He had been ordered to Canada. Hines told Morgan that he had been asked by Jefferson Davis to join Jacob Thompson and Clement Clay, Commissioners in the Confederate Secret Service, in the effort to convince the Copperheads in Illinois and Indiana to throw off the yoke of Union domination.

Morgan may have envied the adventure Hines was undertaking. Morgan himself never regained the old vigor that he had early in the war. When his brother-in-law Duke, who had been exchanged for some Union officers, saw him in early September 1864 for the first time in nearly a year, Duke was shocked at Morgan's appearance: "He was greatly changed. His face wore a weary, care-worn expression, and his manner was totally destitute of its former ardor and enthusiasm."

Several days later, in Greeneville, Tennessee, Morgan's sentries were surprised by Union calvarymen in the predawn darkness as the sentries waited for daylight to clean their weapons of the moisture from the rain that had been steadily falling all night long. When Morgan rushed from the house where he had been sleeping, he was shot down by several Union cavalrymen who had been tipped to his presence by a young slave boy who had heard of the Union patrol.

Once Morgan was shot down, one Union cavalryman shouted, "I've killed the horse thief!" He then jumped down from his horse, retrieved Morgan's body, threw it across the neck of his horse, and paraded it before his commander. The Union commander reprimanded his soldier and had him leave the general's body in Greeneville so that it could be properly buried. Morgan's death shocked the few remaining survivors of the regiments he had formed in the fall of 1861.

"Any one of us—all of us—would gladly have died in his defense, and each one would have envied the man who lost his life defending him. So much was he trusted that his men never dreamed of failing him in anything that he attempted. In all engagements he was our guiding star and hero," wrote Lieutenant Kelio Peddicord.

Hines must have grieved over the senseless murder of his former commander at the hands of jubilant Union cavalrymen who could have easily taken an unarmed man prisoner. But in September 1864, Hines had a mission to complete, so he had no time to consider the death of his friend. Before Election Day in November, Hines wanted to free his old friends from the Second Kentucky Cavalry who were then imprisoned along with seven thousand other Confederates at Camp Douglas, outside of Chicago. In Hines's mind, that would be the best revenge for Morgan's murder: the release of battle-hardened, angry, hungry soldiers into the streets of Chicago.

Up in Canada, other officers who had ridden with Morgan were regularly gathering in their hotel rooms winnowing down the number of Confederate volunteers who were willing to go back into the United States for behind-the-lines missions. By early November, their anger had grown and metastasized into the need for action. The murder of their beloved general coupled with the destruction of the Shenandoah Valley farms and Sherman's burning of the city of Atlanta had given them plenty of motivation for revenge.

Now they would take that revenge. What they imagined was a mission that would express the South's disgust with the Union's wartime tactics, disrupt the reelection bid of President Abraham Lincoln, and strike terror in the hearts of Northern civilians all at the same time.

They reasoned that there was no better way to do all that than attack Northern towns and cities. First on the list would be a training mission on the little town of St. Albans, Vermont, just across the border from Canada. If that mission went well, there were other, much bigger targets that could be hit.

New York City was just 330 miles south of St. Albans. It was an easy train ride from Niagara Falls.

THE
SOUTH'S SECESSIONIST
SISTER CITY

Chapter 1

"Decayed Is Here"

The city smelled. It actually stank as well it might with cabs and omnibuses pulled by hundreds of horses walking the streets every day. Those horses left behind tons of pungent manure baking in the sun for hours before street sweepers came to work each night. Besides the excrement on Broadway, an awful stench came from the meatpacking district where packers dumped offal from the daily slaughtering of ten thousand beeves into the Hudson River.

It was dangerous. At least Charles Dickens thought so in 1842 when he made a famous visit to Five Points in New York City, just northeast of city hall. Dickens returned to London to write, "Other ruins loom upon the eye, as though the world of vice and misery had nothing else to show: hideous tenements which take their name from robbery and murder: all that is loathsome, drooping, and decayed is here."

The year 1863 had been a very deadly year for New Yorkers because of the July Draft Riots. Officials, mindful of the city's image, set the official death toll at one hundred but that number may have been underestimated by ten times. Still, 1863 was an aberration. The most common crime that middle- and upper-class New Yorkers faced in 1864 was pickpocketing while strolling Broadway.

It was crowded. Most of the city's 814,000 residents (one quarter of them Irish immigrants after the potato famine) lived below 26th Street. Lower-class families crowded into single rooms of fifteen thousand dark, dank, and poorly constructed tenant houses, commonly called tenements. So many of these tenements were clustered in the Lower East Side that the neighborhood was considered one of the most densely populated urban areas in the world. Apartment houses built to house twenty people held one hundred. And city building codes did not require fire escapes.

As crowded as the city was, its growth was accelerating at a pace that made even the most ardent boosters nervous. Twenty years earlier in 1844, newspaper editor William Cullen Bryant had said, "Commerce is devouring inch by inch the coast of the island, and if we would rescue any part of it for health and recreation it must be done now."

Bryant's plea was eventually heeded by the city's Common Council. Central Park's construction began in 1858 and continued during the war. The 800-acre construction site itself was a favorite destination for New Yorkers who marveled at the sheer size of the landscaping being undertaken in a city where neighborhood trees were often removed in favor of buildings.

But for all its faults, New York City, in those days consisting only of the population on Manhattan Island, was also the most important city in the United States.

It was larger than Philadelphia, the nation's second largest city by more than 265,000 people. Brooklyn City, the nation's third largest, had 266,000 people, fewer than a third of its neighbor across the East River.

New York had been one of the nation's most active ports since Colonial days, but after the completion of the Erie Canal in 1825 linking the Hudson River with western New York State, the city became even more an export and import magnet. By 1860, more ships were entering and leaving New York's harbor than all the other ports in the nation combined. The Hudson River docks attracted schooners while the East River docks attracted oceangoing ships heading worldwide.

Starting from the southern end, the city sprawled northward rather than growing upward. The tallest structure in 1864 was the top of the 284-foot spire of Trinity Church at Broadway and Wall Street. The spire's tiny observation deck was an attraction out-of-town tourists climbed to when they wanted a bird's-eye view of the city. Most buildings were no taller than eight stories, which was prudent since fire department ladders only reached four stories, and fire hoses threw water no higher than six. Contractors could not build taller buildings because each successive floor added weight to the first floor, increasing the chance of collapse.

Height restrictions on new buildings started to ease in 1848 with the introduction in the United States of cast iron as an architectural choice for commercial buildings. Architects now had the ability to construct structurally stable buildings as tall as people were willing to walk up because cast-iron walls could be bolted to deeply buried cast-iron footers. The city, locked into thirteen miles long by two miles wide Manhattan Island, could now grow up instead of out, though the word "skyscraper" was still years in the future.

Cast-iron buildings, which were fire resistant compared to wood buildings, were often falsely promoted as fireproof. In hot fires, iron melted, allowing flames to seep inside and set the interior wood walls ablaze. Still, cast iron was an improvement over brick and stone buildings as the mortar between bricks melted at much lower temperatures than iron.

The lifestyles that truly set New York City's citizens apart from each other in the mid-nineteenth century were the building of private homes for the upper crust. The vast majority of the city's citizens, even the middle class and wealthy, lived in rented, multifamily structures that could range from luxury-filled hotels to drafty, dangerous tenements.

Money was no object or deterrent to the city's top social class who moved to the northern edge of the city starting in the mid-1830s to build huge houses along Fifth Avenue starting at Washington Square and heading north. Even mayors, who claimed to be just like the men who elected them, moved to the fashionable address of Fifth Avenue, even though the avenue was so far from the center of the city that it had not even been paved until the 1840s.

At all levels of social classes, residents of Manhattan had the best entertainment that could be found in North America. If a famed European singer or actor planned to tour the United States, the citizens of New York saw him or her first.

There was a range of entertainment options. There was the Academy of Music at 14th Street and Irving Place, the city's first opera house, which was a huge 4,000-seat building that took more than two years to construct before opening in 1854. When the newest of the city's wealthy found that the city's old aristocracy would not sell them season tickets for the Academy, they started the Metropolitan Opera House in 1883.

In 1860, four thousand of the city's socialites were invited to a party at the Academy to welcome Edward VII, the 19-year-old Prince of Wales on his first visit to the United States. Queen Victoria's son danced with scores of New York's most eligible young women until he slipped away to visit the city's best-known brothels.

Theaters were a focal point of the city's social life. Prominent New Yorkers packed theaters to see their favorite musicians performing in blackface. It was during such a minstrel show in 1859 that the "walk around" song of *Dixie* was premiered at Mechanics Hall at 442 Broadway by an Ohio banjo player named Daniel Decatur Emmett. Emmett's band stayed booked in New York so long that it was weeks before Southerners even became aware of the song extolling the joy of living "in the land of cotton."

More serious theatergoers visited Niblo's Garden Theatre at Broadway and Prince Street and the even finer Winter Garden Theatre at Broadway and Bond Street. It was at the Winter Garden that famed actor Edwin Booth performed *Julius Caesar* each night for more than one hundred performances. On the night of November 25, 1864, Booth hit on an idea to raise money to erect a statue to William Shakespeare in Central Park. He convinced his brothers, Junius and John Wilkes, to appear with him. The three most famous actors in the nation, all brothers, appeared on the stage together for the first and only time. John Wilkes would eclipse his brothers' fame when he performed a dastardly deed in Ford's Theatre in Washington City, District of Columbia, on the night of April 14, 1865.

Most of the rest of the country did not care about New York City's entertainment options. To citizens who needed bank loans, access to foreign markets, or imported goods and equipment, New York City was all about business. They might never visit what was then nicknamed The Emerald City, but they needed it.

If New York City had a singular focus, it was about making money. Philadelphia was a close and constant rival, but New York was the nation's banking capital. Hundreds of banks were headquartered here. One, the First National Bank of New York City at Broadway and Wall Street, founded by a man named John Thompson, was already changing the way banks did business nationwide. New Yorker Thompson's idea would forever mold the entire economic system of the United States.

Early in the war, Thompson realized how impractical and costly it was for the nation to continue minting metallic coins. He petitioned Lincoln to establish a single national currency based on paper money that banks and merchants would recognize and accept. Instead of putting its gold and silver into circulation, the nation would store the metals in vaults while issuing the paper money that would represent the real value of the money. Thompson believed that the people would have faith that their government could protect their accumulated wealth.

Just as important as the city's individual banks was the New York Bank Clearing House Association at William and Wall streets. Each morning, bank clerks gathered in a large room with a stack of bank drafts drawn on other city banks they had cashed or deposited for their customers the previous day. In turn, each bank's clerk traded the drafts with the other represented banks. Once the trading of paper drafts was completed, cash was exchanged. The process started over again the next morning.

The clearing house was a simple but vital means of making sure that each bank was paid by the end of the day. Banks in distant states established relationships with New York banks to make sure their local banking customers were paid. Southerners particularly depended on New York banks because New York sales agents bought the bulk of cotton and sometimes shipped it from East River ports.

Each night the cash and the paper records of every New York

bank were put into iron safes that bank executives assumed—or at least hoped—were fireproof. No one knew for sure. Nearly thirty years earlier, most of the city's banks as well as the Merchants Exchange had burned, but the city's financial industry recovered. If such a fire occurred again and those safes allowed flames to lick inside, it would be devastating for the city's financial institutions. It could take even more time to recover because the city's financial importance had grown so much in just thirty years.

New Yorkers did not spend much time worrying about such potential disasters. They were too busy generating new ideas that made money.

Alexander T. Stewart, an Irish orphan, immigrated to New York in 1818. By 1828, Stewart had opened a small dry goods store. Stewart kept building larger stores until he realized he was confusing his customers with the sheer volume of goods he was offering. He developed an in-store separation of goods where customers could visit different sections of his stores. He called the sections departments.

Another man who moved to New York in 1858 to try his hand at making it there after failing in his native Massachusetts was a merchant named Rowland H. Macy. After examining the success of Stewart, Macy started the practice of putting price tags on merchandise, advertising those low prices in New York's newspapers, and then promoting holiday sales by hiring Santa Claus to sit in his stores at Christmas. By his death in 1877, Macy had developed another idea, a chain of stores all bearing his name. He created a corporate symbol for his new store chain, another New York idea that had never occurred to any other store owner. Macy chose a red star based on a tattoo he had put on his forearm during his youthful days aboard a whaling ship.

The nineteenth century had been good to New York City. By its midpoint the city was flying high. Only one cloud was on the horizon. New Yorkers were not too worried about it. The same cloud had been on the same horizon for decades. It had never darkened the city's plans for the future. That cloud was the threat of secession by the Southern, slave-holding states.

If the South left the Union, New Yorkers feared the end of good times. The city had grown wealthy trading Southern cotton and financing Southern slave purchases, not to mention buying and selling Africans on their own. What was good for the South was good for New York City.

Chapter 2

"A Traffic in Enslaved Africans"

New York City's acceptance of Southern slavery and its close economic ties with the South came naturally from its own history of being a slave-owning, slave-trading city.

The first black people on Manhattan Island arrived in 1625, just one year before Peter Minuet bought the island from the natives and just five years after the first blacks in America had come ashore in Jamestown, Virginia.

The status of the Africans who landed in Jamestown and Manhattan were different. The twenty-four Angolans who landed at Jamestown, Virginia, were not slaves, whereas those who landed on Manhattan were.

The Jamestown Africans disembarked on the continent with the legal understanding from the white settlers who needed their services that these blacks had the same rights as white English indentured servants who were arriving at the same time. Jamestown settlers paid the Dutch ship captain for the Angolans' passage from Africa in exchange for seven years of service, after which they would have the rights granted to all settlers.

There was no racial color barrier between white and black in 1625 Jamestown. The barriers were social—between master and employee. One of those first black settlers in Virginia, Anthony the Angolan, who later changed his name to Anthony Johnson, worked his way out of his seven years of servitude to become Virginia's first wealthy black man, acquiring as much land as his white neighbors.

While Johnson's white neighbors initially treated him socially as just another landowner, he also infuriated them by his constant use of the courts to sue them over minor disputes. One of Johnson's suits would forever seal the fate of future slaves brought to the continent.

In 1654, Johnson sued his white neighbor, Robert Parker, who Johnson charged was illegally keeping a man named John Castor who Johnson insisted was his slave. Castor insisted he was a former indentured servant who had long ago worked off Johnson's claim on his labor. Castor had gone to the neighbor Parker for protection from Johnson. After a lengthy trial, the colonial court ruled that Castor was Johnson's property, and he could not claim refuge with the neighbor.

For the first time in American history, a court of law had ruled that one man had the legal right to own another man. The court in Jamestown did not find it ironic or even remarkable that the slave owner had once been an indentured servant himself. Nor did it make a difference to the judges that Johnson and Castor were both black.

All the black men who landed on Manhattan Island were owned outright by the Dutch West India Company and their purpose for the past thirty years had been singular—to prepare the colony of New Netherland island and its primary town of New Amsterdam on the southern end of Manhattan Island for more white settlers and more black slaves. The slaves cut timber, built houses and fortifications, and constructed wharves along the Hudson River from which the furs and timber that had first attracted the company to the area could be shipped back to Europe.

In 1653, the colony's slaves were ordered to build a wall around New Amsterdam to protect the development from increasingly irritated and dangerous native tribes who had grown resentful of the encroachment of the white men through the Hudson Valley. Later the slaves would build a road that would run along that wall. History would not remember the names of the black men who built both the wall to protect what would become New York City and Wall Street.

The Dutch view on slavery was liberal, almost an extension of the indentured servitude. The Dutch trusted their slaves to help defend the colony. They set up economic models in which the slaves could work their way into freedom, which, in turn, allowed them to own property, a right that was unheard of in most other civilizations with the exception of Jamestown.

By 1664, Charles II of England had designs on expanding his territories in the New World south of Connecticut. The Dutch West India Company, which had pioneered and financed New Netherland as a colony and New Amsterdam as its capital on Manhattan Island, was caught off guard by the sudden aggressive stance of England.

The company had spent most of its time building relationships with trappers and natives—not in building military fortifications to protect the colony from a seaborne invasion from undetermined enemies. When four British warships appeared in the harbor in the summer of 1664, Peter Stuyvesant, then the governor of the colony, readily capitulated because he had no trained soldiers or enough weapons to fight the British.

One of the first things the new British owners of the colony did was rename it New York. What had been a Dutch outpost in the New World shipping beaver pelts to Europe was now a full-fledged English colony. Among the colonists in New York were about 150 black people, most of whom had not yet worked their way into freedom and likely had no illusions that their state in life would change under new management.

Over the next one hundred years, the British kept the remaining Dutch colonists and the newly arriving British settlers supplied with a steady flow of Africans who were purchased to act as laborers on small farms outside the city and inside the city as trained artisans, craftsmen, and house servants. According to census records, the percentages of blacks to whites in the city crept steadily upward from 14 percent in 1698 to 21 percent by 1756.

While the population of slaves on Manhattan Island steadily increased as the British imported them from Africa, Jamaica, Bermuda, and the Bahamas, the freedoms that slaves had enjoyed under Dutch rule gradually decreased. A 1730 law passed in New York made it illegal for three or more slaves to meet each other under penalty of getting forty lashes on a bare back. Another law, passed the following year, made it illegal for slaves to make noise on a public street. A law passed in 1740 made it illegal for slaves to buy or sell fruit.

What frightened white New Yorkers of the early eighteenth century was the distinct possibility that growing numbers of black slaves in the city and the Hudson River Valley would organize themselves into a formidable armed force. There fears were realized when the first successful slave revolt on the continent occurred on Manhattan in 1712.

On the night of April 6, up to fifty black men and women armed themselves with guns, knives, and hatchets stolen from their masters and then set fire to a farm building on Maiden Lane off Broadway. They lay in the darkness for the white settlers to rush to the scene of the fire. At least nine white settlers were killed in the ensuing melee. Apparently surprised at their easy success, the slaves retreated into the surrounding woods and barns rather than flee the island during the ensuing confusion and terror that now gripped the white community.

The next morning, the colonial militia rounded up virtually all the slaves on Manhattan and arrested and brought to trial more than seventy of them. New York's governor Robert Hunter was sympathetic to what he perceived to be the slaves' main grievances: that some masters had subjected them to "hard use," but he also realized that if he did not punish the blacks, he would have a white revolt on his hands.

Twenty-five slaves were convicted of revolt and executed with twenty being mercifully hanged while three were slow roasted by fire and one was broken on a wheel. So many slaves were executed in such a cruel fashion that Hunter protested that most other civilized societies picked out only the ringleaders of slave revolts and executed them as an example to other slaves. The slave owners ignored their governor's suggestion. They executed all the convicted.

When the slave owners ignored his advice to be lenient, Hunter observed that the only way to prevent future slave revolts in the colony was to stop importing slaves and start building a free white workforce.

That suggestion, intended for both white New Yorkers and New Englanders either who needed free labor or who enjoyed the status symbol of household slaves, was also ignored. Over the next thirty years, the number of slaves in New York City doubled until the slave population made up 20 percent of the population of the city.

Within thirty years, New York City would see—or at least the citizens would think they saw—another slave revolt.

In 1741, New Yorkers who were old enough to remember the events of 1712 must have recognized the similarities of what started happening during March and April. Over those weeks, nearly a dozen fires broke out in the occupied southern portion of the island, including one fire intended to burn the wooden palisades of Fort George (built on the site of today's Battery Park).

White New Yorkers needed little persuasion to believe that the city's slaves were up to their old arson tricks. Some of the fires were being set on the anniversaries of the 1712 fires.

Also fresh on the minds of New Yorkers were terrible stories still told of the 1739 Stono Rebellion near Charlestown (now Charleston), South Carolina. Down south, a mob of fifty rebelling slaves systematically hunted down and killed at least twenty-five whites, some of whom did not even own slaves.

Until the Stono attack, the white slave owners of South Carolina had trusted their slaves so much that they ignored government edicts that forbade the gathering of slaves or allowing them to grow their own food. The trigger for the rebellion was an impending crackdown on slave freedoms because slaves were hearing that the Spanish were granting freedom to any slaves from English Carolina who could make it to their colony in Florida.

Fear of more fires so concerned New York's Common Council that they issued a secret order to search the entire city for "latent Enemies." On Monday, April 13, 1741, the entire city was searched for evidence of fire-making materials or stolen goods. Every citizen (perhaps ten thousand people, both black and white) was accounted for to make sure that no foreign strangers had slipped into New York with the intention of burning it down.

When no strangers were found on whom to blame the fires, that left the people who had been the prime suspects all along—the black slaves. The militia had already rounded up a number of slaves before the search, including some who were the children of slaves who had been executed for the 1712 fires.

During a court inquest, some of the slaves testified that other slaves told them that if they burned down their masters' homes, they would be set free. One of the court's star witnesses was a white indentured servant, Mary Burton, who testified that the fires were the result of a joint conspiracy between black slaves and poor whites to burn down the city and kill the landowning whites so that the poor could inherit what was left.

The chief judge of the panel hearing the cases, Daniel Horsmanden, began to question other prisoners about a conspiracy. Soon the prisoners began to inform on each other and accuse others, white and black, about being part of the conspiracy. Judge Horsmanden accused a newly arrived schoolteacher, John Ury, with being a Spanish spy and the mastermind behind the slave revolt.

Horsmanden did not even wait for everyone accused to be tried before he started executing people. At least thirty blacks were hanged or burned alive. Four whites were hanged. More might have been executed but Horsmanden stopped the trial when his star witness, Mary Burton, began accusing family members of the judges of being in on the conspiracy.

The slave executions demonstrated that white New Yorkers were growing increasingly nervous about the intentions of the black people living among them. While the revolting slaves in 1712 had killed some whites, no white lives were lost at all in this latest conspiracy—if a conspiracy existed at all. The only evidence of a conspiracy were the fires set around the city and the word of Mary Burton, who eventually accused virtually everyone she knew of being behind a plot to burn down the city.

New York governor Hunter's 1712 prediction that using slave labor would only create more slave rebellions had been proven true just thirty years later. Still, that did not lead to the abandonment of the slave trade. In fact, the importation of slaves into New York increased in numbers, but the source of those slaves changed. Three quarters of the slaves imported into the city before 1741 had been from the Bahamas and Jamaica.

Starting after 1741, slave importers increasingly used Africa as a source for slaves rather than the Caribbean islands, believing that slaves taken directly from the continent would speak different languages than those who had lived for years in the Caribbean. Perhaps more importantly, those African slaves would have no knowledge of the Caribbean slave revolts.

The tremendous profits (upwards of 100 percent of an investment for a single voyage) of slaving voyages were a temptation that proved too hard to resist to many New York merchants who had expertise with sailing and shipping. Estimates range as high as one third of the city's merchants being engaged in the slave trade by 1750.

From 1732 through 1754 more than 35 percent of the city's new immigrants were listed as slaves. Since it was a common practice for many slavers to off-load their cargoes on Long Island in order to avoid the colony's tax collectors who were waiting at the official port of entry, it is possible that up to one half of the colony's immigrants in the mid-eighteenth century were slaves.

Slave owners in New England and New York differed from Southern slave owners in their use of slaves. Southern slaveholders looked on slaves as a permanent workforce, a resource to be used until they were too old to work. When that happened, the slaves became house servants. Southern slave women were encouraged to have children who would be born into slavery and eventually grow old enough to work.

While around five hundred thousand slaves landed in all the English American colonies in the 180 years before the slave trade was officially outlawed in 1808, more than 4 million slaves lived in the American South in 1861. Almost all of those were native-born Americans with a tiny fraction arriving from Africa, landed by slavers willing to take the chance on being detected by the United States Navy.

New Yorkers thought of slaves as a disposable commodity. In the late 1990s, Howard University in Washington, D.C., conducted an exhaustive study of the bones found in the African Burial Ground west of Manhattan's City Hall, the traditional burial ground for the city's slaves in the late eighteenth and early nineteenth centuries. The bones revealed that both men and women had lifted heavy weights most of their adult lives, leading to severe bone stresses. That fact indicated to researchers that New York City's slave owners believed the slave population could always be replenished with the arrival of another slave ship as "slaveholders showed no desire to possess young Africans or to 'breed' their captives. They only needed them to keep the market's products and profits flowing."

So many New York slavers got into the slaving business and so many voyages were successful that supply eventually overran demand and the wholesale price of slaves dropped by more than 50 percent by the end of the 1750s. But instead of lessening the demand for slaves, the lower cost encouraged more potential New York owners to make purchases. New York became an even more popular port of call, trailing only Charleston, South Carolina, for the volume of imported slaves.

As the eighteenth century faded and the nineteenth century dawned, so did the senses of lawmakers who questioned the need for domestic slavery and the international slave trade on religious, legal, and economic grounds. The Northern states had begun considering the thorny questions of abolishing slavery within their borders in the mid-eighteenth century, even as they allowed the international trade between Africa, Cuba, and the Caribbean to continue from their seaports. New York State passed a law abolishing slavery in 1799 with provisions that allowed owners to free or sell their slaves slowly so that they would not lose their investment.

Most slaves seemed to have been sold. According to the U.S. Census, the percentage of slaves in New York State in 1790 dropped by more than two thirds by the 1830 Census, indicating a huge transfer of bodies to places where slavery was still legal.

Congress finally passed a law abolishing the slave trade after 1808. Passing the law was one thing; enforcing it was another, particularly since most of the trade had shifted from importing slaves into the

United States to selling them to Caribbean countries. In 1810, President James Madison observed: "It appears that American citizens are instrumental in carrying on a traffic in enslaved Africans, equal in violation of the laws of humanity, and in defiance of those of their own country." Madison had no idea how New York would expand that traffic over the next fifty years.

Chapter 3

"A Great Distribution Point for Cotton"

Had it not been for a free-spending Southern agricultural economy, New York City's mercantile and shipping economy might never have taken off in the nineteenth century.

At first, the South did not need the North. For more than 180 years since 1612 when John Rolfe of the Jamestown colony in Virginia successfully crossbred a native strain of tobacco with a strain the Spanish had developed in the Bahamas, the South's prosperity had been linked to tobacco. Grown, dried, packed in barrels, and then shipped back across the Atlantic from Jamestown, tobacco proved wildly popular with the nicotine-addicted customers in England. More than ten tons of tobacco was shipped to England in 1619.

At the same time Jamestown was thriving with its tobacco exports, the Dutch West India Company in New Amsterdam on Manhattan Island was still figuring out how to secure a steady supply of beaver pelts from the western frontier of their fledgling colony.

Jamestown, which only ten years earlier had almost been starved into oblivion, was proving to be a magnificent investment, whereas the future of the Dutch colony on Manhattan was uncertain.

While tobacco was the crop that made Virginians successful, another plant grew well in the South that had the potential to surpass tobacco in demand among all of Western civilization, not just the

31

smokers. That was cotton, an easy-to-grow fiber that had been spun into thread, woven into cloth, and then cut and sewn into garments since biblical times. The major problem with cotton, however, was removing the seeds embedded in the fiber.

For years English importers had bought bales of cotton from countries like Egypt, broke it up into hundreds of lots, and then delivered the lots to the homes of contract workers who picked out the seeds and then spun the fibers into thread. This "cottage industry" worked, but the huge investment in time of removing the seeds meant cotton was a fiber that only the rich could afford to have made into clothes. Then along came a Connecticut Yankee.

On a visit to a Southern plantation in 1793, Eli Whitney noticed the slaves laboriously picking out the cotton seeds one seed at a time. He watched for a while, grabbed some cotton for himself, and then retired to a workshop. Within months he had developed what he called a cotton engine, a drum studded with metal teeth that easily removed the seeds from the cotton fibers. The work of thousands of fingers that had cleaned the picked cotton of seeds had been eliminated. Those same fingers were now free to pick the cotton from the fields.

At the end of the eighteenth century and the beginning of the nineteenth, the American South was poised to introduce itself to the world's economy as the largest supplier of cotton. This introduction came quickly. Cotton exports from the United States climbed dramatically with eight times the volume of cotton heading for England in 1804 compared with 1796, just three years after the invention of the cotton gin. In 1793, cotton clothes were worn by just 4 percent of the population in Europe and the United States. Over the next one hundred years, that figure jumped to 73 percent.

Sailing directly from the four major cotton ports of Charleston, Savannah, Mobile, and New Orleans to the two major English cotton-milling ports of Manchester and Liverpool would have made the most sense for cotton growers. But that is not how the trade developed. New York may have been far from the Southern cotton fields, but early in the cotton trade in the late 1700s until the 1850s, it became the major port from which Southern cotton made its way across the Atlantic.

All the Southern ports had water deep enough to handle most of the oceangoing ships that could have made it to England safely, but New York had some important, nonnautical advantages over any Southern ports.

Most important of all, the city had financial infrastructure. New York's banks had been dealing with the British textile manufacturers and their system of bills of exchange for fifty years. The city was home base to cotton brokers who visited the South to negotiate both the selling and the buying ends of a cotton transaction. These brokers ingratiated themselves with growers, convincing them there was no need for them to take care of the financial end of the business personally when their time could be better spent managing the slave labor force to grow more cotton.

Besides banks, the city also had scores of maritime insurance companies willing to insure ships and their cargoes on the voyage across the stormy Atlantic. Finally, New York had a long history of building and outfitting ships that could ply the world's seas carrying tons of whatever crops the South wanted to export.

New York's harbor also had a huge advantage over Southern ports in that it already had a long history of handling imports from Europe and a burgeoning population that wanted European imports. The Southern ports might be able to load up a large, heavy ship with cotton bales heading to England, but the South's smaller population meant there was less demand for goods coming from Europe to fill the same ship going back to the same port. In 1860, right before the war, New Orleans, the South's most successful port exported 107 million dollars' worth of goods (primarily cotton) while importing only 22 million dollars' worth of goods.

To handle the trade imbalance, instead of sailing directly to Europe, Southern cotton was loaded in Southern ports, taken to New York, and off-loaded onto larger ships that then sailed to England or New England. The smaller ships that had delivered the cotton to New York then sailed back south loaded with whatever goods Southerners purchased from New York importers.

While the managers of Southern ports could try to argue that it was much easier and less costly to ship cotton directly to England or

New England without the time and expense of off-loading in New York, those port managers had no answer if asked which Southern banks would handle the intricate financial transactions with the final buyers of the cotton who could be six thousand miles away. In 1845, the total number of banks in seven Southern states that produced cotton was 102, with a combined capital of $64 million and loans of $65 million. Alabama had only six banks in the entire state, and Mississippi, one of the major cotton-producing states, did not have a single one.

New York State alone had 150 banks with capital of $44 million and loans of $70 million. Most of those New York State banks were based in New York City.

In the early nineteenth century, within a decade of the invention of Whitney's cotton gin, as much as one quarter of the cotton reaching England came through New York's harbor. Just twenty years into the nineteenth century, cotton accounted for up to 40 percent of the city's exports to Europe. In 1850, the *New York Herald* wrote that New York would be "a great distribution point" for cotton.

Even though shipping their cotton through New York added hundreds of sea miles and weeks of time before their product could reach their customers, Southerners put up with it. Their New York cotton brokers had convinced them the system worked.

While the cotton growers never did a cost-benefit analysis, it was obvious to New Yorkers that the system worked very well for them. A host of intertwined New York businesses fed off the huge profits that moving the cotton through the city's ports generated. Off-loading the cotton from ships coming from the South and then reloading it onto ships bound for Boston or England kept thousands of stevedores employed on the docks. Tracking the handling of those same bales kept clerks employed. Taking the bales to a New England or English port and then returning with agricultural equipment and luxury goods kept shipowners, their captains, and crews employed. Selling the latest Paris fashions to Southern belles kept New York City dry goods store owners employed. Importing the latest English steel plows or selling the more expensive ones manufactured in New England to Southern planters kept the agricultural merchants employed.

Eventually, the New York brokers gave in to the complaints of Southern growers who sometimes watched the price of cotton fall while their crop was still languishing on a New York dock when it could have been already spun into cloth had it sailed directly from Charleston.

The tonnage of cotton actually passing through New York declined in the mid-1850s, but cotton remained the mainstay of Northern trade. The shipowners were New Yorkers; the bankers who advanced Southern plantation owners the cash to plant and raise cotton were New Yorkers; the men who insured the ships and the cargo were New Yorkers; and the merchants who sold Southerners expensive goods and furnishings once the cotton was sold were New Yorkers. About the only New Yorkers who lost out on the slow shift of direct shipping from grower to spinning mill owner were the city's dockworkers. Everyone else continued to make money on the fiber.

Giddy New Yorkers and grumpy Southerners both estimated that as much as forty cents of every dollar exchanged for cotton went to New Yorkers. New Yorkers had not planted, cultivated, picked, or baled any cotton, nor had they taken on any of the risk of flood, drought, wind, hail, or insects destroying that year's crop, but they reaped the lion's share of the profits from cotton.

New York bankers defended their involvement by insisting that were it not for wise New Yorkers handling the financial transactions, the babes-in-the-woods Southerners would be taken advantage of by the wily British textile manufacturers.

"Without the intervention of the great capital and demand at New York, the producer would be entirely at the mercy of the buyer in whatever port abroad his cotton might land, and he would in no case find a greater economy than at present," observed one banking insider.

Other Northerners insisted that Southerners should thank their lucky stars that Northern bankers deemed cotton growers worthy of receiving Northern loans.

"The growth in wealth in the cotton states may be traced almost entirely to eastern capital. Everybody knows that the cotton planters of the Southwestern states procure large supplies of clothing for their slaves and of every article required for their own consumption, upon credit from the neighbouring merchants, in anticipation of the next year's crop," wrote one economist.

And it was not just from raw cotton passing through the city both literally and figuratively that New Yorkers were getting profits. The *New York Journal of Commerce,* a New York City publication, estimated that just in 1849 alone, Southerners had purchased more than 76 million dollars' worth of goods from New York merchants. A decade later, another economist estimated that figure had nearly doubled, and the five major cotton states of the South (Georgia, South Carolina, Florida, Mississippi, and Alabama) had contributed more than $200 million in business for New Yorkers.

Even that considerable sum may be underestimated, as later economists believed that nineteenth century economists had not figured indirect financial benefits such as New York's in-transit trade with New England and Midwestern states. These regions also manufactured considerable goods and foodstuffs that passed through New York on their way to the South. Inevitably, Northern culture and Southern culture began to touch each other, though both would have rejected merging either outright.

Southerners began to think of New York City as a vacation destination to see live theater, buy furnishings, shop for diamonds at Tiffany and Company (founded in 1853), and eat at famous restaurants such as Delmonico's (founded in 1837).

In 1836, a Southern novelist sounded like a member of the New York Chamber of Commerce when he wrote: "Every southerner should visit New York. It would allay provincial prejudices, and calm his excitement against his Northern countrymen. The people here are warm-hearted, generous, and enthusiastic, in a degree scarcely inferior to our own southerners."

Getting a tour of duty at New York's Fort Hamilton was considered a plum assignment for all young officers. Lieutenant Robert E. Lee, U.S. Army, would often take the ferry from Brooklyn to New York City because he enjoyed riding his horse down Broadway.

Lieutenant Thomas J. Jackson would be less interested in the bright lights of Broadway, but more interested in studying religion at his stay at Fort Hamilton. Jackson would be baptized at St. John's Episcopalian church in Brooklyn. Twenty years later when he was a professor at the Virginia Military Institute in Lexington, Virginia, Jackson, twice married, would bring both of his wives at different times to New York City. On one trip, he visited a famed New York hydrotherapist at 47 Bond Street (today's Il Boco restaurant in NoHo). On another honeymoon, Jackson and his second wife climbed Trinity Church's steeple to get a good look at the city.

Professor Jackson remained impressed with New York City for the rest of his life. When he bought a house in Lexington, Virginia, he ordered furniture from a New York City merchant.

In July 1861, Professor Jackson would win the nickname of Stonewall at the Battle of Manassas, Virginia.

Business interests occasionally sent New Yorkers south where they, too, felt welcome. Scotsman Archibald Gracie settled in New York in 1784 where he first found employment as a merchant. Later, he saw the value of New York's harbor and launched a shipping line. Gracie's son, Archibald II, moved to Mobile, Alabama, in order to feed the cotton better from the South to his father's shipping line in New York. His son, Archibald III, continued in the family business of raising and shipping cotton.

The Gracie family made so much money in the cotton trade that they built a large mansion overlooking the East River. In 1942 the City of New York bought the Gracie Mansion that cotton built and made it the official residence of the mayor of New York City.

The business instincts of New Yorkers wanting to please long-term customers came into play whenever there was trouble in the South. When hot climate diseases such as malaria or yellow fever swept through Southern cities that were close to their cotton customers, New Yorkers organized relief missions or sent money. Those gestures were recognized and honored by Southerners who could curse greedy New Yorkers one year and praise the generosity of those same New Yorkers the next year. When yellow fever struck New Orleans in 1853, New York merchants sent money, resulting in a New Orleans city resolution saying, "We thank you for those generous exertions which have enabled us to comfort our sick and bury our dead. May you never need a return of our sympathy, but rest assured our hearts are throbbing with gratitude, and will ever be open to the call of humanity."

It was during the Panic of 1857 that New Yorkers realized how important the South was to the city. A mild nationwide recession in 1856 turned into a nasty and deep recession in 1857. The international causes included a drop in American grain prices when England and Russia reentered the market after ending the Crimean War. Another cause was England pulling most of its cash investments out of U.S. banks to pay its war debts. Domestically, American banks and railroads failed after a rash of land speculation on future rail routes. The final straw came in September when the SS *Central America*, a ship loaded with more than three tons of gold coins, sank off the coast of North Carolina. The loss of that gold, which had been on its way to New York City banks, cast doubt in the minds of investors and merchants that the United States could back up its paper money with hard assets.

Within weeks of the start of the panic, every region of the country was affected except the South. Businesses and banks were failing all over the nation, but cotton prices on the world market remained stable, so the South's economy remained solidly in the black. Southerners continued buying from New York merchants and dealing with New York banks and cotton brokers as if nothing was happening in the economy that could affect their spending.

The successful cotton planters essentially sat out the short-lived severe recession. That meant that the steady infusion of Southern cash kept New York City's merchants and port workers employed, successfully weathering the losses they were suffering from drops in business from other regions.

New Yorkers knew that free-spending Southerners had saved the city, and they were willing to do just about anything to keep the symbiotic relationship between the slaveholding South and the cotton-dependent metropolis intact. That included speaking up for the rights of slaveholders.

As the Panic of 1857 was ending, the nation was seeing a resurgence of abolitionist talk. In 1833, the American Anti-Slavery Society (AASS) was founded in New York by a handful of black and white ministers and a tiny number of merchants either who did not cater to Southerners or who felt compelled to speak out against the immorality of slavery.

Most of the city's businessmen feared what could happen if the abolitionist movement took hold in New York City. According to them, freeing the Southern slaves would mean the end of civilization, at least in New York City.

James Watson Webb, owner and editor of the *Courier and Enquirer*, the largest circulating newspaper in the city and the nation, raged when he heard of the formation of the AASS: "Are we tamely to look on, and see this most dangerous species of fanaticism extending itself through society? . . . Or shall we, by promptly and fearlessly crushing this many-headed hydra in the bud, expose the weakness as well as the folly, madness and mischief of these bold and dangerous men?"

Despite Webb's warnings, the AASS continued to preach against slavery. Two years after its founding, a merchant, identified only as "a partner in one of the most prominent mercantile houses in the city," spoke candidly to abolitionist Samuel J. May at a meeting in May 1835. The man asked May to walk with him so he could quietly deliver a threat that was not even veiled:

> Mr. May, we are not such fools as to not know that slavery is a great evil, a great wrong. But a great portion of the property of the Southerners is invested under its sanction; and the business of the North, as well as of the South, has become adjusted to it. There are millions upon millions of dollars due from Southerners to the merchants and merchants alone, the payment of which would be jeopardized by any rupture between the North and the South. We cannot afford, sir, to let you and your associates endeavor to overthrow slavery. It is not a matter of principles with us. It is a matter of business necessity. . . . We mean, sir, to put you abolitionists down by fair means if we can, by foul means if we must.

Twenty-five years later, attitudes had not changed. Abolitionists who had no ties to the trade in cotton or with the South were continuing to preach that slaves should be freed, even if it meant the collapse of the Southern economy. The defenders of slavery had not given in either. Even on the brink of the American Civil War, New York City's bankers, merchants, and average citizens were still searching for ways to protect the South's institution of slavery.

A prominent Southern journal warned of a New York calamity in very plain language if slavery were abolished. In 1859, months before the November 1860 presidential election, Alfred A. Smith, a South Carolina–based writer for the New Orleans–based agricultural journal *De Bow's Review*, predicted that the South would secede if a "Black Republican" (Lincoln) were elected president.

In making his point that the North needed the South, Smith quoted export records that the South had exported more than 2 billion dollars' worth of goods from 1821 to 1855 compared with only $990 million from the North. Furthermore, Smith found that the Northern textile mills consumed more than 82 percent of the cotton bales produced for domestic use. Smith then made a prediction if pressure on the South to free the slaves forced it out of the Union and into a confederacy of other Southern states:

> What would become of this interest if the supply of Southern cotton should be cut off? What would become of the immense mercantile marine of the country? What would become of the great metropolis New-York? The ships would rot at her docks; grass would grow in Wall Street and Broadway; and the glory of New York, like Babylon and Rome, would be numbered with the things that are past.

New Yorkers were not sure if Smith's predictions were hyperbole or not. They were not willing to take the chance. On the issue of continuing slavery in the South, New York would support the South.

Chapter 4

"Money Is Plenty, Business Is Brisk"

Throughout most of the eighteenth and early nineteenth centuries, New York's political leaders knew that the cotton enriching the city was directly linked to Southern slavery. They praised the crop and the city's ability to turn it into cash, while trying their best to ignore the working conditions of the labor force that produced it.

Philip Hone, the city's mayor from 1826 to 1827, kept a detailed diary from 1828 to 1851, the year of his death, noting the daily social and economic conditions of the city. On October 3, 1833, Hone noted that he was irritated to find out that Clinton Hall, the location of the fledgling New York University, had been rented out to a meeting of some abolitionists.

"I expressed great dissatisfaction that the hall should be let without my approbation for any purposes not immediately connected with the objects of the institution, and my decided opposition to its being used for the agitation of this most mischievous question," Hone wrote.

When other concerned New Yorkers wanted to hold a meeting to decide what to do about the abolition movement that was moving into New York, Hone noted that he would attend because "I am desirous that persons of character should be present in the greatest possible numbers, with the twofold object of convincing the people of the South that the incendiaries constitute an inconsiderable portion of our citizens."

On April 9, 1835, Hone noted that "money is plenty, business is brisk; the staple commodity of the country [cotton] has enriched all whose hands it has passed. The merchant, mechanic and proprietor all rejoice in the result of last year's operations."

During the recession of 1837 on July 4, Hone noted that "with the aid of one or two cotton crops, and the realization of the present glorious prospects for the harvest, we shall not only get right, but the character of our merchants will stand higher than ever among the nations of the earth."

Hone was an instinctive politician who recognized that big issues often led to big problems. On November 17, 1837, he made a prediction about the future of abolition that he had earlier described as "the enemy of mankind": "The terrible abolition question is fated to destroy the Union of the states, and to destroy the peace and happiness of our western world."

Throughout the first half of the nineteenth century, New York's mayors and the city's Common Council representing the city's wards remained concerned about the growing abolition movement. The mayors were concerned because they were almost all merchants or industrialists whose businesses could be affected if their Southern customers grew irritated.

In October 1833, Democratic mayor Gideon Lee and other prominent business leaders of the city gathered at Tammany Hall before rushing off to break up the antislavery meeting mentioned by former Mayor Hone. The Democrats, led by editor James Watson Webb, ran into the abolitionist meeting shouting that a reward of $10,000 would be given for anyone who harmed Arthur Tappan, the editor of the *Journal of Commerce*, who had organized the meeting. Tappan and most of the other abolitionists had wisely left out a back door when they heard the mob was approaching.

Mayor Lee organized a meeting later that same week denouncing abolitionists. One of the speakers at the meeting was U.S. senator Theodore Frelinghuysen of New Jersey who told the assembled crowd of businessmen that the abolitionists were trying to "dissolve the Union" and, besides, "nine-tenths of the horrors of slavery are imaginary."

On July 4, 1834, when Lee was still mayor of New York City, several days of antiabolitionist riots were staged with mobs attacking the abolitionists in their homes. The city's police force, under control of the mayor, did little to prevent the violence.

At the same time that New York's public officials and politicians were struggling to deal with abolitionist organizing, Southerners were shrewdly instituting an informal public relations campaign to show Northerners that slavery was not as bad as they may have heard. The August 29, 1854, *New York Times* republished an article from the *Mobile* (Alabama) *Tribune*, supposedly written by a slave describing his recent trip to New York City with his master.

"In my strolls of three days in that city [New York], I saw more evidences of destitution—more ragged, half-clad, miserable, beggarly looking people than in all of Virginia and Alabama. I met beggars and loafers at every corner and a cent is as gladly received by these poor creatures as a dollar would be by any servant in Mobile," wrote the supposed slave. Even the *Times* did not question how a slave could write such a vivid description of the city when it was against the law in all Southern states to teach slaves to read and write.

Even those Northerners who had freed their own slaves decades earlier and who were now sympathetic to abolitionists had to admit to themselves that slavery still played a large role in the economy of their region.

The outfitting and home port docking of slave ships in New England and New York ports was openly practiced for more than fifty years after Congress officially abolished the slave trade in 1808. The only true change that slavers made to their routine after the supposed abolition of the American slave trade was to change their final ports of call from Southern ports to those in the Caribbean, principally Havana, Cuba. New York's mayors, aldermen, police, marshals, state and federal prosecutors, and state and federal judges all knew which New York City–based ships were slavers. They just chose to ignore them.

Remarkably, even known criminals and gang leaders could wrangle appointments as U.S. Marshals who had the responsibility to enforce federal laws against slaving. Such was the case with Isaiah Rynders, a former leader of the Five Points street gang, who had a history of roughing up abolitionists like Frederick Douglass and Wendell Phillips when they came to visit New York's abolitionist societies. In 1857, President James Buchanan appointed Rynders U.S. Marshal, the perfect position from which to continue to collect protection money and to ignore rumors of slave outfitting. Rynders employed his nephew as an assistant marshal. When the nephew was accused of taking a bribe of $1,000 to let a slaver leave port, he vigorously insisted that the accusation was wrong. The bribe was, in fact $1,500.

If the men entrusted with enforcing U.S. law in New York City were not inclined to stop slavers, neither was the U.S. judiciary. Of 125 slave traders tried for slave trading in the city's courts from 1837 to 1861, just twenty were given prison sentences of two years, even though they had been caught with slaves in the holds of their ships on the open seas by the United States Navy. While the men in jail for two years might have considered that just punishment, federal law provided for the execution of slavers. The federal judiciary in New York City was not about to stop the slave trade.

In 1848, the crew of the ship *Mary Ann*, operating out of New York City, mutinied off the coast of Africa when they realized that their captain intended to take on a cargo of slaves rather than goods. The crew sailed the ship back to New York City, confident that they would be hailed as heroes for foiling at least one slaving voyage. They sued the ship's owner for the weeks of wages that they had been promised for what they had been told would be a legitimate voyage.

The crew of the *Mary Ann* went before federal judge Samuel Rossiter Betts, who shared the Southern District of New York bench with Judge Samuel Nelson. Betts, who was often called the father of Admiralty Law and who one biography claims was never overruled on appeal, ruled that the crew of the *Mary Ann* were not entitled to the wages that they had expected for a legitimate voyage, and that "by absconding with the vessel and bringing her to the United States from the coast of Africa, they have been guilty of a violation of their duty to the ship and to the owner, and deprived themselves of all rightful claim to wages for any portion of the time they were connected to her."

Instead of awarding the men wages from the owner, Betts ordered them to pay the slave ship owner for the costs of the unsuccessful voyage to Africa.

In another case the *Catherine* was boarded by suspicious U.S. Marshals in New York harbor before even reaching the Atlantic Ocean. Even though the Marshals found items on board that clearly demonstrated that it was intended to be a slave ship, such as a large cooking pot, a huge cistern of water, and hundreds of wooden spoons, Betts ruled that no outfitting could be considered suspicious unless a crew member was willing to testify once the ship was captured with slaves aboard that the outfitting was used in slaving.

For years the city's newspaper editors were all well aware that the city's politicians and its marshals and judges were allowing the slave trade to operate out of New York City. But these men were not crusading journalists. Perhaps out of fear for their lives, the newspaper editors only made vague protests about what they knew was happening.

"It is known that there are in this City several mercantile houses extensively engaged in the slave trade, and that half a dozen vessels have recently left this and other American ports, for the African Coast. . . . Our Authorities would do well to exercise more than ordinary vigilance in regard to vessels clearing for Cuban ports," intoned the *New York Times.*

The next year the *Times* wrote:

This City and Baltimore are now, and have been for years, the great headquarters of the African Slave-trade. In the face of our laws, in defiance of our treaty stipulations and in contempt of armed cruisers and men-of-war, that piratical traffic is largely carried on by ships fitted out in American ports, and under the protection of the American flag. If the authorities plead that they cannot stop this, they simply confess their own imbecility. If they will not do it, the moral guilt they incur is scarcely less than that of the Slave-traders themselves.

None of the daily newspapers ever had the nerve to name names, even though they were accusing public officials of corruption, as opined by the *New York Daily News*: "The price for the clearance of a slaver [from the port of New York] is as well-known to those in the trade as the price of a barrel of pork."

Horace Greeley of the *New York Daily Tribune* wrote:

> The traders engaged in this traffic are known; the men who supply their vessels with stores, who fit them with sails, who provide them with sailors, are known also. That knowledge, and much other that is curious and interesting in relation to this subject, awaits the Government, whenever the Government chooses to seek for it. It does not seek for it. It does not choose to have it. It will not thank us even for hinting that it can be had, or for providing any portion of it.

Not only were New York City's politicians unwilling to stop the slave trade operating out of their port, but they were even willing to increase the number of slave states. In March 1859, the Democrats of the Tammany Hall political machine, including Samuel Tilden, the future New York gubernatorial and presidential candidate, voted for a resolution calling on the United States to buy Cuba and annex it into the nation as a slave state. Among the big proponents of that idea were New York's sugar refiners, who believed that the slave labor cutting the sugarcane in Cuba would continue to do so if it became a state. They were very interested in lowering and stabilizing the price of sugar.

New York's public officials and political leaders did not want to offend the South in any way. It was not about hurt feelings. It was about money. By 1860, on the eve of the war, the spinning mills of New England produced nearly 75 percent of the nation's cloth, including the rough-textured mix of wool and cotton called negro cloth that plantation owners bought to clothe their slaves.

Even on the eve of war, New York's officials turned a blind eye to the slave traders heading out from New York City to Africa. On December 1, 1860, within three weeks of South Carolina seceding from the Union, the *New York Times* listed eight different ships that had been seized in the port of New York on suspicion of being bound for a slave voyage. All the ships would be released by the court to their owners.

As war became inevitable, some cracks began to show in the North's wall of resistance on dealing with its own slave trade issues. On December 26, 1860, Judge David A. Smalley convened a grand jury in New York in the same Southern District that was home to judges Betts and Nelson, the two judges known to be lenient with slave ship outfitters, captains, and owners.

Smalley apparently did not consult with his fellow judges because he charged the jurors that it was their duty to "investigate infractions of the laws for the suppression of the slave trade."

Later in the charge, Smalley told the jurors:

That the laws for the suppression of the Slave trade have been often grossly violated in this port, and in other places within the Federal Courts in this District, is a fact too notorious to admit of dispute or question. That this unchristian [*sic*] and inhumane traffic has greatly increased within the last few years, and is still increasing, and that principally from vessels fitted in and cleared from this port, does not admit of a doubt. . . . It has at home and abroad, become a stigma and reproach upon this, the great commercial and maritime metropolis of the Western Continent, that this has been permitted. The laws against it are sufficiently plain, explicit and severe to put a speedy end to it, if vigorously and vigilantly enforced.

The next day, the *New York Times* reacted with:

Such an announcement as this, and from such a source, cannot fail to cause a wholesome terror amongst those commercial houses whose names are invariably found connected, in some mysterious manner, with the fitting out and clearance of vessels subsequently arrested in the Slave-trade, or known to be burned on the coast of Cuba, after having made a successful voyage. . . . If we understand Judge Smalley rightly, he means not to rest satisfied with the trial and punishment of the poor, ignorant seamen who are actually engaged on board the slave-ships; but will also do his utmost, within the limits of his of-fice, toward directing the attention and action of the Grand Jury against the millionaires and wealthy merchants who have ac-cumulated, and are still trying to increase their fortunes in this unholy business.

Smalley's grand jury was apparently dissolved early in 1861 with-out rendering any opinions. The judge's name, though praised so highly by the *New York Times*' editors, does not appear in the news-paper's columns after March 1861.

One explanation for why Smalley's bold charge to his grand jury never resulted in any bolder indictments may be that New York City's mayor might have stepped into the breach. The South had many pow-erful political friends in the North in the nineteenth century, but none of them were as bold as Mayor Fernando Wood.

Had Wood had his way, New York City would have left the Union just after South Carolina and maybe even before Mississippi and Florida, the second and third states to secede from the Union.

Born in Philadelphia in 1812, Wood moved to New York City at nineteen years old and found work as a salesman and bartender. Tall and handsome and anxious to get involved with the local politi-cal bosses, he soon gained the attention of Tammany Hall's political machine. He rose so quickly that other Tammany Hall Democrats disliked him as a rival. Another future mayor, sugar merchant Wil-liam F. Havemeyer, said that Wood was "without character or conse-quence, yet shrewd & Subtle, a cunning politician."

In 1841, Wood was elected to the U.S. Congress but served only two years. He came back in 1854 to be elected mayor of the city with the help of the working classes and new immigrants who recog-nized that he did not come from money.

Even though he fell out of favor with the Tammany Hall machine, Wood was reelected in 1857. His term was marred by the constant clashing of two different police forces, the New York Municipal

Police (which had been authorized by the New York State legislature) and the Metropolitan Police (who were aligned with Wood). The two police forces often fought each other in open riots, much to the glee of the street criminals and the gangs who took the opportunity to steal from citizens while the police force was in disarray.

Wood was out of office for one term and then returned to run for mayor in 1859 for a two-year term running from 1860 to 1862. He ran on a platform of standing up for the working class and for accommodation with the South. That second campaign plank pleased the merchants.

"The South is our best customer. She pays the best prices and pays promptly," Wood said at one campaign rally. He easily won, the first man in New York history to serve two nonconsecutive terms as mayor.

Starting almost as soon as he was inaugurated early in 1860, Wood plunged himself into national politics by giving speeches around the Northeast calling for the nation to elect Democrats because the election of a Republican president in 1860 would lead to disunion. He tried to appeal to the average voter by warning them that freeing the slaves would mean blacks would compete for their jobs. His speeches so pleased Southern power brokers that they began to mention his name as a potential vice president. That Wood dream, however, ended when the Democratic Party split into Northern and Southern factions and put up two different presidential candidates. Taking advantage of the split vote, Abraham Lincoln was elected in November 1860.

Still convinced that states rights were preferable over national power and still convinced that abolitionists were pushing the nation closer to war, perhaps being pushed by the city's merchants, Wood kept his Southern sympathies.

On January 6, 1861, three weeks after South Carolina had seceded from the Union, but before all the other ten states that would eventually make up the Confederacy had even voted themselves out of the Union, Wood launched into a lengthy speech to the Common Council on the state of the city. Within the first few paragraphs, Wood addressed the national crisis.

"It would seem that a dissolution of the Federal Union is inevitable" was the opening line of the second paragraph. Wood then went on to say that if a separation of states did occur, "momentous considerations will be presented to the corporate authorities of this city. We must provide for the new relations which will necessarily grow out of the new condition of public affairs."

The Common Council members started to listen more closely to understand just what Mayor Wood was proposing:

With our aggrieved brethren of the Slave States, we have friendly relations and a common sympathy. We have not participated in the warfare upon their constitutional rights or their domestic institutions. While other portions of our State have unfortunately been imbued with the fanatical spirit which actuates a portion of the people of New England, the city of New York has unfalteringly preserved the integrity of its principles of adherence to the compromises of the Constitution and the equal rights of the people of all States.

Having just heard the mayor insult upstate New York and New England, the Common Council members wondered what Wood was going to say next. They were shocked to hear him say that if the South were to leave the Union, so too would California "and her sisters of the Pacific" and the "western states" (the midwest).

Wood continued:

Then it may be said, why should not New York City, instead of supporting by her contributions in revenue two-thirds of the expenses of the United States, become also equally independent? As a free city, with but nominal duty on imports, her local Government could be supported without taxation upon her people. Thus we could live free from taxes, and have cheap goods nearly duty free. In this she would have the whole and united support of the Southern States, as well as all the Other States to whose interests and rights under the Constitution she has always been true. . . .

[If] . . . the Government is dissolved, and it behooves every distinct community, as well as every individual, to take care of themselves.

When Disunion has become a fixed and certain fact, why may not New York disrupt the bands which bind her to a venal and corrupt master—to a people and a party that have plundered her revenues, attempted to ruin her commerce, taken away the power of self-government, and destroyed the Confederacy [meaning the Union] of which she was the proud Empire City? Amid the gloom which the present and prospective condition of things must cast over the country, New York as a Free City, may shed the only light and hope of a future reconstruction of our once blessed Confederacy [Union].

Wood then told the Common Council how much tax money the city had contributed to the state but for which the city had gotten little in return. He ended his speech by reiterating something he had said earlier. He insisted that he was not suggesting that people use "violence" to free the city itself from New York State and the Union. Instead, he hoped that the people of New York State would allow New York City to go peacefully.

Wood had not pledged the city's allegiance to the Southern states, which would soon name itself the Confederate States of America and the Confederacy. Instead, Wood had suggested that New York City itself secede from the state of New York and the Union. The mayor imagined that if New York City were "free," it would be able to trade with the Union and the South, as well as all the other countries in the world.

The Common Council did not vote on the mayor's idea, and some newspapers criticized him with the *New York Sun* writing: "Mayor Wood's secessionist Message has sounded the bathos of absurdity."

After the firing on Fort Sumter in April 1861, Wood objected to the seizing of a shipment of muskets destined for Georgia. It was then that some citizens began to think of him as a traitor to the Union.

Wood had misjudged the mood of the average person in the street when it came to what they thought of the South.

But behind the scenes and without publicly defending their mayor, the wealthy merchants and industrialists of New York City still were looking for a way for the North to avoid going to war with the South. If that happened, they feared, the warning that "grass would grow in Broadway and Wall Street," would come true.

Chapter 5

"The Meetings of These Madmen"

Nothing irritated New York's leading citizens more in the 1850s than abolitionists. In 1850, the *New York Herald* urged that abolitionists be barred from holding meetings in New York City—something merchants had been trying to do for more than fifteen years since the first major abolitionist meeting in the city was shut down in 1834 using the threat of violence against its organizers.

The editor, James Gordon Bennett, Sr., wrote:

> The merchants, men of business, and men of property in this city, should frown down upon the meetings of these madmen. . . . What right have all the religious fanatics of the free States to gather in this commercial city for the purposes, which, if carried out, would ruin and destroy its prosperity? Will the men of sense allow meetings to be held in this city, which are calculated to make our country the arena of blood and murder, and render our city the object of horror to the whole South?

Bennett was reacting to an upsurge of abolitionist protests after Senator Daniel Webster of Massachusetts suggested in a Senate speech that some permanent compromise be reached with the South over the future of slavery.

Within a week of Webster's speech, New York's merchants were raising money to reprint the speech and gleefully quoting it to each other as they met in the streets, banks, and stock exchange. They felt Webster's speech was evidence that few in Congress wanted to rock the boat when it came to the question of Southerners owning slaves or, for that matter, Northerners transporting slaves.

The New Yorkers underestimated the determination of abolitionists to make the holding of slaves on the American continent unpalatable to the average American. Webster's speech did not deter the abolitionist movement in the least. Nor did it stop other politicians, who may well have respected Webster's efforts, from thinking about how they could end slavery and the slave trade in all its forms.

In August 1858, William H. Seward, one of the U.S. senators from New York and, at that time, the supposed frontrunner for the 1860 presidential nomination for the Republicans, bitterly complained that his efforts in the Congress to control the slave trade had been regularly thwarted by his own constituents.

"The root of the evil is in the great commercial cities, and I frankly admit, in the City of New York. I can say also that the objection I found to that bill came not so much from the Slave States as from the commercial interests of New York," said Seward.

Seward's homegrown problem was that the acceptance of slavery had been ingrained in the city's culture since its creation as a Dutch colony two hundred years earlier. Between January 1859 and August 1860, at least eighty-five slaving voyages originated from New York's harbor transporting between 30,000 and 60,000 slaves from Africa to Cuba.

The city's newspaper editors were not all like the *Herald*. Some tried to shame the city's business leaders into ending their association with slavery.

The August 10, 1859, *New York Times*, apparently bored with describing how slavers were outfitting in its home city, used a correspondent to track down two slavers that were being outfitted in faraway Portland and Salem, Maine.

"The business is so very dangerous a one, and has been organized so long in the lesser New England seaports, whether by merchants resident, or by a skillful use of the facilities of those ports for the purposes of New York houses, that it is difficult to track the guilty parties. The Government treats the whole matter with indifference," wrote the *Times* correspondent.

The *Journal of Commerce*, founded by the abolitionist Tappan brothers, Arthur and Lewis, and their partner Samuel F. B. Morse, railed in 1857, "[D]owntown merchants of wealth and respectability are extensively engaged in buying and selling African Negroes, and have been, with comparative little interruption, for an indefinite number of years."

Horace Greeley, editor of the *New York Tribune* complained, "The most successful of the Merchant Princes; those who show the most courage in mercantile venture, those who best succeed in the speedy acquisition of wealth, are those who supply the markets of the world with slaves."

New York City's most influential businessmen were shrewd enough to keep secret any direct interests they had in the slave trade, but some of these men must have been the subject of whispers.

Jacob Westervelt, the city's mayor from 1853 to 1855, was a partner with his brother in building fine sailing ships that crossed the oceans. While his name and ships were not mentioned in contemporary newspaper accounts as being slavers, one of his relatives, Minthorne Westervelt, was tried in 1862 for being third mate on a captured slaver. His first trial ended in a hung jury, and the judge released him with the remark that he was "too good a man to be kept in confinement with criminals."

William Havemeyer, who served as mayor of New York City from 1845 to 1846 and then again from 1848 to 1849 (and then again from 1873 to 1874) was a sugar refiner who purchased hundreds of tons of Cuban and Southern grown sugarcane that depended on slave labor. Slaves working in sugarcane had much worse working conditions than the average slave on a cotton plantation did. Sugarcane slaves could cut themselves on the cane itself or with the knives used to slash the cane. Snakes that lived in the same wet, boggy conditions in which the cane grew could bite the slaves. Finally, the slaves had to work in hot, humid conditions caused by the tall cane stalks stopping the breezes from reaching the workers.

Moses Taylor was one of the busiest men in all of New York. He acted as a sugar broker for the sugarcane coming into the city's ports, so he was a supplier to Havemeyer, the sugar refiner. Taylor was also a board member of the City Bank of New York (predecessor to Citibank). His role as banker allowed him to give loans to sugar growers in Cuba to expand their slave labor force. Taylor was so tied to the Cuban sugar growers that he offered to help their children find internships in the city so that they could learn more about how to run the family businesses.

One of New York's elite was caught red-handed not only supporting the South but also trying to arm it when war was imminent. He was Gazaway Bugg Lamar, a Georgia native who understandably went by his initials of G. B., who founded the Bank of the Republic in New York City, in the 1840s in a prime location on the corner of Broadway and Wall Street. When the Confederacy was still forming early in 1861, Lamar was in New York writing his political contacts in the South urging them to adopt a free trade policy. Lamar believed Mayor Fernando Wood's suggestion of setting up New York as a "free city" was still possible even though the Common Council had initially rejected the idea.

Lamar said:

> The difference between the rates of the tariffs North and South are creating great discontent already at the North, and they will in the North have to call an extra Congress to repeal their Morrill tariff. . . . With free trade at the South, all the imports would be diverted to the Southern ports until New York City could redress herself either by dissolving the relations she holds to the Union and adopting free trade or by bringing all of the other states to do it.

Lamar, staying true to his home state of Georgia, which seceded from the Union, would eventually be forced to leave the city in 1861 when he was caught trying to ship a load of muskets to the governor of Georgia. Earlier Lamar had used some New York City printers to print bonds for the Confederate government. Those beautifully detailed certificates successfully made their way south before the Union confiscated the printing plates in New York City less than two weeks after the firing on Fort Sumter on April 12, 1861.

Not withstanding the occasional man in their midst like Lamar who let his ties to the South become too well known, New York City's businessmen knew how to use public relations to try preempting any separation of North and South. One successful method was publishing economic predictions on the disaster that would occur if the Union split. In 1856, Thomas Kettell, a New York City economist and magazine editor with ties to the New York business community, published a book called *Southern Wealth and Northern Profits, As Exhibited by Statistical Facts and Official Figures: Showing the Necessity of the Union to the Future Prosperity and Welfare of the Republic.*

By page two of the preface, Kettell made it clear what he thought of "agitators," his name for abolitionists:

The national prosperity, the domestic peace, the safety of life and property, the very existence of the nation, are jeopardized by an idea that is admitted by the agitators to be fruitless. The agitation at the North has no practical application whatsoever while at the South it has in the background servile insurrection, bloodshed and annihilation of person and property, involving ultimately the ruin of the North.

On page seven of the 143-page book, Kettell laid out how New York depended on the South: "All the profitable branches of freighting, brokering, selling, banking, insurance, etc., that grow out of the Southern product are enjoyed in New York."

Though the language is dense and the charts comparing crop yields even denser, Kettell finally ends his book with a warning of dire economic consequences if the South is forced to free its slaves: "The depreciation of property which would follow at the North is a matter for serious contemplation, and it well behooves those who are interested to guard against it."

Despite such efforts to show the South that New York's merchants were behind them, increasing numbers of Southerners were beginning to associate the abolitionist movement with all of the North—including New York. Some Southern newspapers lumped the Northern abolitionist activities together with long-held animosities about how much money New Yorkers skimmed off the top of cotton sales forced through the city's ports and banks. The editors knew how Southern trade kept the city afloat during the panic of 1857, and they took offense that New York was not more appreciative, even though New Yorkers had often expressed appreciation in print and by action such as sending money south during such disasters as yellow fever epidemics.

In October 1857, the *Charleston Mercury* asked:

Why does the South allow itself to be tattered and torn by the dissensions and death struggles of New York money changers? Why not trade directly with our customers? What need is there of this going between to convey to the markets of our world our rich products, for which the consumers stand ready, gold in hand, to pay the full value?

In December 1857, the *New Orleans Crescent* lashed out with a startling description of her Atlantic port rival:

New York with her rotten bankruptcies permeating and injuring almost every solvent community in the Union. New York, the centre of reckless speculation, unflinching fraud and downright robbery. New York, the prime cause of four-fifths of the insolvencies of the country; New York, carrying on an enormous trade with capital mostly furnished with other communities.

If they were not subscribers of the Louisiana newspaper, New York merchants might have missed the editorial, but the *Herald* reprinted it.

New York's merchants might have been fuming at the verbal and written attacks from their supposed Southern friends, but most of them bit their lips and did not respond. They did not want to anger their best customers any further, particularly now that it appeared that the South had entered its own recession in the summer of 1860 after years of steady buying, including right through the Panic of 1857. Newspapers speculated that Southern purchases from New York merchants in 1860 were between one third and one half of what they had been in 1859. The merchants were already nervously eyeing 1861 because they expected the Morrill Tariff to pass and take effect the following year.

Designed to protect the Northeast's manufacturing industry and force the rest of the nation to buy American by putting European goods out of reach, the Morrill Tariff, introduced in Congress by Vermont representative Justin Morrill, was born out of the Panic of 1857 when some Northern economists blamed free trade for causing the deep recession. The Republicans, eager to establish themselves as a force in the Congress, championed the bill because it would protect virtually every American industry from iron to textiles by increasing the tariffs on similar imported goods by as much as 100 percent.

The House of Representatives passed the bill in May 1860 with nearly 90 percent of the North's representatives supporting it and only one Southern representative supporting it. The bill was tabled in the Senate until after the presidential election of 1860, allowing Lincoln to use its future passage as a campaign tool in states where manufacturing was important, such as Pennsylvania, New Jersey, and Massachusetts. Lincoln muted his support for the bill when he visited New York City because he knew the merchants opposed it.

Lincoln's dual campaign strategy did not really fool anyone. Both Southern consumers of imported goods and the New York City merchants who imported those goods knew that Lincoln would sign the bill once it passed the Senate.

Southerners, who often exchanged their cotton in England for everything from cloth to plows, were outraged that the U.S. government was promising to double the cost of those goods.

On November 19, 1860, U.S. senator Robert Toombs from Georgia made a speech where he incorrectly lumped together all Northerners as being in favor of the Morrill Tariff, charging that the "free-trade abolitionists became protectionists; the non-abolition protectionists became abolitionists. The result of this coalition was . . . the robber and the incendiary struck hands, and are united in joint raid against the South."

Robert Barnwell Rhett, a Charleston newspaper editor who had been pushing for the South to secede for years and to form a "Confederacy of slave holding states" made a speech to South Carolinians where he charged: "For the last forty years, the taxes laid by Congress of the United States have been laid with a view of subserving the interests of the North. The people of the South have been taxed by duties on imports, not for revenue, but for an object inconsistent with revenue—to promote, by prohibitions, Northern interests in the production of their mines and manufacturers."

New York City's merchants shared the South's anger at what the bill would do to New York's import and export business. With Southern trade already off by 50 percent with New York due to the Southern recession, the city's merchants feared the Morrill Tariff could send New York into the same recession early in 1861.

The *Journal of Commerce* laid out in print what most of the merchants were thinking, "The merchants are waking up to the fact that a tariff bill is hanging over them and likely to prove disastrous to their trade."

"The passage of the Bill in its present shape will bring ruin and disaster upon a very large class of merchants," wrote an importer in the *Herald*.

Already too late with their protests since the bill had overwhelming support among the legislators in New England and the western states (today's Midwest), New York's merchants vainly explained to anyone who would listen that the Morrill bill would be bad for New York. It would double the cost of some goods coming into the port, which meant customers would stop buying imported goods from New York merchants. It would be complicated and time-consuming to enforce, as separate items in an entire shipment would be taxed at varying rates. Just sorting through what tariff rates applied to which goods would take days to accomplish, which meant ships would be backed up in the harbor waiting to unload on the city's wharves.

The New York City Chamber of Commerce predicted that "the commerce of the City of New York would shrink into one-tenth of its present compass. . . . This measure is known to be obnoxious to the Southern States. To pass it when a part of them are not represented in Congress could scarcely fail to widen the existing breach and present a new and serious obstacle to reconciliation."

After Lincoln was elected, the entire delegation of Southern senators (with the exception of Senator Andrew Johnson of Tennessee) and representatives walked out of Congress early in 1861. With a Senate made up entirely of Northerners, the Morrill Tariff sailed through with no opposition. Ironically, the bill was signed into law, not by Republican Lincoln who had made signing it a campaign promise, but by outgoing Democrat James Buchanan, whose Pennsylvania congressional delegation had been strong supporters.

As important as the problem of the impending Morrill Tariff was for New York City's merchants, it paled beside the election of Abraham Lincoln as president.

Chapter 6

"The City of New York Belongs
to the South"

Until Lincoln was actually nominated, the idea that an unpopular, one-term congressman from Illinois who last held office in 1847, and who had been defeated for a United States Senate seat in 1858, might be elected president of the United States had not crossed the minds of New York City's merchants, bankers, industrialists, and millionaires. They never thought that a politician who aroused the South's suspicions so much about the future of slavery could ever get his party's nod to run for high office.

What the New Yorkers did not count on was the nation's rapidly changing political landscape from the fall of 1859 to the summer of 1860.

"The City of New York belongs almost as much to the South as to the North," observed the editor of the *New York Post* in the spring of 1860, just three months before Lincoln would win the Republican nomination for president.

The businessmen were not as much caught off guard politically during this national election as they were simply disgusted with the machinations and backstabbing games played by both the Democrats and Republicans down in Washington City. For the previous five months, the U.S. House of Representatives had been without a Speaker of the House thanks to a coalition of Democratic representatives who joined with some minor parties to stave off electing a Republican to the post. The House had been paralyzed in passing any legislation that the business community wanted.

On October 20, 1859, New York City's merchants were reminded of how outside events could affect their businesses when abolitionist John Brown briefly captured Harpers Ferry, Virginia (now West Virginia). Brown, a New York State native, had hoped to launch a Southern slave revolt, but he was captured and executed after a swiftly conducted trial.

New York City's merchants, supremely conscious of not offending their best customers, reacted quickly through the Democratic Vigilant Association. The association not only condemned the violence at Harpers Ferry but financed their own investigation of it to prove to Southerners that they still had a friend in New York City.

The South was not impressed. When Republicans won a number of statewide political offices in a November 1859 election, Southern vote counters noted that a majority of residents in New York City had not voted at all. In the eyes of Southern planters and newspaper editors, this lackadaisical attitude of New York City's merchants toward keeping the Republicans in check in their own state signified enmity toward the South.

"New York City, the emporium of trade, the city supported by Southern productions, her merchants enriched by our traffic, her vessels freighted with our produce, the grass kept growing from her streets, and the bats and owls from her warehouses by Southern trade, has not even made a decent effort to defeat her enemies, as well as those of the South," wrote the editor of the *Richmond Enquirer.*

Some Southern newspapers and magazines began to compile blacklists of merchants they felt were not doing enough to protect the South. Other irritated Southerners began canceling long-standing orders with Northern merchants and warning their personal friends in the city that "the trade of Southern merchants and planters in New York will be greatly diminished in the future if not entirely clogged."

Desperate to show how much they cared, New York City's businessmen held a meeting at the Academy of Music attended by several thousand men on December 19, 1859. One of the evening's speakers was former U.S. district attorney for the Southern District of New York Charles O'Conor. O'Conor was not at all shy about giving his opinion on slavery. He was often interrupted by applause when he made comments such as these:

> I maintain that it is ordained by Nature—that it is a necessity of both races. . . . As to the Negro, we allowed him to live under the shadow and protection of our laws. We gave him, as we were bound to give him, protection; but we denied to him political rights or the power to govern. . . . To that condition the negro is assigned by nature. . . . Experience has shown that his class cannot prosper save in warm climates. In a cold or even a moderately cold climate he soon perishes; in the extremely warm regions his race is perpetuated, and with proper guardianship, may prosper. He has ample strength, and is competent to labor, but nature denies to him either the intellect to govern or the willingness to work.

O'Conor's language may have been blunt and breathtaking in its racist views on the intellectual capacities of black people, but the opening sentence of the final paragraph of his speech made clear the purpose of the meeting: "Let our brethren of the South alone, gentlemen." Though a few people had hissed O'Conor's racist statements, sustained cheering followed the end of his speech.

The meeting may have mollified some Southerners when they read newspapers accounts, but others reminded each other that forty cents of every dollar of cotton sales stayed in New York. The New Yorkers were only friends with Southerners because they needed their trade.

New York City's merchants missed an opportunity to end the future career of Lincoln when he gave his most famous election campaign speech at New York City's Cooper Union hall on February 27, 1860.

Coming to New York City more than two months before the Republican nomination, Lincoln was still considered a regional candidate from the distant western state of Illinois. His chances of winning the nomination from better-known politicians such as Senators William H. Seward of New York and Salmon Chase of Ohio were long. Still, Lincoln was the man running for president so many New Yorkers turned out to hear what he had to say.

If many or any Democratic merchants attended that night, they did not try to interrupt Lincoln's speech that concentrated on how the federal government should prevent slavery from being introduced into the western territories. Lincoln tried to mollify the South by emphasizing that the federal government had no right to interfere with slavery as it existed in the Southern states. He even insulted John Brown, the hero of the abolition movement.

"It [Brown's attempt to capture the U.S. arsenal at Harpers Ferry] was not a slave insurrection. It was an attempt by white men to get up a revolt among slaves in which the slaves refused to participate. In fact, it was so absurd, that the slaves, with all their ignorance, saw plainly enough that it could not succeed," said Lincoln.

Lincoln tried to both reassure the South and reward the abolitionists in the same paragraph when he quoted Southerners as saying:

"Leave us alone. Do nothing with us, and say what you please about slavery. But we do let them alone—have never disturbed them. . . . Wrong as we think Slavery is, we can yet afford to leave it alone where it is because that much is due to the necessity arising from its actual presence in the nation, but can we, while our votes can prevent it, allow it to spread to the National Territories, and to overrun us here in the Free States?"

Lincoln also bolstered the mood of the attending Republicans by telling them that the party was the wave of the future.

After Lincoln finished the speech, which was often interrupted by applause, he was given three rousing cheers. The *New York Tribune*'s editor, Horace Greeley, came onto the stage after Lincoln finished. According to the *New York Times*' reporting on the speech, Greeley "came forward and assured the audience that the orator of the occasion was a specimen of what free labor and free expression of ideas could produce."

Curiously, that single article in the *Times* was the only time the newspaper, still yet to be recognized as the city's premier newspaper, would mention the Cooper Union speech over the coming weeks. Lincoln himself was not mentioned in a *Times* headline again until he won the Republican nomination in May.

Greeley's *Tribune* coverage started by calling the speech "one of the happiest and most convincing political arguments ever made in this City and was addressed to a crowded and most appreciative audience. . . . The vast assemblage frequently rang with cheers and shouts of applause, which were prolonged and intensified at the close. . . . No man ever before made such an impression on his first appeal to a New York audience."

The *New York Evening News* gushed that "the speaker places the Republican party on the very ground occupied by the framers of our constitution and fathers of our republic, strikes us as particularly forcible."

Even the Democratic newspaper, *New York Herald*, reported positively on the speech, though it also pointed out that Cooper Union was only three quarters filled, perhaps because the organizers charged each person twenty-five cents to attend.

Word of Lincoln's positive reception by New York Republicans and the enthusiastic reporting of his speech by the pro-Republican newspapers spread to western newspapers. Because he had been warmly welcomed in the nation's largest city, the failed congressman and defeated senatorial candidate from Illinois was suddenly a viable presidential candidate even though he was running against better-known candidates like Seward and Chase.

By the summer of 1860, when Lincoln was the candidate, the political landscape for the South and its friends in New York City had deteriorated even more from the previous summer.

In April 1860, the city's probusiness mayor, Fernando Wood, had gone to the Democratic National Convention in Charleston, South Carolina, thinking that his pro-South business stance could result in his nomination as vice president to the expected presidential candidacy of Senator Stephen A. Douglas from Illinois. Instead, the Southern Democrats, who Wood thought would back him, walked out of the convention when the Northern delegates firmly refused to support allowing slavery in the western territories.

In June, dual Democratic conventions resulted in the Northern Democrats nominating Douglas for president and the Southern Democrats nominating John C. Breckinridge, the current U.S. vice president in the Buchanan administration.

As if that were not already complicated and contentious enough for the American people, remnants of the old Whig Party formed the Constitution Party, which nominated former U.S. senator John Bell from Tennessee for president.

What in February had shaped up to be an expected showdown between two candidates had grown by June to be a showdown between four candidates.

Complicating the political strategy of the city's merchants even more was the problem that both of the state's United States Senators, Preston King and William Seward, were Republicans. Neither was from New York City. Neither had close ties to the city. Seward, in fact, was an outspoken critic of the merchants' involvement in the slave trade. For their part, the merchants were constantly accusing Seward of leading the nation down the path of disunion if he continued to talk of freeing the South's slaves.

Neutralizing King and Seward was a problem because there were at least three distinct political groups among the Democrats that had only one thing in common—they were anti-Republican.

Over the summer, the merchants settled on promoting a fusion ticket, a complicated agreement that relied on all the anti-Republican groups to agree that their supporters would vote for a single slate of electors who would split their electoral college votes among Douglas, Breckinridge, and Bell. Bell, little known outside of Tennessee, soon agreed to throw his support over to Douglas in New York State, but Breckinridge's and Douglas's electors squabbled with each other right up until the November election. The disagreements kept the fusion campaign from getting traction and, more importantly, raising campaign money from the wealthy merchants.

Not all the city's prominent businessmen were convinced that a fusion ticket was good for the state—or even something that they entirely understood. George Templeton Strong, a New York City lawyer who kept a detailed diary of his life, recorded his thoughts on September 14, 1860, on the presidential campaign. Strong's own rambling diary entry indicates just how confusing trying to promote a fusion to the public could be.

Last night's Republican turnout is the town talk. . . . Certainly, all the vigor and enthusiasm of this campaign are thus far confined to the Republicans. . . . Their adversaries are disorganized, divided, and discouraged. In this state, there is a fusion (worse confounded) of the Union Party (Bell and Everett) with the Squatter Sovereignty Democrats (Douglas and Johnson), and a sort of feebly coherent composite electoral ticket. They are trying to coalesce with the Breckinridge people so as to include in one ticket all the anti-Lincoln elements. But that seems as yet beyond the powers of political synthesis.

I don't know clearly on which side to count myself in. I've a leaning toward the Republicans. But I shall be sorry to see Seward and Thurlow Weed with their tail of profligate lobby men promoted from Albany to Washington. I do not like the tone of the Republican papers and party in regard to the John Brown business of last fall, and I do not think rail-splitting in early life a guarantee of fitness for the presidency.

I could vote for Bell and Mr. Orator Everett. But I can't support them in their partnership with Douglas, the little giant, for I hold the little giant to be a mere demagogue. As to Breckinridge, the ultra Southern candidate, I renounce and abhor him and his party. He represents the most cruel, blind, unreasoning, cowardly, absolute despotism that now disgraces the earth.

Strong's diary entry demonstrated the Republican strategy to overcome the potential huge vote of New York City. The Republicans wanted to convince some independent-minded city residents and the rest of New York State's voters that a fusion vote forced people to vote for someone they did not like. Sometimes without any subtlety, the Republicans also wanted New York State voters to believe that the city's power mongers did not have the rest of the state's interests in mind when they came up with the idea of a fusion vote.

"There is no virtue in Pearl Street, in Wall Street, in Court Street, in Chestnut Street, in any street of great commercial cities," said New York's own senator, William Seward, when he was campaigning for Lincoln in Madison, Wisconsin.

Upstate New York newspapers followed the same reasoning as Seward. The editors could not resist getting in a few digs at their state's largest city.

The *Rochester Union* suggested: "Manhattan Island does not comprise quite all there is of the State of New York. The Democracy of the rural districts have an idea that they and their principles should be consulted as well as the merchants and millionaires of New York City."

Even as late as the summer of 1860, the merchants and industrialists still had hope that Lincoln could be stopped. Some of the wealthiest, most powerful men in the city met in the home of August Belmont early in August 1860 to figure out what else their money could do to prevent Lincoln's election. They were determined to "save the federal Union from the calamities which would become the inevitable consequences of the election of Lincoln and Hamlin."

August Belmont, a former chairman of the Democratic Party, immigrated to New York City from what is now Germany when he was twenty-five years old in order to take care of the Rothschild banking interests. One of his favorite ideas was buying Cuba so that it could be admitted into the Union as a slave state. During the 1860 campaign, Belmont threw his support to Douglas and remained committed against the Republicans. In a speech at Cooper Union in October 1860, Belmont said that Republicans held "principles incompatible with the sacred obligations of the Constitution and arrayed in open and unrelenting hostility against the property and the institutions of the fair portions of our common country."

William B. Astor, owner of the Astor House hotel, which his father had built, was one of the largest landowners in New York City, holding title to more than seven hundred houses on Manhattan. He was also one of the city's most generous philanthropists, donating money to build and stock the Astor library, the city's leading research library in the 1850s. Eventually, it would merge with two other collections to form the New York Public Library.

Erastus Corning was a rarity among the other merchants. Though his fortune was tied up in New York City businesses, he spent most of his time in his hometown of Albany. Over the course of several decades, he had made a fortune by expanding his hardware business into holdings in an iron foundry. Most of his fortune grew from his early involvement in chartering railroads, including the New York Central, which grew into the largest corporation in the nation.

But by October, just days before the election, some merchants and bankers, John Jacob Astor among them, had switched sides. They signed letters to each other that they would reluctantly vote for Lincoln in order to elect a clear winner as president rather than have the U.S. House of Representatives select a new president. Some Republicans, seeing the crack in the merchant ranks, made speeches insisting that Lincoln had no intention of calling for the abolition of slavery. Others held firm.

Four days before the election, Belmont sent a letter to the city's businessmen in which he made a prediction: "The election of Lincoln to the presidential chair must prove the forerunner of a dissolution of this confederacy [meaning the Union] amidst the horrors of civil strife and bloodshed."

To help convince them to vote Democrat on November 6, most merchants gave their clerks the day off with strong hints as to how their bosses would vote and how employees were expected to follow that lead.

The merchants were successful in their strategy of convincing city residents to vote against Lincoln. Douglas, the fusion candidate, received 62,482 votes to Lincoln's 33,290 votes. But the merchants had focused their get-out-the-vote campaign entirely on their own city and not the rest of New York State. The final vote count for New York State was Lincoln 362,646 and Douglas 312,510. The upstate counties of New York, far from Manhattan, had all come out for Lincoln.

The *New York Times*, making no mention of the fact that Lincoln lost the city by nearly two to one, claimed that it was New York State that won the nation for Lincoln: "It has been universally conceded that the issue lay with New York—and New York casts her vote for Lincoln. . . . The contest, on the part of the Republicans, has been throughout one of principle; on the part of their opponents it has been waged almost exclusively on the basis of fear."

With the election of Lincoln, few in the North doubted that the Southern states would carry out their threat to leave the Union. New York City's merchants were in instant, deep trouble, and they knew it.

Within days of Lincoln's election, Southern newspapers were reporting laws were being introduced in Southern legislatures to halt any debt repayments owed to Northern creditors. The New York Chamber of Commerce estimated that Southerners owed Northern merchants more than $200 million, and $150 million of that was owed to New Yorkers.

The merchants scrambled to write letters and resolutions to their Southern friends insisting that Manhattan was still a friend of the South and the city would do all it could to neutralize the Republican administration.

At the same time as they were pleading with Southerners to give them time, the merchants, most of whom had campaigned against Lincoln, were pleading with the Congress and president-elect to "do everything short of the sacrifice of a vital principle of the government" to answer the concerns of the South.

On January 29, 1861, a delegation of New York's businessmen arrived in Washington with a plan for peace that had been signed by more than 40,000 businessmen, almost five percent of the entire population of the city of more than 800,000. The plan excluded slavery above the 36th parallel (roughly the line between Virginia and North Carolina extended out to California) and would allow future states below that line to decide by vote if they wanted slavery while protecting slavery where it already existed.

The new Congress was not in a mood to compromise with anyone, and the New Yorkers returned to the city in a fit of depression.

"The refusal at Washington to concede costs us millions daily.

It is opening up our nation to every conceivable mischief and danger," said A. T. Stewart.

Dozens of merchants began closing their shops, convinced that the combination of angry Southerners refusing to pay their bills or order new merchandise and the coming high costs of the Morrill Tariff would ruin them. Mayor Wood's suggestion that New York turn itself into a free city, separate from both New York State and the Union, got fresh attention from merchants.

"We learn that in consequence of the dissatisfaction occasioned by the injurious and inexplicable Morrill tariff, there has been an association, consisting of prominent merchants, citizens, etc. started in this city, for the purpose of uniting Staten Island, Long Island, and Manhattan Island, and incorporating the three into a free city," wrote Greeley of the *Tribune* on April 8, 1861.

This plan would be forgotten by the time the boroughs of New York consolidated into one city in 1898, but the idea first came up in 1861 as a means of aligning the city with the emerging Confederacy.

Dark rumors even swept the city that a force of New Yorkers planned to seize Fort Hamilton and Fort Lafayette, two forts guarding the entrance to New York's harbor, and turn them over to Southern sympathizers. Federal authorities were so concerned about the wild story that they warned the post commanders to be vigilant.

To the dismay of Southerners, they soon learned that New Yorkers' sentiments could quickly change. When word reached New York that the Confederates had fired on Fort Sumter on April 12, 1861, talk among the merchants of finding a peaceful resolution with the South ended. On April 19, the Chamber of Commerce held a meeting, including all the merchants and industrialists who had spent the last thirty years courting the South and the last two years begging the federal government to find a way to protect slavery.

"We are either for the country, or we are for its enemies," said Chamber president Pelatiah Perit.

The warm, close relationship New York City had maintained with the South for more than a half century had ended. Now it was time for war.

Chapter 7

"That Which Comes Easy Goes Easy"

For years before the war, New York City's reputation was probusiness, pro-South, proslavery, pro-compromise, pro-free trade, and anti-Republican. When Lincoln emerged as a viable presidential candidate, the city also became anti-Lincoln. The city's political leaders, bankers, merchants, and industrialists did not want anything or anyone, particularly a man most suspected was an abolitionist in disguise, to rock the boat when it came to the city's relationship with the South.

When word reached the city about the Confederate bombardment of Fort Sumter on April 12, 1861, the city's political and business leaders abruptly about-faced. After a symbol of the power of the United States was attacked, they immediately switched their allegiances from the South to the Union. They now wanted federal protection of the city's war-related industries. They wanted the South defeated. They did not necessarily want Lincoln as their president, but the nation and the rest of their own state had elected him. The city's businessmen determined that they would try to work with anyone who had the potential of bringing them business.

They had no choice. Now that war had been declared, their trade with the South was wrecked.

New York City's businessmen immediately stopped promoting

the South and started promoting the Union. Within a few days of the attack on Fort Sumter, the city's businessmen had pledged tens of thousands of dollars to equip fully the city's Seventh New York Militia Regiment so that it could march off within the week to defend Washington City from any attack that might come from Virginia. The New York City regiment, made up of so many young protégé bankers and assistant managers that it was called "The Silk Stocking Regiment," was one of the first regiments to respond to President Lincoln's national call for seventy-five thousand volunteers to put down the Southern "rebellion." The New Yorkers wore the same natty gray uniforms they had always worn during drill.

By June, before any major battles had been fought, the Seventh New York Militia was back home in the city and mustered out. It would be called up two more times, but powerful men with connections made sure the regiment was kept from having to do any real fighting. Those bankers were just too valuable to the city's elite to send to war.

On April 20, just one day after the Seventh Regiment had boarded a ferry to take them south, a huge crowd of New Yorkers, variously reported at between 100,000 and 250,000, jammed Union Square to rally for the Union cause. After watching the natty Seventh Regiment march away and after attending the rally in Union Square, patriotic young men jammed the recruitment centers that sprang up around the city.

Recent immigrants from eastern and western Europe, who had been unable to find jobs in the depressed economy, jumped at the chance to earn eleven dollars a month for what they assumed would be only a few months' service before returning to the city as war heroes. Many of the German, Polish, Hungarian, and Italian recruits did not even speak English, so they were formed into regiments with other immigrants from the same country and commanded by bilingual officers.

Among the most famous of the city's immigrant regiments was the Sixty-ninth New York Volunteers, made up of Irish immigrants who joined several other Irish immigrant regiments from New York,

Pennsylvania, and Massachusetts to form the Irish Brigade. The Irish, at the low end of the city's status ranking, did not have the political connections of the Seventh New York Militia to protect them from overuse on the battlefield. The Irish Brigade, numbering five thousand at its largest, would take part in so many battles and would lose so many men that it was dissolved in 1864 with its survivors being transferred into other units.

In the spring of 1861, before any fighting had actually taken place, the lure of adventure also sounded good to more than 1,100 of the city's 4,000 volunteer firefighters. They joined the Eleventh Regiment New York Volunteers. So many trained firefighters joined the army that lesser-trained men, once rejected by the volunteer companies for being unsavory characters, were given slots in the city's fire department.

The Eleventh Regiment, also known as the First Fire Zouaves, first won fame not on the battlefield but in downtown Washington when they put out a fire at the Willard Hotel while Washington's own firefighters slept off a typical night of drinking. They won even more fame when its commander, Colonel Elmer Ellsworth, was killed ripping down a Confederate flag flying from an Alexandria, Virginia, hotel, just days after arriving in Washington. One of the Zouaves killed Ellsworth's attacker, making both him and Ellsworth instant heroes back in New York City.

But while the Fire Zouaves proved to be good firefighters, they proved less than effective soldiers. Routed by Virginia's Black Horse Cavalry at the Battle of First Manassas in July 1861, many in the regiment deserted and headed back to New York where they hoped they could brawl their way back into the ranks of the volunteer firefighters. The Eleventh was never again a fighting force.

The Seventy-third New York Regiment, also raised in 1861 from among the Bowery fire stations and called the Second Fire Zouaves, proved to be better soldiers. So too were the Fifth New York and the Ninth New York, both organized as Zouaves and recruited from New York City. All three of these regiments, made up of working-class men, would fight in many more battles and would prove more valuable to the Union army than the wealthy dandies in the Silk

Stocking Regiment, which first won the city's admiration. More of these working-class soldiers would also die.

More than 475,000 men from New York State eventually joined the Union army, the largest contribution of troops by any Union state. That figure was also three times the number of North Carolinians who served, the Confederate state with the highest enlistment figures. By the end of the war, more than 50,000 New Yorkers would be dead from war injuries and sickness.

While the human cost of the war could not be ignored, the city's businessmen were pleasantly surprised at its impact on them. They had needlessly worried that their businesses would sink into a depression once trade with the South was cut off. Instead, a wartime economy swept over the city, spreading wealth and power over the same men who had enjoyed the same during the heyday of the South.

While the cotton exports to England understandably dried up, failure of wheat crops in Europe created a huge market for that crop, raised in a number of states, to be exported from New York.

The need for ships to enforce the blockade of Confederate ports created a building boom for the city's shipyards, as well as that of neighboring Brooklyn, where the ironclad USS *Monitor* was launched in less than ninety days from model to launch. The demand for shallow draft boats to patrol Southern coastal waters and rivers was so great that some New York City double-ended ferries were pressed into service without even modifying them for military service.

The city's iron works shifted from manufacturing iron for all types of civilian industries to a higher grade of iron used for cannons. Even manufacturers of fine, delicate carriages, whose primary customers still lived on Fifth Avenue, hired more workers to build big, bulky, ugly wooden ambulances for the Union army.

Clothing merchants like A. T. Stewart, who had sold clothes through his department stores, grew even richer when they fulfilled military contracts to provide uniforms. Stewart continued to sell clothes to the wealthy in his department stores, including one that he built during the war that was a block long on Broadway between 9th and 10th streets. One of Stewart's best customers was First Lady Mary Todd Lincoln who spent more than $20,000 with Stewart.

Mrs. Lincoln so overspent her clothing and furnishings budget that she begged for a bailout from Congress and a promise from them not to tell her husband what she had done. Lincoln found out and upbraided his wife for spending the nation's money on frivolous things when its sons were at war with each other.

The business boom proved some of the city's elite could not resist cutting corners. Early in 1861, Brooks Brothers, the clothier of choice for the city's business class from its store on Broadway and Grand Street, won a government contract to provide uniforms for the United States Army. Instead of sticking to the high standards of sewing and materials their wealthy clients expected in their own fancy suits, Brooks Brothers substituted a type of reclaimed rag cloth mixed with glue they called shoddy when manufacturing its Union army uniforms. While the uniforms looked fine when delivered and inspected in the sunshine, the shoddy cloth melted when worn in a rainstorm.

By July 1861, news of how the high-society Brooks Brothers had taken advantage of battlefield-bound soldiers from New York was all over the newspapers. The word shoddy, the name Brooks Brothers gave their new miracle cloth, entered the American lexicon as a word meaning inferior quality.

No class of people benefited from the war more than New York City's bankers, the same men who had benefited for more than fifty years by loaning money to Southern cotton planters. Since the federal government's main source of income, taxes collected on the export of cotton and import of goods heading south, had disappeared, Washington had little choice but to turn to the bankers to figure out how to finance the war.

Over the course of the war, the government came to the bankers to issue bonds and take out loans. Lincoln and Congress also borrowed money from average citizens by issuing war bonds. These could be bought in small enough denominations that the middle-aged middle class considered it their patriotic duty to finance the war their sons were fighting.

Lincoln and Congress held no grudges against the men who had been working against them before war was declared. Some of the city's merchants went on to play valuable roles in the war effort, though they remained Democrats.

August Belmont, who stubbornly lobbied for Southern concessions right up until Fort Sumter, immediately raised and equipped a German regiment for the Union. He then volunteered for overseas missions to dissuade European bankers from financing the Confederacy. Ironically, one of Belmont's relatives by marriage, John Slidell of Louisiana, was taken off a British ship by a zealous Union naval officer when Slidell was on his way to Europe to do his own lobbying for the Confederacy. The Union navy's boarding of a British ship at sea, known as The Mason-Slidell Affair, was a major international incident that Lincoln had to defuse to keep England from siding with the Confederacy.

Erastus Corning, a hardware merchant, was expanding into iron production and had gone to Washington in February 1861 with a delegation of merchants to urge the government to concede to the South's demands that slavery be untouched in the existing slave states. Within weeks of failing to convince the government of that plan, Corning's ironworks company was selected to manufacture the iron deck plates and side skirt for the USS *Monitor*.

The most successful of Lincoln's former opponents from New York City must have been John A. Dix, a Democrat who had served as a United States Senator, secretary of the treasury, and New York's governor. Dix had also been one of the organizers of the fusion ticket that pushed Douglas for president. Despite that history, Lincoln appointed Dix a general early in the war. Dix returned the favor by arresting most of the Maryland legislature so it could not vote on a bill that would have taken that state out of the Union.

The war further enriched the already established merchants. It also created a new class of wealthy men.

"Things here at the North are in a great state of prosperity. . . . The large amount expended by the government has given great activity to everything and but for the daily news from the War in the papers and the crowds of soldiers you see about the streets, you would have no idea of any war," mining industrialist William E. Dodge wrote a friend.

The existing old wealthy class did not welcome this new wealthy class with open arms. Instead, they and the newspapers proclaimed the newcomers war profiteers and dubbed them the "shoddy aristocracy," hinting that the word first applied to the low-quality Brooks Brothers uniforms could also be applied to businessmen whose ethical standards were lacking when compared to the more established businessmen.

Harper's Magazine sneered at the new rich in an 1864 article: "The old proverb says: 'That which comes easy goes easy.' The suddenly enriched contractors, speculators, and stock-jobbers illustrate its truth. They are spending money with a profusion never before witnessed in our country, at no time remarkable for its frugality. Our great houses are not big enough for them. They pull them down and build greater."

By 1863, the average workingman, particularly the Irish immigrant who was at the lowest rung of New York society, had had enough of both the old rich and the new rich.

The attitudes of average New Yorkers about the war had changed since that huge Union Square rally in April 1861. The short war Lincoln and the army recruiters promised had been a lie. Instead, New Yorkers had been ground up in battles like First and Second Manassas, Sharpsburg, and Fredericksburg. Then in the fall of 1862, Lincoln announced that he would free the Southern slaves on January 1, 1863, something that he had previously told the nation he had no constitutional right to do and no personal intention of doing.

In a letter to Horace Greeley of the *Tribune* on August 22, 1862, Lincoln said:

My paramount object in this struggle is to save the Union, and is not either to save or to destroy slavery. If I could save the Union without freeing any slave I would do it, and if I could save it by freeing all the slaves I would do it; and if I could save it by freeing some and leaving others alone I would also do that. What I do about slavery, and the colored race, I do because I believe it helps to save the Union.

Lincoln's unexpected action of announcing the freeing of Southern slaves while leaving in bondage slaves owned by Northern-loyal Border States shook up the political landscape. Some Peace Democrats were swept into power, including Horatio Seymour, who replaced a Republican governor who had helped Lincoln win the state. The city's secessionist former mayor Fernando Wood won a seat in Congress. While Lincoln's political tactic of changing the war's goals from preserving the Union to freeing Southern slaves had given the war a new purpose, his actions once again alienated New Yorkers.

Even August Belmont, who had gone to Europe on a mission for Lincoln in 1861 to convince England and France to ignore the Confederacy, once again turned against Lincoln and the Union. Belmont formed yet another businessman's committee that wrote tracts saying freeing the slaves would forever damage the South's economy, even when it came back into the Union. Belmont quietly began looking for a Democrat he thought would be a strong candidate to run against Lincoln in 1864.

Further irritating the workingman of New York City that summer of 1863 was the implementation of the National Conscription Act, which called for a draft lottery for all men between the ages of 20 to 35.

The purpose of the act seemed fair enough—fill the ranks after the devastating losses the Union army had suffered the previous summer, fall, and winter. But closer reading of the law showed that it reemphasized what Lincoln's critics had been saying for two years— that he was waging a rich man's war and a poor man's fight. The law allowed for anyone who fell into that age range to pay a fee of three hundred dollars to get out of the draft. Alternately, the draft-eligible man whose number had come up in the lottery could hire his own substitute to go into the army in his place.

Few workingmen had the luxury of three hundred dollars sitting in a bank account, so they were immediately subject to the draft. The wealthy of New York could easily pay the fees to keep their sons cozy at home on Fifth Avenue. The inequity in how young men were to be drafted into service was obvious to everyone, particularly the new immigrants who arrived without a dollar in their pockets.

One group of men found out that the law specifically included their profession in the draft. They were volunteer firefighters. Earlier laws had singled firefighters out as a class of municipal workers who were too valuable to the city to be used to fill military ranks. It had been understood for two years that firefighters were exempt from all military duty unless they specifically volunteered as had the two regiments of Fire Zouaves early in the war. Now they too would be eligible for the draft unless each man paid three hundred dollars to the federal government to stay out of it.

News of the Union's victory at Gettysburg filtered into the city on July 4, 1863. The good news of the Confederacy being stopped in its tracks just two hundred miles to the west was tempered by the bad news that thousands of Union soldiers had been killed in accomplishing that goal. Within a few days, the casualty lists of the dead, wounded, and captured New Yorkers arrived and were posted in public places.

On July 13, 1863, just over one week after the Union victory at Gettysburg, the first draft lottery to select about two thousand young men to serve from New York City was held on the northern edge of the city at a draft office located at Third Avenue and 47th Street. Wary draft organizers had intentionally held the lottery far away from the city's population center to lessen the chance that the men who were drafted would be in the audience to hear their own names. The draft organizers figured there would be less chance of protests or resistance if the draftees read their names in the newspaper after the fact rather than heard their names read aloud.

The city's draft quota of more than 2,000 men took so long to draw from a drum that only 1,200 had been drawn on the first day. When the draft officials returned the next day to draw the final 800 names, a large protest crowd was waiting for them. Mingling with the crowd was the famed Black Joe Engine Company 33. The firefighters had boldly decided over the weekend that they would confiscate the records of the first draft to destroy the slips of paper with the names of anyone from their fire company who had been drawn.

This was more than a protest of U.S. government policies. These average citizens of New York City were challenging the power of the

federal government to draft them and their friends. They were looking for a fight with the U.S. government. Black Joe started the ruckus
that would become known as the New York City Draft Riots.

The firefighters drove off the police who had been assigned to protect the draft officials and then set the building on fire. When other
firefighters arrived to put out the fire, Black Joe firefighters refused to
let them fight the fire at the draft office.

A small unit of veteran soldiers tried to disperse the growing
crowd, but they were swept aside. Then the city's police superintendent John Kennedy arrived, thinking his authority would be enough
to impress the draftees. Kennedy waded into the crowd calling for
them to disperse. Instead of listening to the city's top police official,
they beat him until he was almost unrecognizable. Other squads of
police were beaten when they tried to stop the flow of the crowd. A
full-scale riot now erupted that would last for three days.

Virtually every street and avenue from 47th Street south was
roamed by the crowd of people who first attacked what they considered Republican targets. When not enough of those kinds of targets could be found in the Democratic city, the crowd focused on the
homes of the wealthy who had moved in recent years from downtown
to Fifth Avenue.

Diarist George Templeton Strong, the wealthy lawyer, had no
doubt who the rioters were, though it is unlikely he had ever met
any of them. "The rabble was perfectly homogeneous. Every brute in
the drove was pure Celtic—either hod-carrier or pure loafer," wrote
Strong, who also noted that the mob included Irish women whom he
described as "low Irish women, stalwart young vixens and withered
old hags egging their men on to mischief."

While Republicans and wealthy whites had been the first targets
of the rioters, the chance meeting of some blacks turned it into a race
riot. The crowd attacked the Colored Orphan Asylum on Fifth Avenue and 43rd Street, screaming, "Burn the niggers' nest!" Random
black men walking the streets were attacked. They hung some from
lampposts and their bodies set afire.

That night the rioters moved farther downtown to target the offices of the *New York Tribune* and *New York Times*. Putting aside

the old saying that "the pen is mightier than the sword," the owner of the *Times,* Henry Raymond, joined with stockholders and employees to man three Gatling guns (six-barreled forerunners of machine guns) that they had appropriated from one of New York's armories.

Seeing that the *Times* owners were taking advantage of the Second Amendment to keep and bear arms in defense of one's self and property and were quite prepared to mow down scores of readers with a few cranks of a brass handle, the mob wisely turned instead to the *Tribune.* Its editor, Horace Greeley, had done little more to protect his newspaper than barricade his building with bales of newsprint. The mob used the newsprint to set the building afire. Squads of police officers ferried over from Brooklyn put out the fire before it could do serious damage.

On the second day of the riot, the mobs once again concentrated on attacking the wealthy who were not affected by Lincoln's draft law. Brooks Brothers' store was sacked. The mob considered attacking Wall Street, but the sight of bank tellers standing in windows armed with rifles and bottles of acid deterred them. The mob did capture, torture, and kill Colonel Henry O'Brian, a veteran of the Eleventh New York Regiment, who had survived the Battle of First Manassas, only to die a slow, horrible death in the backyard of his own house on the Upper East Side. The crowd had recognized O'Brian from the day before when he had used a howitzer (low-trajectory cannon) to clear Second Avenue of rioters. A woman and child were killed in that incident.

The mobs, who were protesting the idea that they should join the Union army, showed remarkable talent at quickly organizing their own riotous army. They built barricades to protect their home bases, sent out scouts to find human and property targets, and organized intelligence to monitor the opposing police forces.

New York City's authorities were at a loss to figure out how to deal with their own murderous citizens. The politicians preached peaceful, nonviolent intervention as a way to quell the riots. Democrat governor Horatio Seymour rushed to the city and told the rioters that he understood their grievances. He spoke from the front steps of City Hall to the crowd of people who had spent two days murdering their fellow citizens. Seymour addressed the incredulous rioters as "My Friends" and assured them that he would do what he could to end the draft.

The merchants and their very rare allies in the press had their blood up. Raymond (the *Times* owner), the man who had been willing to kill scores of his readers and fellow citizens with three machine guns, wrote that ending the riot had a simple solution. "Crush the mob!" read the July 14 headline with Raymond endorsing Mayor George Opdyke's plan to arm and deputize volunteer policemen.

Finally, at noon on the second day of the riot, Opdyke telegraphed Washington asking for federal troops. Secretary of War Edwin Stanton rushed five regiments, about four thousand men, directly from the Gettysburg battlefield that same evening.

It took twenty-four hours before the battle-weary Union soldiers arrived in New York. During that third day, Wednesday, July 15, the mobs had been mopping up enclaves of black and Republican homes that they had missed on the previous two days. Even with the arrival of soldiers armed with rifles and sixty rounds each in their cartridge boxes, the mobs were defiant. They had faced down the city's police. They figured to do the same with the Union's soldiers. The mob was mistaken.

The Union troops, including hundreds of men from New York State, were angry that they had been fighting Confederates as volunteers for more than two years. Now here they were fighting their own kind who had refused to come onto the battlefield to help them. Led by capable officers who knew how to assault fortified positions, the soldiers attacked the rioters' barricades with the same cannons loaded with canister shot (small projectiles) that they had used against the Confederates at Gettysburg. While they had been willing to give the Confederates at Gettysburg a break a few days earlier, these Union soldiers were disinclined to take prisoners on the Upper East Side of New York City.

"Some of them [rioters] fought like incarnate fiends, and would not surrender. All such were shot on the spot," said Captain H. R. Putnam, commanding about 160 soldiers.

The arrival of the Union soldiers with their rifles and cannons finally put an end to three days of lawless rioting. A complete and thorough accounting of the death toll was never completed. Some estimates range as high as 1,100, counting victims of the rioters as well as the rioters themselves who were shot down by the military. The city's official estimate was around 100, a low figure thrown out to mask the fact that New York was ruled by mobs for more than three days.

The blame for the riots fell on the Irish Catholic laboring class, the recent immigrants who American-born whites despised. In an effort to make sure rioting did not reoccur, city officials demanded the Catholic archbishop of the city address a post-riot gathering of Irishmen. The archbishop pointedly told the gathering that he did not believe they were rioters, but he urged them to refrain from participating in any violence. Union army soldiers waited out of sight around the corner from the speech, ready to attack if the Irishmen showed any signs of continuing the violence.

The *New York Times* did not mention the Irish in its first assessment of the causes and participants. Instead, the newspaper called the riots "a conspiracy."

"The late outbreak was a deliberate plot, devised and managed by men of talent, who did not at all appear on the scene." The *Times* blamed "Copperhead leaders," including Democratic governor Seymour who it claimed made a speech "to excite passion against the National government." The *Times* further charged that there was a "well-concocted plan" to get New Yorkers to protest the draft violently, and it called for a committee to investigate the newspaper's charges that the riots were planned and carried out "by men of talent." The editors were confident they were right in their assessment even without any committee fulfilling an investigation. The Confederate newspapers seemed to hint that they, too, believed the riots were not spontaneous.

With the headline of BEGINNING OF CHAOS, the *Richmond Enquirer* described how "Riot, murder and conflagration have begun in New York City." Later, the newspaper mentioned that the riots were

This excellent outbreak [which] may be the opening scene of the inevitable revolution which is to tear to pieces that most rotten society, and leave the Northern half of the old American Union a desert of blood-soaked ashes. . . . We shall see the giant, but hollow bulk of the Yankee nation bursting into fragments, and rushing down into perdition in flames and blood. Amen."

The *Richmond Dispatch* was more circumspect, but it seemingly called for more attacks on Northern cities by people angry about the draft:

Let us have more of these outpourings—a few more great cities on the mourners' bench—some more gutting and sacking of houses, and hanging and mutilating of men. It saves the Confederate troops a deal of marching and fighting, and lops off many a dreary month of this war. The sacking and burning has been heretofore at the South. Our compliments to our Northern 'brethren,' and may they enjoy their turn.

The Confederate newspapers made it seem like some other plans to attack the North were waiting to be implemented.

THE SOUTH SEETHES

Chapter 8

"How Sad Is This Life"

The South never saw the war as civil war, defined as two warring sides trying to take over one government. All it wanted was to be independent of the rest of the United States. The Confederacy's president Jefferson Davis had no desire to occupy Washington, the capital of the Union, or sit in Abraham Lincoln's chair in the Executive Mansion. The representatives and senators sitting in the Confederate Congress did not want to occupy the same seats in the U.S. Capitol. Some of them had just left that building. Nor did any of the state judges in the South want to move up to the United States Supreme Court.

"If the Northern states . . . desire to inflict injury upon us . . . a terrible responsibility will rest upon it, and the suffering of millions will bear testimony to the folly and wickedness of our aggressors. . . . All we ask is to be left alone," said Davis in his inaugural address in Montgomery, Alabama, on February 18, 1861.

As mentioned earlier, some states had a hard time deciding sides. General John Dix, Lincoln's new friend in New York, arrested the Southern-leaning members of the Maryland state legislature to prevent them from taking the state out of the Union.

Kentucky, the home state of both Lincoln and Davis, had strong sentiments for both the Union and the Confederacy. When Lincoln sent Governor Beriah Magoffin a note requesting troops, the governor of the state where Lincoln had been born replied, "I will send not a man nor a dollar for the wicked purpose of subduing my sister Southern states." Magoffin tried on at least two occasions to hold a statewide vote on secession, but the state's Union-leaning legislators refused out of fear that the voters would approve taking the state out of the Union. Unionists eventually captured more seats in both houses of Kentucky's legislature, rendering the governor ineffective in pushing a Southern agenda. The state would still send thousands of its men to fight with the South, most notably former U.S. vice president John C. Breckinridge who became a Confederate general and later Secretary of War.

Among the units formed in Kentucky was the Second Kentucky Cavalry, recruited by John Hunt Morgan, the Lexington hemp farmer who had opposed secession and who thought well of Lincoln when he was elected in 1860. Morgan had remained a Union man right up until Lincoln's call for the volunteers to invade the other Southern states.

Though Morgan himself would never get within five hundred miles of New York City during the war, he would be on the thoughts of men operating on Manhattan Island.

If the Civil War was not a textbook definition of two sides fighting to gain control of one government, neither was it a war conducted by two armies fighting each other while protecting the civilian population. Early in the war, the Union made it clear that attacks on cities and towns were permissible.

On February 18, 1862, Colonel Rush C. Hawkins, commander of the Ninth New York Zouaves, a regiment raised from New York City, loaded his men on a tug and took them up the Chowan River in North Carolina to the town of Winton. Hawkins narrowly avoided an ambush from the bluffs above the town. The next day, an angry Hawkins returned to Winton over a land route and burned and sacked the town. This was the first instance of the war when Union soldiers attacked civilians and private property.

By the next year, Union attacks on the civilian populations of towns and cities had become common. At first, the Union army attacked towns that had some kind of military value.

In the spring of 1863, Vicksburg, Mississippi, a town of five thousand located on high bluffs above the Mississippi River, was the last place on the river held by the Confederates. With their heavy guns pointing down on the river, the Confederates held up Union river traffic that normally could have gone all the way to New Orleans, which had been captured a year earlier. Vicksburg had to be captured.

In early May 1863, the army of General Ulysses S. Grant twice attacked the town's military defenses. Frustrated and angry that his men had failed to breach the Confederate defenses, Grant settled on a strategy of shelling the town to force both the army and the civilians into submission. In two months, nearly fifty thousand artillery shells were thrown into the town.

The civilians in Vicksburg suffered from the constant shelling. Most abandoned their houses, which made easy targets for Federal artillery, and moved into caves that they dug in the hillsides. When shelling destroyed the wells, the civilians resorted to sopping up rainwater from shell holes and squeezing the mud through muslin to strain it. When the beef supply ran out, they ate mules. When the mules ran out, they ate dogs. When the dogs ran out, they ate rats.

Vicksburg's civilians came to expect death, though they also kept a sense of humor about their plight. One wag wrote a song called "Listen to the Parrott (a type of cannon) Shells" that was sung to the popular tune of "Listen to the Mockingbird."

"How very sad is this life in Vicksburg. I endeavored by constant prayer to prepare myself for the sudden death I was almost certain awaited me," wrote one woman who then described the sound of a Union artillery shell descending toward her. "The noise became more deafening; the air was full of the rushing sound; pain darted through my temples; my ears were full of the confusing noise; and, as it exploded, the report flashed through my head like an electric shock, leaving me in a quiet state of terror."

Finally, on July 4, 1863, the Confederate commander of Vicksburg, Philadelphia-born John C. Pemberton surrendered his 30,000-man army, ending the siege. When Lincoln heard what happened, he remarked that "The Father of Waters [the Mississippi River] now flows unvexed to the sea." Lincoln made no mention of the months-long suffering of the civilians who had been targeted by his army.

Emboldened by its success at Vicksburg, the Union army threatened to start shelling Charleston, South Carolina. On August 21, 1863, the Union commander of the region, General Quincy Gilmore, sent a note to Confederate General P. G. T. Beauregard demanding the immediate surrender within four hours or the city would be shelled.

Beauregard replied:

> Among nations not barbarous the usage of war prescribes that when a city is about to be attacked, timely notice shall be given by the attacking commander in order that noncombatants may have an opportunity for withdrawing beyond its limits. . . . It would appear, sir, that despairing of reducing these works, you now resort to the novel measure of turning your guns against the old men, the women and children, and the hospitals of a sleeping city, an act of inexcusable barbarity.

To his credit, Gilmore gave Beauregard two more days to allow civilians to leave the city. The bombardment started on August 22, 1863.

Charleston was shelled every day for 587 days. The number of shells falling on the city would vary with one of the heaviest times coming in January 1864 when 1,500 shells landed over nine days. Civilians and the military quickly figured out the Union artillery's range, so they simply abandoned the city below Market Street and moved all essential services to above Calhoun Street. Because the land north of Charleston was still in Southern hands, the Union army could not surround the city. Charleston's civilians did not suffer as much as the people in Vicksburg.

The taking of Atlanta, Georgia, in the summer of 1864 set new guidelines for what Union armies were allowed to do with civilian populations. On September 7, Union general William T. Sherman ordered all civilians to leave the captured city. When the mayor and city council protested that forced evacuation would cause suffering among the elderly and pregnant women still in the city, Sherman replied, "My order was not designed to meet the humanities of the case. . . . You cannot qualify war in harsher terms than I will. War is cruelty, and you cannot refine it."

Sherman then explained why he was treating the civilians of Atlanta harshly. It was for the good of the Union. If he had to destroy Atlanta for the good of the rest of the Union, he would do it.

In a letter to the mayor and a representative of the city council of Atlanta, Sherman wrote:

The United States does and must assert its authority, wherever it once had power; for, if it relaxes one bit to pressure, it is gone, and I believe that such is the national feeling. This feeling assumes various shapes, but always comes back to that of Union. Once admit the Union, once more acknowledge the authority of the national Government, and, instead of devoting your houses and streets and roads to the dread uses of war, I and this army become at once your protectors and supporters, shielding you from danger. I want peace, and believe it can only be reached through union and war, and I will ever conduct war with a view to perfect an early success.

When Sherman left Atlanta on his march to Savannah on November 11, 1864, he set one of the largest intentional fires in American history. More than five thousand buildings, at least two thirds of the city of Atlanta, were destroyed. Initially, Sherman had ordered the entire city burned, but the entreaties of a Catholic priest convinced him to try to spare the churches and private homes. Still, witnesses reported that most of the churches and a number of private homes were caught in the flames.

Sherman was satisfied with his treatment of the city. In his postwar memoirs, the general remembered what he saw as he rode out of the city on his way toward Savannah: "Behind us lay Atlanta, smoldering and in ruins, the black smoke rising high in air, and hanging like a pall over the ruined city."

Cities and towns were not the only targets of the Federal army in the summer of 1864. What Southerners knew were farms. There were few true cities in the South. Nearly everyone in the Confederacy made his living in some fashion by working the soil. It could be rocky land in the Appalachians, rich bottom lands in the deltas of the region's many rivers, or coastal salt marshes where sea island cotton grew. The soil could be clay, loam, or sand, thick with rich topsoil, or thin and poor. Southerners always figured out something that would grow in it. They knew the land. They knew how to make it produce a living for themselves and their families.

Southerners grudgingly understood how their few cities and towns had some kind of military value that made them military targets. Cities were where the factories, mills, and warehouses were located. They were situated on rivers and beside ports leading to the sea. Railroads that took food and ammunition to far-flung battlefields crossed in cities. Cities, at least capital cities, were where politicians met and made decisions. All those were fair targets for the Union.

But farms were different in the eyes of the Southern soldier. Farms were populated mostly by wives and children and by men too old to join the army. Farms had no garrisons, no rail stations, no warehouses. The land produced food, not weapons or gunpowder.

President Lincoln and his war planners disagreed. In their view, Southern farms were legitimate military targets because the food produced by them found its way into the stomachs of Southern soldiers. Civilian farms were no different from the blockade-runners plying the Atlantic Ocean and the Gulf of Mexico and running their way into Southern ports loaded with supplies for the Confederacy. It was simple war strategy. If the Union navy could capture or sink the blockade-runners and the Union army could wreck the farms, the Confederacy would starve and be forced to rejoin the Union.

One particularly rich area of farms in the Confederacy drew the acute attention of the Union army. While both Union and Confederate leaders could not know it at the time, attacking this peaceful, productive, rural valley would play a major role in convincing the Confederacy to attack the largest city in the United States.

The Shenandoah Valley of western Virginia is a twenty-mile-wide valley stretching more than one hundred miles north and south between the Blue Ridge Mountains on the east and the Appalachian Mountains on the west.

Militarily, the Shenandoah Valley forms a natural, screened byway for any army heading north or south. Confederate general Thomas J. "Stonewall" Jackson with just 10,000 men had beaten several Union armies in the valley in the spring of 1862. Robert E. Lee had used the valley to march his 80,000-man army rapidly to Gettysburg in June 1863.

But as important as the valley was to the generals as a means of moving their men, it was vital to the existence of the Confederacy itself. Ever since the war began, the Shenandoah Valley was a major source of foodstuffs for the Confederate armies thanks to the hundreds of farms raising wheat, fruit, vegetables, cattle, sheep, and goats.

At first, the Union war planners did not recognize that the valley had that kind of value. They still thought of the targets as the armies operating in the valley. Union general David Hunter pushed farther south than any other previous Union force in May and June 1864 when he was chasing a small Confederate army.

Hunter occupied Lexington, at the upper or southern end of the valley, taking time to burn the Virginia Military Institute, which had trained scores of Southern officers the Union army was now fighting. Stonewall Jackson had been a professor of physics and artillery at the Virginia Military Institute before the war. Just for spite, Hunter also burned the home of the governor of Virginia, before pushing on to the southeast toward Lynchburg. Hunter's attacks on civilian property would come to haunt him.

By delaying several days so his men could burn and loot civilian homes, Hunter unwittingly allowed Robert E. Lee time to move an entire corps under General Jubal Early out of the trenches around Petersburg to rush to Lynchburg to confront the unaware Federals.

Hunter was routed by Early and summarily relieved of command, even though he had accomplished more penetration of the western part of Virginia than any previous Union general.

The real reason Hunter was relieved of command was that his loss to Jubal Early created a situation that deeply embarrassed Union general-in-chief Grant. Grant had never believed that the force Hunter faced was part of Lee's army. Grant had convinced himself he had bottled up all of Lee's men. In reality, Early had left Petersburg right under the nose of Grant.

Instead of returning to Petersburg after defeating Hunter, Early's men used the valley to rapidly march north in an effort to attack Washington City from an unexpected direction—the west. After being held up for a day of fighting a ragtag defensive force thrown together at Monocracy, Maryland, on July 9, 1864, Early's men marched to less than six miles from Lincoln's Executive Mansion.

There they were stopped by a far superior force rushed to Washington from Petersburg by Grant who finally realized that Lee had duped him. Early really was in Washington. Lincoln himself could have been captured because of Grant's laxity in protecting Washington from an attack launched from the Shenandoah Valley.

An angry Grant, ready to exact revenge for his mistakes in allowing Early to attack Washington, looked for a target. He saw one, the Shenandoah Valley.

In September 1864, just two months after Early and his men had used the valley to stage a sneak attack on Washington, Grant issued an order to his cavalry commander, Major General Philip Sheridan. Grant ordered: "In pushing up the Shenandoah Valley . . . it is desirable that nothing should be left to invite the enemy to return. Take all provisions, forage and stock wanted for the use of your command; such as cannot be consumed, destroy."

Grant was not solely targeting the civilians of the valley for his own mistakes. He had a two-pronged strategy: defeat Early who had remained in the valley since he had retreated from Washington, and destroy the supplies and means of replenishing those supplies that were being shipped out of the valley to Lee at Petersburg.

Sheridan's officers and men, including a newly minted brigadier general named George Armstrong Custer, carried out Grant's order that "nothing should be left to invite the enemy to return" with a vengeance.

Barns, stacks of hay in the fields, supplies of oats, and stockpiles of food were all destroyed, usually by soaking them in turpentine and then setting them ablaze. Horses were carried off to be used for cavalry mounts. Colts and ponies that had no military use were shot. Pigs and chickens were either shot or carried off to be eaten later in camp. Private homes were ransacked as the soldiers were allowed to search for food and valuables.

After meeting some resistance from civilians, Sheridan issued an order that any male found with a weapon on his person was to be executed as a guerrilla. Several civilians, including one man who was described as "simple" by his neighbors, met that fate. In retaliation for the deaths of the civilians and some of their own men, Confederate partisan rangers under John Singleton Mosby executed captured Union soldiers. For every Southerner executed, one Union soldier was executed in an eye-for-an-eye retaliation for the harsh policies Sheridan and Custer were practicing.

Union authorities used one battlefield encounter as an excuse to start what valley residents would remember forever as The Burning. Lieutenant John Meigs, son of Union general Montgomery Meigs, was riding a scout one night when he encountered several other men. He pulled his revolver, and was shot from his horse by the men, who turned out to be Confederate on their own scout. Even when Meigs's body was found next to his fired revolver, Sheridan declared that he had been bushwhacked and murdered.

Based on the death of a single soldier riding behind enemy lines and encountering Confederate soldiers, Sheridan ordered the town of Dayton, Virginia, and all the farms in a three-mile circle of the spot where Meigs was found to be burned.

Custer rode away with the order telling Sheridan to "watch for the smoke" to know that his order was successfully carried out.

The order to burn Dayton was rescinded by a reluctant Sheridan when a Union cavalryman who had been with Meigs arrived in headquarters to explain that Meigs had died in a fair fight. Even knowing that Meigs's death was a legitimate battlefield casualty and he had not been murdered, Sheridan let the order stand to burn all the outlying farms. Grant did nothing to countermand Sheridan's order. So many farms and homesteads were burned that the area acquired the wartime and postwar nickname of The Burnt District.

One Union soldier was so impressed with the number of fires that he could see from one point that he counted them. He stopped counting at 167.

One embarrassed Union soldier wrote:

Such wholesale incendiarism could not have been pursued, however, without undue license being taken by the worst class of soldiers, and there have been frequent instances of rascality and pillage. . . . The poor, alike with the rich, have suffered. The wholesale devastation of the valley from mountain to mountain, with the intent to render the entire region a desert, embittered the inhabitants to the last degree.

Confederate resistance in the valley ended on October 19, 1864, when Early's forces surprised Sheridan's men in camp in a daylong Battle of Cedar Creek, fought just south of Winchester, Virginia. Early's men won the first part of the day with an early-morning rout of Sheridan's men. Thinking they had won, Early's men stopped chasing Sheridan's men. Then Sheridan himself rode onto the battlefield and rallied his men. They turned around and won the second part of the battle in the afternoon.

Early's men retreated from the battlefield, never again to play a major force in the valley.

In under three months, the Shenandoah Valley had changed from a prosperous valley filled with working farms to a desolate region filled with starving people who would always remember and hate the names of Sheridan, Custer, and Lincoln.

All that remained for the devastated residents of the valley was the hope and wish that someone would avenge them somewhere. In Canada, the Confederate Secret Service was planning to do just that. They were looking at and thinking about attacking New York City as a just revenge for what had been done to Winton, Vicksburg, Charleston, Atlanta, and the Shenandoah Valley.

Chapter 9

"A Fire in the Rear Will Be Opened"

Lincoln knew that New York City residents did not like him. He had lost the city's 1860 vote by more than two to one. He may have been surprised that large numbers of residents of the states where he had spent his youth and early career also disliked him.

The southern parts of Indiana and Illinois had been heavily settled by former Southerners who had left their home states to find their own pieces of ground. These people, particularly those who did not live near any large towns or cities, usually retained their common Southern political opinions that state governments were more important than federal government. They were suspicious of a strong federal government, which Lincoln favored.

A large number of the remaining residents of these Southern-leaning Northern states were recent Irish or German immigrants who were politically savvy enough to remember that the Republicans had grown out of a branch of the Know-Nothing Party of the 1850s. Although Lincoln claimed he rejected the nativist, anti-immigration, anti-Catholic preachings of the Know Nothings and he had been a member of the Whig Party, the Republicans' association with the Know Nothings made these new Americans suspicious of Lincoln's true political nature.

The election of 1860 proved what many had suspected. Lincoln did not carry the southern border counties of Ohio, Indiana, or Illinois, which was his own state of residence. Those people seemed to side with the South. In any war, that could be troubling to a federal government unsure of whether it had the support of its own residents in its rear if it had to wage a war on the South.

Just as Lincoln feared, some western newspapers, including those in counties and states he carried, even newspapers that he had expected to support him, told him to make concessions to the South.

The Belleville, Illinois, *Democrat,* one hundred miles south of Springfield and just east of St. Louis wrote that "the North is hopelessly abolitioinized. To submit then, or secede is forced upon the South. That their rights have long been disregarded, and now defiantly trampled under foot, by the North is true."

The *Chicago Times and Herald* wrote: "When the hearts of the people of any great section are permanently alienated, the Union is already practically dissolved. . . . The Union is valuable only so long as its services to the people make it dear to them."

The Kenosha, Wisconsin, *Democrat*, north of Chicago, noted: "The right of secession inheres to the people of every sovereign state. . . . South Carolina voted herself into the Union; she can vote herself out. . . . [The Founding Fathers] declared any state had an inherent right to secede at pleasure, and a forcible union would be an invasion of that right."

Some western newspapers, hundreds of miles north of any extended Mason-Dixon Line into the west, threatened war in the North if the Union invaded the South.

The *Detroit Free Press* made a remarkable threat on January 29, 1861, when its editors wrote: "If troops shall be raised in the North to march against the people of the South, a fire in the rear will be opened upon such troops. . . . There are some sixty-five thousand able-bodied men, voters at the late election, citizens of this State, who will interpose themselves between any troops that may be raised in Michigan and the people of the South."

Republican newspapers had a word for the Democratic politicians and newspapers who opposed the president. They were Copperheads.

The origin of the word is murky. Some Democrats subtly protested Lincoln's election by substituting their coat buttons with those made from Lady Liberty copper cents. The word also appeared in print and in editorial cartoons associated with the copperhead snake, a poisonous reptile that has no rattle, allowing it to strike prey without warning.

On April 10, 1861, two days before the firing on Fort Sumter, the *New York Times* reported that a box mailed to Washington City had broken open in the post office and two copperhead snakes fell out, with one being a healthy and angry three feet long. The *Times* hinted that the snakes had been mailed to the Executive Mansion and were intended to kill Lincoln.

"What are we to think of a people who resort to such weapons of warfare?" asked the *Times*.

The *Chicago Tribune* did not buy the *Times'* explanation that the snakes were meant for Lincoln. "The specimens had probably been originally addressed to the Smithsonian Institution, which frequently receives such objects by mail," wrote the *Tribune*, which playfully took a slap at its big city rival by saying it had "taken some pains to inquire into the truth of the story." It seems that the *Chicago Times* had just accused the *New York Times* of reporting news that was not fit to print.

After South Carolina's firing on Fort Sumter, many westerners who had considered the North to be the aggressor reversed their opinions. Some newspapers that had considered secession legal now called for the Union to take action against the South, which had fired the first shot.

Lincoln's presidential opponent, a very generous Stephen Douglas, conducted a whirlwind tour of the southern parts of the western states, urging them to support the man who had defeated him in the November election and to reject any affinity with the South. An exhausted Douglas would die of typhoid fever in June 1861, just before any combat broke out.

Despite Douglas's call to his fellow Democrats to unite behind his Republican rival, not everyone did. Some Congressmen and newspapers continued to stay firmly in the Democratic opposition camp. By July 1861, the month when Manassas was fought and lost by the Union, Republican newspapers around the nation were routinely calling Peace Democrats Copperheads.

These Democrats freely admitted that they opposed Lincoln, but they also claimed they had a reason to do so—Lincoln was in violation of the Constitution. All throughout the war, the Democrats would question if the United States had a legal right to keep the South in the Union and if Lincoln was violating the Constitution by waging war against the South. It made no difference if the war was doing well or poorly for the Union. The Democrats, some of whom were openly Copperheads and openly antiadministration, questioned if the war was necessary.

Many of New York City's and New York State's leading citizens, including the governor and some of its congressmen, remained convinced that the war was wrong. As time would show, they were willing to work secretly with the Confederacy to end the war one way or the other.

From the beginning of the war, Lincoln's adherence to the U.S. Constitution was questioned by the Democrats starting with his April 15, 1861, call for seventy-five thousand volunteers to "suppress" seven Southern states and to "cause the laws to be duly executed." Article 1, section 8 of the Constitution grants Congress the power to declare war, but Lincoln had issued an executive order calling for the volunteers.

Lincoln said he needed the volunteers because seven named states were acting "in combinations too powerful to be suppressed by the ordinary course of judicial proceedings." With that explanation, Lincoln used the very words President George Washington used in calling for a volunteer army to put down the Whiskey Rebellion among Pennsylvanians in 1794.

Lincoln asked the "persons composing the combinations" to "retire peaceably to their respective abodes within twenty days from this date."

In this first communication with the nation about the need for war, Lincoln did not use the word "rebellion," which would become his most commonly used term for the war. Nor did Lincoln mention the Southern state legislatures and secession delegations that had met with the consent of their citizens to vote on leaving the Union.

The governor of North Carolina, the next to last state to leave the

Union and one that had opposed secession for months, responded with a telegram back to Lincoln: "I regard the levy of troops made by the administration for the purpose of subjugating the states of the South as in violation of the Constitution, and a usurpation of power. I can be no party to this wicked violation of the laws of the country, and to this war upon the liberties of a free people. You can get no troops from North Carolina."

Only on rare occasions would Lincoln use the word "Confederate." When he had to, he would say "the so-called Confederate States of America." He believed that recognition of any kind of the Confederacy gave it legitimacy as a separate nation. Lincoln believed it impossible for any state to declare itself free from the Union.

The South's reading of the Constitution was that it was a voluntary association of states that could be broken apart if the federal government began acting in ways that were detrimental to the health of the states. The Southern states, as had all Northern states, voluntarily ratified the Constitution, and they believed they could also voluntarily exit the contract if their citizens agreed.

Lincoln's ordering of a blockade on Southern ports in April 1861 was also considered by his critics to be a violation of the Constitution's article 1 section 9, which restricts the government from giving "preference" to any one state's ports over another. Closing all the Southern ports to commerce with each other as well as foreign ports while Northern ports were kept open was clearly unconstitutional in the eyes of Democrats. Some politicians also feared that foreign powers would consider Lincoln's actions of blockading Southern ports as a de facto declaration of war against them if those nations tried to continue or open trade with the South. The taking of Confederate commissioners Mason and Slidell from a British ship by a Union warship had already enraged England.

On July 1, 1861, Lincoln addressed Congress, where he patiently, but adamantly, explained that it was his opinion that the president could exercise power normally reserved to the legislative branch when the nation faced an emergency. Immediately on beginning the speech, Lincoln, speaking in the third person of himself, blamed South Carolina for the conflict by its firing on Fort Sumter.

That this was their object, the Executive well understood; and having said to them in the inaugural address, 'You can have no conflict without being yourselves the aggressors,' he took pains, not only to keep this declaration good, but also to keep the case so free from the power of ingenious sophistry, as that the world should not be able to misunderstand it. By the affair at Fort Sumter, with its surrounding circumstances, that point was reached. Then, and thereby, the assailants of the Government, began the conflict of arms, without a gun in sight, or in expectancy, to return their fire, save only the few in the Fort, sent to that harbor, years before, for their own protection.

These measures, whether strictly legal or not, were ventured upon, under what appeared to be a popular demand, and a public necessity, trusting, then, as now, that Congress would readily ratify them. It is believed that nothing has been done beyond the constitutional competency of Congress.

Not all Northerners believed Lincoln when he said that the Constitution allowed him to do what he had just done and what he planned to do. New York City mayor Fernando Wood and New York governor Horatio Seymour did not. A number of congressmen and state legislators believed he was breaking the law, as did a number of newspaper editors. More ominously for Lincoln, the chief justice of the United States Supreme Court, Roger Taney, also believed Lincoln had overstepped his authority.

Lincoln's solution to dealing with people who opposed his policies was to threaten them with arrest. He tried to buy off or ignore more high profile opponents such as Governor Seymour and Mayor Wood. Lincoln chose a different tact with Chief Justice Taney. He ordered him arrested.

While asking for volunteers, declaring war, and blockading the South without congressional discussion or approval deeply angered the Copperheads, what enraged them more was the president's suspending the writ of habeas corpus.

Habeas corpus is a legal term demanding that the authority that has arrested a person deliver that person in front of a court so the court can determine if the arrest was legal or if the person should be released because the arrest is illegal. It is allowable for the president to suspend habeas corpus in the event of a rebellion (article 1, section 9), but before Lincoln, no president had tried to arrest a large portion of the nation's population.

On April 27, Lincoln issued an executive order that said in part: "All rebels and insurgents, their aiders and abettors within the United States, and all persons discouraging volunteer enlistments, resisting militia drafts, or guilty of any disloyal practice affording aid and comfort to the rebels against the authority of the United States, shall be subject to martial law, and liable to trial and punishment by courts-martial or military commission."

Within hours, people who had expressed dissatisfaction with Lincoln were being arrested. When Chief Justice Taney heard about one Southern sympathizer under arrest in Maryland, John Merryman, Taney sent an order to Lincoln to release Merryman. Lincoln responded by giving an order to a U.S. Marshal to arrest the chief justice. The Marshal, a close friend of Lincoln from Springfield, convinced Lincoln that he would only make matters worse if Taney was actually taken into custody. Lincoln agreed and Taney was not arrested. Merryman stayed in jail.

During the course of the war thousands of people, most prominently the Southern-leaning members of the Maryland legislature, were arrested when military officers suspected those people had Southern sympathies. One prominent former Ohio congressman, Clement Vallandigham, made such noise opposing Lincoln that he was arrested on May 5, 1863, tried quickly by a military tribunal, and imprisoned. When citizens and newspapers protested that the congressman had been practicing his right to free speech under the First Amendment, they too were threatened with military arrest.

Two-time New York governor Horatio Seymour was not arrested, but some Lincoln supporters may have wanted him in a jail cell for his public call to action for an event that took place hundreds of miles to the west from his governor's mansion in Albany.

Seymour, a lawyer and native of Utica, in upstate New York, had little in common with the merchants of New York City other than he was a Democrat. He had already served one term as governor from 1853 to 1854, but was out of office when the war began. He quickly gained the attention of the incoming Republican administration, however, when he spoke at a February 1861 convention of Democrats and observed: "All virtue, patriotism, and intelligence seem to have fled from our National Capitol; it has been well likened to a conflagration of an asylum for madmen—some look on with idiotic imbecility, some in sullen silence, and some scatter the firebrands which consume the fabric above them, and bring upon all a common destruction."

Likening the incoming presidential administration to a flaming insane asylum did not win Seymour any friends in Washington. Lincoln once tried to buy Seymour off with the promise that he would support the governor for president at some point in the future if he would publicly support the Republican administration on its war effort. Seymour scoffed at the idea of a Republican ever endorsing a Democrat. The governor continued his public pronouncements against the war, though at his address to the New York legislature on January 7, 1863, he said that "under no circumstances can the division of the Union be conceded. . . . We will guarantee them [South] every right, every consideration demanded by the Constitution."

Seymour was consistent in his beliefs though they angered the Republicans. He did not want the Southern states to leave the Union, but he also rejected what he considered the federal government's unconstitutional efforts to keep them in the Union.

When Vallandigham was arrested, Seymour responded in public by charging that the Lincoln administration violated the Constitution by infringing on the congressman's free speech and that his military trial was a "mockery."

Said Seymour on May 16, 1863:

If this proceeding is approved by the government, and sanctioned by the government, it is not merely a step toward revolution, it is revolution; it will not only lead to military despotism, it establishes military despotism. . . . If it is upheld, our liberties are overthrown; the safety of our persons, security of our property, will hereafter depend upon the arbitrary will of such military rulers as may be placed over us; while our Constitutional guarantees will be broken down. The action of the administration will determine in the minds of more than one half of the people of the loyal States, whether the war is waged to put down the rebellion at the South or destroy free institutions at the North.

The following month on June 3, there was a meeting at Cooper Union in New York City, the same place that had made Lincoln a national name. It was a packed house that heard Seymour call for "peace and reunion."

The Republican newspapers made no distinction between Peace Democrats like Seymour and more subversive Copperheads who talked of helping the Confederacy win their war of secession.

The September 19, 1863, issue of *Harper's Weekly* featured a front-page editorial asking some rhetorical questions:

Whose phrase is that the Union must fall rather than slavery? Horatio Seymour's. . . . Whose opinion was it, when the rebels "seceded," that the Government could not "coerce" States? Horatio Seymour's. . . . Whose election would help to secure the triumph of the rebels? Horatio Seymour's. . . . Whose position beside that of his old political companion General Dix is that of a Copperhead beside a patriot? Horatio Seymour's.

While Seymour was in Albany, former mayor Fernando Wood was in Washington, having been elected to the House of Representatives in 1863. While he no longer advocated radical ideas such as making New York City a free city that could trade with any country, including the Confederacy, he remained pro-South in all of his congressional dealings. When the Confiscation Act of 1862 was introduced, Wood tried to argue before Congress that the Union could not simultaneously insist that the Southern states had not left the Union while also taking and selling captured property in those same states as if the property was spoils of war captured from foreign nations.

Fernando Wood's brother Benjamin attracted more rancor from the Lincoln administration, and Benjamin came closer to arrest than his brother. Benjamin was owner and editor of the *New York Daily News*, the city's largest daily newspaper, which was also its most fierce critic of the Lincoln administration. His early editorials so angered the Lincoln administration that the U.S. Postal Service was authorized to refuse to deliver the newspaper to other cities. When Benjamin tried to transport his newspapers by rail, the administration confiscated those too. Benjamin finally ceased publication for eighteen months while he waited for the administration to cool off.

In July 1863, just before the riots broke out, Benjamin charged: "The miscreants at the head of the Government are bending all their powers . . . to secure a perpetuation of their ascendancy for another four years, and that triple method of accomplishing this purpose, is to kill off Democrats, stuff the ballot boxes with bogus soldier votes, and deluge recusant districts with negro suffrage."

Benjamin remained a thorn in the side of the administration, both as a congressman and as a newspaperman. He was investigated several times by House committees looking for connections to the Confederacy but never formally charged with any crime such as treason.

Benjamin was a bold man who made little effort to conceal his connections to true Copperheads dedicated to helping the Confederacy. While his brother Fernando was a Peace Democrat who wanted the North to compromise with the South, Benjamin always felt betrayed by what he considered the Union's attempt to subvert the Constitution and subjugate the South.

In January 1864, Benjamin hired a man as editor who was a member of the Sons of Liberty, a known Copperhead organization. Benjamin was so wrapped up in his principles that his Peace Democrat newspaper did not come out for War Democrat George McClellan for president in 1864 because McClellan called for continuing the war against the South.

The Peace Democrats and the Copperheads would be blamed for supporting what happened in New York City on November 25, 1864. It was true. They were involved.

Chapter 10

"State Governments Will Be Seized"

The Confederate States of America in April 1861 did not have much going for it. It was a thrown-together nation with a hastily written constitution modeled after the U.S. Constitution. It had to create its own banking and credit system overnight; these functions were something the South's prewar political leaders had been content to leave in the hands of New York bankers for the previous fifty years.

The South's entire economy had always been based on two agricultural crops: first tobacco and then cotton. Immediately before the war, the South was a net importer of food because most of its agricultural resources were growing its two money crops.

The new Confederate nation had no currency. Neither did it have any gold or silver reserves to back up any currency that would be created.

Now, thanks to some shortsighted, fire-eating, speechifying politicians who had fired on Fort Sumter rather than force the United States to fire on them, the Confederacy had talked itself into a war with an industrial giant of a nation that had four times the South's population.

The Confederacy's inventory of military advantages was slim, whereas the ledger sheet column for disadvantages was prodigious.

Under advantages, the South had a long coastline with several deep-water ports at Charleston, Mobile, and New Orleans. Even four years after Lincoln's blockade of those ports, the vast majority of blockade-runners still were able to slip past Union blockaders and deliver their cargoes. It also had an impressive roster of military and naval officers who had resigned from the services of the United States to cast their lots with their home states.

Under a shared category of advantages and disadvantages, the South had a large-scale, modern factory in Richmond called the Tredegar Iron Works that had developed a solid, prewar reputation with the U.S. government for delivering quality products on time and on budget.

The huge disadvantage for the South was that Tredegar was the lone large factory in the South. For decades, the region's political leaders insisted that the South needed no manufacturing and that building factories would only distract the region from its agriculture. So while the Confederacy had Tredegar to build cannons, it had no existing factory to make gunpowder that would go into those cannons.

Under advantages, the South had captured the machinery of the musket factory at Harpers Ferry, Virginia, but it was a disadvantage that many of the factory buildings and stocks of completed arms had been ruined by a retreating force of U.S. soldiers.

It was an advantage that thousands of small arms had been captured from the U.S. arsenals in each of the Southern states, but the disadvantage was that almost all those weapons were outdated smoothbore muskets. The effective range of the 1842 Springfield smoothbore musket was only 100 yards compared with the 400-yard range for the 1861 Springfield rifled musket that would soon be pouring out of the factories and into the hands of eager Union volunteers.

It was a huge advantage for the Confederacy to capture the U.S. Naval Shipyard at Portsmouth, Virginia, including tons of gunpowder and naval cannons that could be transferred as far away as the Tennessee River to be used in forts. It was a disadvantage that Portsmouth was the only place in the South with a history of shipbuilding. The North's coasts and ports were dotted with scores of shipbuilding operations employing men who simply changed their skills from building whaling and slaving ships to warships.

The list of disadvantages that the South faced was daunting. It had a poorly developed system of railroads where gauges varied from one line to the next. The North had seven times the miles of track that existed in the South. The South had some mills to make cloth for uniforms, but nothing like the spinning mills that drove the New England economy. The South had little experience manufacturing drugs that could be used in battlefield hospitals. It did not even have factories to mass manufacture canteens. Many of its first soldiers marched off with canteens made of wood or handcrafted by tin smiths in their small towns.

The South did have one advantage over the North, one that Lincoln had never anticipated when he predicted an early and short war that would not need any volunteers for longer than ninety days. Confederates were innovative. When they had nothing, they made something.

At Manassas in July 1861, they used signal flags to warn an exposed portion of the battle line that a Union force was moving unseen on its flank. At New Orleans in September 1861, they converted a former ice-breaking ship into the CSS *Manassas,* the war's first ironclad, which damaged several wooden ships on the Mississippi River. At Portsmouth in April 1862, they converted the hulk of the USS *Merrimack* into the ironclad CSS *Virginia*, which smashed the Union's wooden warships like matchsticks. During the Peninsula Campaign in June 1862, they developed torpedoes or land mines that could be deployed on land or in water. In February 1864, they converted a steam boiler into the hand-cranked submarine *H. L. Hunley* that sank a Union warship in Charleston, South Carolina's harbor. In August 1864, they developed a clock-powered time bomb to blow up a Union ammunition barge at a huge munitions depot at City Point, Virginia. The barge exploded so close to Union general Grant that he was showered with wooden splinters and human body parts.

While Union war planners were bogged down in bureaucratic arguments about equipping their soldiers with repeating rifles out of fear that the men would waste ammunition, Confederates were thinking about how to use what few resources they had to win the war.

If the Confederacy could not outmanufacture the Union, the South's war planners believed they could outthink it by using ingenuity, espionage, and subterfuge. Thus, a secret group of the Confederate government was created.

All the activities of the Confederate Secret Service will never be known because its official records and the personal papers of its chief were burned to keep them out of Federal hands once Richmond fell on April 2, 1865. But what is known is that the Confederate Secret Service was more than a collection of spies keeping tracking of Union army movements.

Operating under the management of Secretary of War James Seddon starting in 1863, the Secret Service actively worked to undermine the Union's currency, promoted Democrats for high office, and attacked the Union public's confidence that the war could be won. Most ambitiously, the Confederate Secret Service planned to create an army of angry Northerners wanting to overthrow their own President Lincoln.

The commissioner of the Confederate Secret Service was Jacob Thompson, a 53-year-old native of North Carolina who had moved to Mississippi as a youth. After becoming a planter, Thompson served six terms in the U.S. House of Representatives. Out of politics for a while after losing a bid for the United States Senate seat in 1855, Thompson was tapped for U.S. interior secretary by President James Buchanan.

While serving in Buchanan's cabinet, Thompson saw the gathering clouds of war. He pleaded with officials he knew in both the North and the South to cool their talk of abolition and secession. After Lincoln was elected, he resigned his post and returned to Mississippi. Thompson, middle-aged, without military experience and largely without political significance, served as a general's aide during the first two years of the war. Early in 1864, President Davis, who had run against Thompson for political office in Mississippi, added his former rival to his team to act as a commissioner of the Confederate Secret Service. Thompson's vague assignment was to do what he could to help the Confederate cause while operating from the neutral country of Canada.

Thompson's second in command was Clement Clay, a former United States senator from Alabama, who had most recently served in the Confederate Congress. Like Thompson, Clay was middle-aged, had never served in the military, and had no clue how to go about creating a spy agency. He was also a thin, sickly man who had no business living in a country with a cold climate like Canada.

Davis's and Seddon's inexperience in trying to set up an espionage and intelligence network immediately showed with the selection of Thompson and Clay to head it. Thompson and Clay did not know each other well and did not seem even to enjoy each other's company. Before the Confederate outpost was even established, the two men were feuding over how to keep in touch with each other as Clay did not want to be even based in the same city as Thompson.

"Clay was not a practical man. He lacked judgment and was in ill health, was peevish, irritable and suspicious," noted Major John Castleman, the former commander of the Second Kentucky Cavalry of Morgan's command and one of the agents under Thompson's command in Canada.

The opinion of the agents who worked with Thompson was not much higher. To their astonishment, Thompson regularly gave money to characters that the agents were not even sure were fellow Confederates. It seemed that anyone with good salesmanship skills could get some cash from Thompson to finance a real or fake scheme to further Confederate goals.

Not long after he arrived in Canada, Thompson discovered that a shadowy man named George Sanders, who had served as a revenue agent in the port of New York City before the war, was also claiming to be working for the Confederate Secret Service. Thompson remained suspicious of Sanders during his stay in Canada, though Federal officers always associated Sanders with the Confederate Secret Service. Sanders seemed to have some sort of personal magnetism that captivated some of those within his sphere.

Castleman wrote in his memoir, *Active Service*: "In my long life, I have known no counterpart to this man. Commissioner Clay soon yielded entirely to his influence, most men were swayed by his plausible theories and he was a constant menace to the interests for which the commissioners were responsible. He controlled Mr. Clay."

While any specific instructions they were given must have been among the records destroyed at the end of the war, it is clear that the Confederacy had high hopes for its Canadian outpost. On leaving Richmond, Thompson was issued more than $1 million in gold and silver to put on deposit in Montreal to finance whatever operations seemed promising.

At least Thompson and Clay had one experienced military mind in Canada on whom they could rely. Captain Thomas Hines, a member of General John Hunt Morgan's cavalry command who had escaped with him from the Ohio State Penitentiary, was ordered from Richmond to Canada in March 1864 to lay the groundwork for the pending assignment of Thompson and Clay.

While Thompson and Clay had been given verbal orders, Seddon gave Hines a letter instructing him: "In passing through the United States you will confer with the leading persons friendly or attached to the cause of the Confederacy, or who may be advocates of peace, and do all in your power to induce our friends to organize and prepare themselves to render such aid as circumstances may allow."

Hines was a bold man. He wagered a friend that on his way to Canada he would visit Washington City and shake hands with President Lincoln himself. After the war, Hines claimed he collected on the wager. Hines may have been able to get an audience with the president by impersonating Lincoln's favorite stage actor, John Wilkes Booth. Contemporary photos of Hines show a remarkable resemblance to Booth.

Hines and Thompson agreed on duties at their first meeting in Toronto. Hines would recruit what military men he needed for any missions from among the Confederates who had made their way across the border after escaping from Northern prisoner-of-war camps in Illinois, Ohio, and New York. Thompson would develop the schemes that would need those men.

What seemed ripe for exploitation was matching experienced Confederate leaders with angry Copperheads. Just what such a combination would do to help the war effort was still to be determined, but the South did know one thing: tens of thousands, perhaps hundreds of thousands, of U.S. citizens were angry with their own president and his war policies.

In the fall of 1862, Lincoln expanded his 1861 suspension of habeas corpus for Southern sympathizers in Maryland by issuing an executive order covering the entire country suspending habeas corpus for anyone protesting the administration's war policies. Just to play it safe, Lincoln pushed a law through Congress in March 1863 codifying his right to arrest anyone who complained about his war policies, which he likened to being a traitor to one's country.

"Must I shoot a simple-minded soldier boy who deserts, while I must not touch a hair of a wily agitator who induces him to desert? . . . I think that in such a case, to silence the agitator, and save the boy, is not only constitutional, but, withal, a great mercy," said Lincoln in commenting on the arrest of Ohio congressman Vallandigham, the Ohio congressman who had been a war critic.

Acting on Lincoln's orders, the military stuffed county jails with war dissidents. During the war more than thirteen thousand citizens, most of them Northerners, were arrested on charges as minor as drunkenly shouting: "Hurrah for Jeff Davis" or as major as writing editorials questioning if the president had the constitutional right to do what he was doing. At least one Episcopal priest was arrested because he did not include a prayer for the president in his Sunday service.

Within weeks after the army began arresting dissidents, Secretary of War Stanton suggested to the U.S. attorney general that the administration allow a habeas corpus case to come before the United States Supreme Court so that the public would see that Lincoln's unpopular order was constitutional. Stanton felt confident that the Supreme Court would rule in the administration's favor as Lincoln had appointed three of the justices.

Attorney General Edward Bates said that putting any such case before the Supreme Court would be a bad idea because the judges would likely support a view of the Constitution supporting individuals' right to free speech under the First Amendment, as opposed to

Lincoln's view that suspending habeas corpus was allowed during wartime under article 1 of the Constitution.

Losing the case before the Supreme Court "would inflict upon the Administration a serious injury, and would do more good to the rebels than the worst defeat our armies have yet sustained," said Bates.

Davis and his war planners knew that the suspension of habeas corpus could cause anger among citizens. Davis himself had issued a similar suspension in the fall of 1862, though relatively few citizens and no newspaper editors had been arrested.

Letters and reports from the western states of Ohio, Indiana, and Illinois regularly arrived at Richmond describing how Copperhead groups such as the Sons of Liberty and Knights of the Golden Circle were simply waiting for some overt action to rise up and rebel themselves. Believing those reports, Davis and his cabinet began musing about what they called The Northwest Confederacy.

The Confederate cabinet imagined that if these secretive would-be rebel groups would rise up, the Union-loyal state legislatures of Ohio, Indiana, and Illinois might be overthrown and replaced with members more interested in joining the Confederacy. That could force nearby Border States like Kentucky and Missouri to join this sudden extension of the Confederacy rather than be cut off from the Union.

The cabinet reasoned that if the Confederacy grew by at least five states with some states being far north of the traditional South, virtually all the Union armies operating in the western part of the Confederacy would have to withdraw and return north to address the sudden threat in their rear. At the very least, the Confederate leaders imagined, desertions in the Union armies would soar as men either would change their loyalties to go with their home states or would be anxious to return home to protect their families from this new war front.

The Confederate cabinet was so excited about the reports of the supposed hidden groundswell of support in Union states for the Confederacy that they did not take time to evaluate the fabulous claims. One letter sent to Jefferson Davis assured him that 490,000 men in those three states were secretly members of the Knights of the Golden Circle and were ready to take over when the time arrived.

Manhattan's 1835 fire destroyed nearly 700 buildings in 17 blocks.
Library of Congress

Man-powered pumps were the norm through the 1850s.
New York Public Library

New York's firefighters resisted adopting steam-powered engines until 1859, fearing the machines would lessen the need for volunteers.
New York Public Library

New York's most experienced volunteer firefighters marched out of the city in 1861 as the New York Fire Zouaves infantry regiment. They would perform poorly in combat, damaging their reputation as brave men.
Library of Congress

Manhattan Mayor Fernando Wood suggested just before the Civil War started that the city secede from the Union to become a "free city." *Library of Congress*

New York Governor Horatio Seymour was a man Confederate agents believed could be persuaded to support them. *Library of Congress*

Former U.S. Interior
Secretary Jacob Thompson
headed the Confederate
Secret Service in Canada.
Library of Congress

C. Clement Clay was
Confederate second in
command in Canada.
Library of Congress

Jefferson Davis's
knowledge and control of
Confederate Secret Service
operations is still unclear.
Library of Congress

James Seddon, Confederate
Secretary of War, created
the Confederate Secret
Service. *National Archives*

Union General John A.
Dix was a Democrat, but a
general Lincoln trusted.
His orders to pursue
Confederates into Canada
almost caused an
international incident.

New York Police
Superintendent
John A. Kennedy correctly
pegged the attack as a
Confederate plot.
Library of Congress

Astor House at Broadway and Vesey Street, just south of City Hall, was
where Abraham Lincoln stayed while visiting New York.
New York Public Library

The Fifth Avenue Hotel at Fifth Avenue and 23rd Street, across from
Madison Square, was finished in 1859, becoming the city's most
elegant hotel. *New York Public Library*

Looking east, south, and west from the steeple of St. Paul's Church,
between Fulton and Vesey Streets. This area could have been engulfed
in flames as six hotels within a six-block area were targeted.
Library of Congress

Morgan's cavalry early in the conflict were brave, well-armed, and well-mounted young men who loved the adventure and danger of war.
New York Public Library

The St. James Hotel at Broadway and 26th Street was the target farthest north. *New York Public Library*

Captain Robert Martin of Kentucky, leader of the attack, would be freed from prison by a general amnesty given Confederates in 1866.
New-York Historical Society

Lieutenant John W. Headley of Kentucky would write a book about the attack.
New-York Historical Society

Confederate General John Hunt Morgan of Kentucky had been the beloved commander of all but one of the Confederates who attacked New York. He was murdered by Union soldiers in September 1864.
Library of Congress

Captain Robert Cobb Kennedy, a Louisianan, pictured just days before his death, was the only man executed for the attack on New York City.
Courtesy of the LaFleur family of Lafayette, Louisiana

Washington Square.

A chemist working near Washington Square prepared the Greek fire.
New York Public Library

On December 17, 1864, *Harper's Weekly* printed this accurate, if melodramatic, image of how the Confederates set their hotel fires by stacking up furniture and bed clothes, then pouring Greek fire over the stack. *Library of Congress*

Union General Ben Butler flooded the city's polling places with 3,500 troops on election day, which postponed the Confederate attack. *Library of Congress*

Former Union General Edwin Stoughton defended his doomed West Point classmate Captain Kennedy in his secret military tribunal trial for spying. *Library of Congress*

North

**November 25, 1864
Targets**

Map by Patrick Hart

Locations of all of the fires set.

That number had to be wildly inflated, but the Confederate cabinet did not dispute it.

Ohio, Indiana, and Illinois contributed a combined total of 753,000 troops to the Union armies. Subtracting that number from the 1860 population of those three states and assuming 25 percent of the male population at that time was under 18 years of age in 1860 and would not be fighting, the Sons of Liberty were claiming that they represented 30 percent of the 1,581,000 men at home in those three states. More importantly, the Sons of Liberty were claiming they had a hidden army that was five times the size of Robert E. Lee's Army of Northern Virginia at its strongest.

By June 1864, Thompson and Hines had met on several occasions with Vallandigham, now living in exile in Canada but also playing the role of commander of that secret army of Copperheads. Thompson was impressed by the tall, handsome orator with the flowery talk. Hines, who had seen men killed on the battlefield, thought less of him, commenting that "he [Vallandigham] believed all that was told to him."

Still, Vallandigham eventually convinced Hines that a force of Copperheads numbering 2,000 in Chicago was ready to surprise the Union garrison at Camp Douglas and free the 10,000 Confederate prisoners of war there. Another 3,000 Copperheads were ready to free the 7,000 Confederate prisoners at the Rock Island, Illinois, prison camp.

"State governments of Indiana, Ohio, and Illinois will be seized and their executives disposed of. By this means, we hope to have, within ten days after the movement has begun, a force of 50,000 men," Hines wrote in a coded report to Secretary of War Seddon.

In a separate report to Secretary of State Judah P. Benjamin, Thompson confidently predicted: "Although intending this as a Western Confederacy and demanding peace, if peace be not granted, then it shall be war. . . . All that is needed for our success is unflinching nerve."

Both men had been blinded by their desire to do something quickly for the Confederacy. They bought the idea Vallandigham apparently planted in their heads that fifty regiments of Midwestern men, who had not signed up for service for the Union, were ready and willing to fight for the Confederacy.

Neither Thompson nor Hines thought through how such an army, equivalent to nearly three Civil War era corps, could be equipped with muskets, cartridges filled with black powder and Minié balls, and all the food necessary to feed such a force. At that time of the war, most of that sort of war material was being shipped to Union armies fighting in the South.

The logistics of commanding such an unorganized, secret army never crossed Hines's mind. He was too intent on recruiting officers for it.

Hines searched for officers for his army in the only place that made sense to him: a bar in Toronto favored by escaped Confederate officers who had successfully broken out of prison camps in Illinois and Ohio. They had made their way north to Canada in hopes that they could figure out a way to get back south by means of a blockade-runner.

Also hanging around the bar were Union spies who easily kept track of which Confederates were coming and going. It must have been comical with Federals and Confederates watching each other over their glasses of beer and whiskey. Everyone in the bar either knew or suspected everyone else they did not know personally of being an enemy.

One man who showed up in Canada to sign up with Hines was an old comrade from Morgan's cavalry, George St. Leger Grenfell, a 62-year-old soldier of fortune from England, who had been fighting in foreign wars for more than forty-five years. Grenfell was a natural at espionage. Just before reaching Canada, he had a personal audience with Union secretary of war Stanton after convincing the Union War Department head that he had retired from service in the Confederacy. Grenfell told Stanton fantastic tales of how strong the Confederate army still was, and the only reason he had left it was that he was growing too old to fight. According to Grenfell, Stanton bought every word.

Grenfell threw in with the Confederates in Canada because he loved fighting for the underdog and operating as a spy and agitator in

Canada. At least this work put his aging body into a warm bed every night, something he did not have when he was in the saddle with Morgan's cavalry.

In addition to interviewing potential officers in Canada, Hines also made secret trips to secure arms and equipment. He would claim that two of the men helping him with this task were the brothers Fernando and Benjamin Wood. If such a meeting did occur and if they had been caught, both of the Wood brothers, both United States congressmen representing New York State, could have been tried and executed for associating with a known Confederate spy.

The *New York Daily News*, owned by Benjamin Wood, had always been an anti-Republican newspaper. In its later years, it may have received money to be just that. Hines claimed that he paid Benjamin $25,000 to continue to print anti-Republican stories in the *Daily News*.

Reporting on an apparent separate meeting between Clay and Benjamin, Clay wrote to Thompson that Benjamin virtually guaranteed an uprising in New York City when the fighting in Ohio, Indiana, and Illinois was launched. This claim, attributed by Thompson to Benjamin, would help make New York City a target in November 1864.

"If there is an insurrection in the West, a riot in New York would checkmate any attempt to suppress it. You will understand without further explanation. Holcombe [another Confederate agent in Canada] agrees with me that we can invest twenty thousand dollars in New York with profit, especially to assist the other operation in the West. The former will secure the fruits of the latter," wrote Clay to Thompson.

If Hines's story is true, former New York City mayor and current congressman Fernando Wood committed an even bigger crime than his brother Benjamin, who apparently suggested that New York City be targeted.

Hines said he traveled to New York City where Fernando put him in touch with a man in a small violin shop off Washington Square in New York City. That man assembled a cache of pistols and ammunition that were slipped aboard a ship and smuggled to Canada for use by the expatriate Confederate agents Hines was assembling.

For all the planning and all the hundreds of thousands of dollars in gold and silver that were expended, the Confederacy's plans to create an uprising in the Midwestern states were never fulfilled.

Though Hines, Grenfell, and Castleman traveled to Chicago in August 1864 just before the Democratic convention in order to make the attack on Camp Douglas to free its prisoners, the Copperheads never delivered that secret army to him. The trained Confederate soldiers sat in a Chicago hotel room for days waiting for Copperhead commanders who never came.

Disgusted with the lack of cooperation by the Copperheads, Hines and Grenfell went back to Canada. Thus, the plans to free the prisoners at Camp Douglas and open a new front in the Northwest were undone on two fronts:

On one front, there simply never was a huge secret army of Northerners who wanted to join with the Confederacy. They never existed except in the fertile imaginations of committed Copperheads who sold their existence to real Confederates. Men like Vallandigham were politicians who believed their own speeches but who never offered any proof that they had the backing they claimed. Thompson and Clay were similar types, politicians used to believing the bluster and boasts of fellow bloviators, so it is understandable that they would have fallen for such stories.

Hines, however, was a military man who had seen hard fighting. He should have known better than to trust the words of men who were not military and who had never looked down the barrel of a gun.

On the second front was a double agent named Felix Stidger who reported whatever plans he discovered to his commanding officer in Indianapolis, Indiana, and had long ago infiltrated the Northwest Confederacy Conspiracy. Stidger, who was described as looking no more harmless than a store clerk, was able to wheedle his way into the confidences of the various splinter organizations that claimed to be forming the Northwest Conspiracy.

Hines and Grenfell would return once again to Chicago to try to rally the Copperheads. Stidger would be waiting for them. Stidger would be the star witness at the Indianapolis trials of the Copperhead he supposedly caught in the act of disloyalty. Those trials were notable for how the judge manipulated the testimony to win convictions from the military tribunal.

The Northwest Conspiracy that was supposed to have launched itself in August 1864 to create the Northwest Confederacy never really advanced beyond the planning stages in a few hotel and barrooms in Canada. Middle-aged Midwestern farmers who read newspaper editorials raging at Lincoln's crackdown on dissent never knew that politicians they had never met counted them as would-be soldiers in a secret army ready to fight the Union.

Still, some elements of the Northwest Conspiracy survived into November 1864. The plans to disrupt the American Midwest had included trying to influence the presidential and congressional election of 1864. If it proved possible, the largest cities in the United States would be attacked at the same time.

Hines had come up with the idea. Other men he had recruited in Canada would carry it out.

Chapter 11

"The People Have Lost All Confidence in Lincoln"

The year 1864 did not start well for Lincoln. In addition to the Copperheads who were still complaining about the draft, one of Lincoln's own cabinet members was trying to replace him on the presidential ticket.

Early in February, the allies of Secretary of Treasury Salmon Chase distributed an anonymously authored pamphlet that claimed: "The people have lost all confidence in his [Lincoln's] ability to suppress the rebellion and restore the Union."

The brochure blamed the Union army's failure to defeat the Confederates on Lincoln's "feebleness of will" and his "wont of intellectual grasp." Instead of the rail-splitter, the nation needed "an advanced thinker; a statesman profoundly versed in political and economic science, one who fully comprehends the spirit of the age."

Even worse than sponsoring a brochure that made Lincoln look simpleminded and ineffective, Chase cooked up a conspiracy with two Union generals to steal the 1864 Republican nomination for himself.

In the fall of 1863, Lincoln signed an amnesty bill calling for the readmittance into the Union of any seceded state that produced the signatures of 10 percent of its voters agreeing to sign a loyalty oath to the United States. At the time the law was passed, Lincoln imagined that he could collect the electoral votes of now captured Confederate states such as Louisiana, Arkansas, and Tennessee.

Chase, still smarting from being outmaneuvered in 1860 for the nomination that he was convinced was rightfully his, had other ideas of how to get those Southern states to vote for him.

As secretary of the treasury, Chase could appoint tax commissioners in occupied Confederate states with the power to tax captured property and sell it when the taxes were not paid. Chase selected a Vermont lawyer named Lyman D. Stickney as his main contact in Florida, granting him the power to appoint other tax commissioners. Chase imagined that if Florida was captured early in 1864, by the June Republican convention, Stickney would have built a network of tax commissioners who would be beholden to Chase. Those Chase men would then use their influence over high-ranking politicians and taxpayers to deliver Florida's nomination to their boss. Using Florida as a model, Chase figured he would be able to appoint tax commissioners in other former Confederate states trying to reenter the United States. With the former Confederacy controlled by his tax commissioners and his friends in Congress already organizing Union states for him, Chase saw a way to remove Lincoln painlessly from the picture before the nominating convention was even held.

There were two glitches in Chase's plans to use Florida as a stepping-stone to the presidency: First, Lincoln had heard about Chase's maneuvering. Second, Florida was still a Confederate state. Jacksonville and St. Augustine had been captured, but the Confederacy still controlled the state capital of Tallahassee and most of the interior of the state. The state's meager military forces would still have to be defeated in order to readmit it into the Union.

Two Union generals who commanded the military district that included the captured parts of Florida, Quincy Gilmore and Truman Seymour, both had ties to Chase. Apparently, at Chase's suggestion, but without mentioning his name as the inspiration for the suggested campaign, Gilmore and Seymour sought permission from the War Department to move west from Jacksonville toward Tallahassee. A suspicious Lincoln approved the Florida invasion, but also sent his personal secretary John Hay down to Jacksonville with thousands of loyalty oath forms for Floridians to sign. Hay's other job was to keep his eye on Seymour, who would be the general leading the invasion.

Lincoln and Chase were now in a race to capture Florida: Lincoln by signing up voters from captured cities who were now supposedly loyal to the Union, and Chase by using generals to capture territory so he could appoint tax commissioners to do his bidding.

Seymour and five thousand Union troops, the majority of them U.S. Colored Troops, started marching west from Jacksonville in February 1864. On February 20, 1864, Seymour ran into an entrenched force of Confederates at a pine swamp known as Ocean Pond, near the train depot of Olustee. Within hours, more than a third of Seymour's men were killed, wounded, and captured. The remainder frantically ran all the way back to Jacksonville. While the battle pitting five thousand men on each side against each other was hardly even a skirmish compared with the huge battles that had been fought in Virginia, Tennessee, and Mississippi earlier in the war, Olustee, expressed as a percentage of losses of men engaged, was the most crushing defeat the Union army suffered during the entire war.

Both Lincoln and Chase lost in Florida. Hay could not find enough defeated Confederates in Jacksonville willing to pledge loyalty to the Union, so he could not fill his quota. Seymour's defeat meant that Chase's cronies would not be able to hire that duplicitous web of tax collectors.

When yet another anti-Lincoln brochure that could be tied to him surfaced, an embarrassed Chase formally withdrew his name from presidential consideration on March 5, 1864. It was barely two weeks after the Union's debacle at Olustee.

Chase had been relatively easy for Lincoln to outmaneuver to assure himself the Republican nomination for president, but the Democrats remained a stubborn obstacle to any easy reelection bid in November 1864. New York's governor Seymour complained that it was ludicrous to claim that 10 percent of a state's voters who pledged loyalty to the Union really represented the voters' intentions in a majority of the state. He pointed out that under Lincoln's version of electoral math, 70,000 votes in the reconstructed Southern states was the equivalent of 16 million votes in the eight largest Union states with New York being the largest.

More darkly, Seymour and others pointed out that captured Confederate territory was under military control. In Seymour's view of the coming fall election, Lincoln would use the military to set up martial law governments in each of the captured Southern states. Seymour insisted that since Lincoln controlled the military, he was planning to control the votes where the U.S. Army was in control.

Even though Chase had taken himself out of the running, Lincoln still had another political opponent besides the Peace Democrats. It was his own Republican Party.

By 1864, the Republican party had split itself into two camps: One group consisted of congressmen and senators who supported the president's war efforts and his desire to bring the rebellious states back into the Union as quickly as possible. These politicians followed Lincoln's every wish.

The second group enjoyed the label of Radical Republicans because they admitted that they were radically opposed to showing any leniency toward a defeated Confederacy. The Radicals believed in subjugating the Southern states: treating them as conquered territories where white-owned land would be confiscated and given to freed slaves.

Most important of all, the Radicals believed it was the duty of Congress, not the president, to set any political policies to reconstruct the South after the war was over. Lincoln even had Radicals in his own cabinet including Secretary of War Stanton who was forever pushing Lincoln to pound the South into dust.

As 1864 dawned, Lincoln was fighting not only the Confederates but also his own party and the Peace Democrats. He claimed he was too busy to plan even for a second term. He was tired. He was distracted. And even putting Chase in his place did not seem to brighten Lincoln's mood by much.

Maybe the pressures of the office combined with the pressure to run for election while fighting both the Democrats and members of his own party caused Lincoln to make a horrendous mistake in judgment.

In February 1864, the president of the United States of America may have either expressly ordered or tacitly approved a full-scale military assault on Richmond with the purpose of assassinating the Confederate cabinet, including Jefferson Davis, the president of the Confederate States of America.

The thought of capturing Davis had occurred to Lincoln on other occasions. The president even encouraged just such an expedition. In early May 1863, Union general George Stoneman was sent rushing south toward Richmond with a force of cavalry in an attempt to capture the attention of Robert E. Lee's Army of Northern Virginia, which was then on the south banks of the Rappahannock River at Fredericksburg. Union general Joseph Hooker hoped Stoneman's cavalry raid would distract Lee while he crossed the Rappahannock and hit Lee on the left flank. Lee was not fooled and did not send his army after Stoneman. The Battle of Chancellorsville, fought on May 10, 1863, turned out to be a huge Confederate victory.

But while Stoneman's raid on Richmond was considered a failure in distracting Lee, one of its cavalry commanders, Judson Kilpatrick, came within a few miles of the Confederate capital before pulling back to rejoin the Army of the Potomac. Lincoln heard about this missed opportunity to have ridden into the Confederate capital. In a personal conversation with General Hooker, Lincoln said that Richmond must have been so defenseless of troops that the cavalry expedition "could have safely gone in and burnt every thing & brought us Jeff Davis."

Lincoln kept that thought. Nine months later, in early February 1864, Union general Ben Butler, then on the peninsula of Virginia east of the Richmond, received approval from Lincoln for another raid into the city. Butler went over the raid's objectives with its commander including objective number 3: "To capture some of the leaders of the rebellion, so that at least we can have means to meet their constant threats of retaliation and hanging of men white and black. If any of the more prominent can be brought off, I believe a blow will be given to the rebellion from which it will never recover."

Butler's raid was called off when the approach toward Richmond was found to be heavily fortified. Belatedly, Butler sent a note to his commander telling him to destroy the paper with the raid's objectives, but the instructions had already been filed, and Butler's admonition was not followed. The orders were later preserved in war archives.

Three weeks later, the War Department, with the express approval of Stanton, approved yet another cavalry raid into Richmond. Its commander was General Kilpatrick, the same man who had claimed to have almost reached the streets of Richmond eight months earlier. The supposed objective of the raid would be to free the Union prisoners being held at Belle Isle prison camp and Libby Prison.

Leading part of the 3,600-man raid was handsome, 21-year-old, one-legged Lieutenant Ulric Dahlgren. Like Colonel Elmer Ellsworth before him, Lincoln had taken a personal interest in advancing the career of young Dahlgren, son of Union navy admiral John Dahlgren, Lincoln's close friend. When Dahlgren walked into Kilpatrick's office asking to be a part of the upcoming raid, he may have brought with him a letter of introduction from the president himself. Kilpatrick readily put Lincoln's young friend in command of part of the raid that would try to slip in from Richmond's undefended southwest side while Kilpatrick's larger force approached from the north.

Though the raid had been approved at the top, no one including Lincoln, Stanton, or Kilpatrick wrote down any orders or the objectives of the raid. That was an unusual occurrence for an army steeped in bureaucracy. All of those who knew better forgot to tell Dahlgren, who had never before held any sort of command, to do the same.

Dahlgren, a young man anxious to prove himself to his famous father and to make a place for himself in the history of the war, wanted to remember all the details of the raid that he believed would make him a war hero. In a letter to his father before leaving, Dahlgren hinted at the raid's objectives: "If successful, it will be the grandest thing on record; and if it fails many of us will 'go up' [die]."

He wrote down his orders plus an address that he would say to his men once they got close to their target and put them in his coat pocket. It never occurred to him that he could be captured, wounded, or killed and that his orders could be found and read by Confederate authorities.

Both Kilpatrick's large force to the north of Richmond and Dahlgren's small force southwest of Richmond floundered around in the darkness, unable to cross the James River, which was running higher than they had expected. Instead of waiting for or trying to find Dahlgren, Kilpatrick pulled away to the north, leaving an unknowing Dahlgren on his own. Before even coming close to their objectives of downtown Richmond, Dahlgren's men were discovered. Dahlgren was shot and killed on March 2, 1864, and most of his men were captured. When the young officer's body was searched, a sheaf of papers, the orders he had written to himself, was discovered.

The orders and address shocked the Confederates who read them: "We hope to release the prisoners from Belle Island first & having seen them fairly started, we will cross the James River into Richmond, destroying the bridges after us & exhorting the released prisoners to destroy & burn the hateful City & do not allow the Rebel Leader Davis and his traitorous crew to escape."

A second document written in the same hand also suggested the same: "Jeff Davis and Cabinet killed." A notebook on the body had yet another diary entry: "Jeff Davis and Cabinet must be killed on the spot."

Davis at first laughed off the implication that Lincoln had sent mounted assassins after him, but his cabinet was not amused. After a few days of contemplation and examination of the documents to make sure they were authentic, the cabinet called in the Richmond newspapers. The newspapers published the content of the Dahlgren papers, charging that the North had embarked on a new kind of war where killing political leaders was now sanctioned.

Most of the Northern newspapers reacted with shock that Southerners would even think that the Union would participate in assassination. The *New York Times* responded to the South's charges with: "No officer of the American army would ever dream of putting to death civil officers taken captive in such a raid."

There was a problem with the Northern newspapers' shocked reaction. At least one newspaper had prior knowledge that the raid was going to take place and that the raid had a purpose other than attacking military targets.

The *New York Herald*, a Democratic newspaper, could have published details of the raid on the day it left thanks to a source either within the War Department or from the vainglorious

Kilpatrick himself. The newspaper's editors chose to wait a few days so as not to reveal a military secret. The newspaper assumed the raid's success when it printed on February 29, three days before Dahlgren would be killed, that "Kilpatrick started to make a dash upon Richmond, for the purpose of releasing our prisoners there, sacking the rebel capital, and effecting such other laudable purposes as might be within his power."

Southern newspaper editors thought they saw clearly through what was meant by the vague "laudable purposes." Those were code words for assassination, and the Southern papers more than hinted that it was time for retaliation.

The *Richmond Sentinel* wrote:

Man proposes but God disposes. LINCOLN, through his armed emissaries, has told us what he would *like* to do, and he has made the *attempt* to do it. Morally, therefore, he and his officers are guilty of the crime. . . . Let LINCOLN and KILPATRICK remember that they have bidden their subordinates give no quarter to the Confederate chiefs! Perhaps even a Scotch cap and military cloak will not prevent a just and stern vengeance from overtaking them for this revolting outrage on civilization and the rules of war. . . . What course should our Government pursue under this revelation of the enormous infamy of our enemies? It is a question not to be put aside; nor is it a question to be answered under impulse. We commend it to the attention of our authorities; for it is of a nature that requires a prompt decision.

Two days later the same newspaper continued: "He [Dahlgren] was the willing instrument for executing an atrocity which his superiors had carefully approved and sanctioned. Truly there is no depth of dishonor and villainy to which Lincoln and his agents are not capable of descending."

The *Richmond Daily Dispatch* also hinted at retaliation:

The chief criminals are Lincoln, Seward, and the Black Republican crew at Washington—men who have deliberately planned and directed the commission of one of the most gigantic crimes in the annals of human warfare. Upon them let the execrations of all civilized men descend, as well as upon their miserable tools, some of whom have been sent to that great tribunal where all must one day stand and receive the just reward of their deeds.

The Northern newspapers never asked Lincoln, Stanton, or Kilpatrick if they had ordered such a raid. Lincoln, who met with young Dahlgren on February 1 and Kilpatrick on February 13 before sending Kilpatrick to meet with Stanton on the same day, never publicly addressed the Confederacy's assertions that he had personally approved the raid. Lincoln did send Admiral Dahlgren a personal note expressing his sadness at the loss of Ulric.

Historians have never determined if Lincoln and Stanton approved the assassination of the Confederate cabinet as an object of the Dahlgren raid. After the war was over in December 1865, Stanton specifically requisitioned the orders and the notebook Dahlgren was carrying on the day he was killed. Those papers had been in the Confederate archives that had been captured when Richmond was captured on April 3, 1865. What Stanton did with the Dahlgren papers and any orders he had in his file cabinets relating to the raid will never be known. Nothing related to the raid that Stanton had access to was ever delivered to the National Archives, nor do any specific orders from Stanton to Kilpatrick mentioning assassination appear in the 128 volumes of the Official Records of the War of the Rebellion that were published after the war.

The Confederates did not need a specific admission of guilt from Lincoln or Stanton that they ordered a presidential assassination. They believed the orders Dahlgren was carrying and the handwritten notes he had added as an address to his men. How to deal with an opposing government that had such murderous ideas was something still to be figured.

Just months before the Republican National Convention scheduled for June, some of New York City's newspapers were still looking for a president they liked. It was not Lincoln.

In February 1864, James Gordon Bennett's *New York Herald* called Lincoln "a joke incarnated. . . . The very idea that such a man as he should be President of such a country as this is a very ridiculous joke. . . . The hopes he appears to entertain of a re-election are, however, the most laughable jokes of all."

Just two weeks later, the same newspaper would hint at the goals of the Dahlgren raid while it was still in progress.

Horace Greeley's *New York Tribune*, which had supported Lincoln for most of the war, now turned against him with Greeley searching the ranks of politicians and military leaders alike for a man to replace the president. At one time the previous fall, Greeley had written Secretary of State William Seward a note saying that no one was "better qualified for President than yourself, nor one whom I would more cordially support."

Now that Chase had taken himself out of the presidential race, Greeley was trying to postpone the Republican convention from June until September in hopes that something would happen on the battlefield that would remove Lincoln from consideration. The strongest candidate waiting on the sidelines appeared to be John C. Fremont, the 1856 Republican presidential candidate and a general Lincoln had fired in 1862 for issuing his own order freeing slaves in the district under his command in Missouri.

Only Henry J. Raymond's *New York Times* liked Lincoln and predicted that he would be the nominee at the June convention: "Mr. Lincoln will surely be the Union [Republican] candidate, when the Nominating Committee meets, as the sun will rise on that day."

None of this dissatisfaction with Lincoln went unnoticed in the South. Southern newspapers called for their armies to renew attacks against the Union in hopes that its soldiers would grow tired and vote Lincoln out themselves. One newspaper editor wrote that the way to win the war with the North was "carrying a sword in one hand and an olive branch in the other."

The Confederate government did not hold out much hope that Lincoln would not be renominated by his own party, but the Davis cabinet did have high hopes that a Peace Democrat could defeat Lincoln in November. If that happened, the Confederate leaders imagined the new president would sit down at the bargaining table to talk about a peaceful parting of the two regions.

It was to that end that Davis sent Thompson, Clay, and Hines to Canada. If the establishment of a Northwest Confederacy by enlisting armed Copperheads did not work out, then at least the Confederacy could try to influence the Democratic Party to put up a candidate who would push for a negotiated settlement of the war.

Greeley's hope that change on the battlefield would decide the Republican nomination did come true, but not as he expected, and not as soon as he wanted. While Grant was stalled in his attempt to destroy Lee, Sherman slowly but surely continued to close in on the vital Georgia railhead in Atlanta. Assuming Sherman would succeed, the very heart of the South now had a dagger poised over it.

To throw both the Radical Republicans and the Democrats into a state of confusion just before the national convention in Baltimore in June, the Republicans renamed their party the National Union Party and selected a Democrat as President Lincoln's vice-presidential candidate. That was Tennessee senator Andrew Johnson, the only Southerner not to resign his seat and vacate Washington once the South seceded. The Radicals, irritated that Lincoln had brought a Democrat onto the ticket, held their own convention, nominating Fremont.

When the Democrats met in Chicago for their convention in late August, the Peace Democrat faction was in charge. Peace with the South so dominated the work of the convention that the song "Dixie" was played and cheered by the delegates while Union songs were met with silence.

Remarkably, Vallandigham, back from Canada, was put in charge of writing the party's platform, which included a plank assuring voters that a Democratic president would seek peace with the South. The Ohio congressmen knew about the plot to liberate Camp Douglas, and he may have waited to see men in gray rags running through the streets of Chicago, but by this time the plot had fallen apart.

After the Democrats announced their platform that called for an immediate cessation of hostilities so both sides could meet, diarist George Templeton Strong remarked that the Democratic Party platform seemed so pro-Southern that "Jefferson Davis might have drawn it."

Strong was not far off the mark. Vallandigham had been in regular contact with Confederate commissioners Jacob Thompson and Clement Clay while in exile in Canada. They had been in regular contact with Davis. Davis certainly knew that the Democrats would offer a peace plank at its convention. He was counting on it to be the backbone of the Democrats' fall campaign and the key to it winning the national election.

Curiously, even though the Peace Democrats had written the party plank for making peace with the South, the Democrats' presidential candidate was Union general George McClellan of New Jersey. McClellan had twice been commander of the Union Army of the Potomac and twice fired by Lincoln for inaction in that role. New York governor Seymour was available, a Peace Democrat to run on a peace plank, but he was never seriously considered when compared with McClellan.

Several days after the Democratic convention, word came that Sherman had captured Atlanta. Just a month earlier Admiral David Farragut had captured Mobile, Alabama. With the war going so well for the Union now, McClellan rejected the peace plank and promised to prosecute the war just as Lincoln had done.

In September 1864, after the Democratic convention, the Confederate cabinet in Richmond and the Confederate commissioners took stock of everything.

The military situation on land looked grim. Sherman had defeated the Army of Tennessee and now possessed Atlanta. Grant was still trying to close a circle around Petersburg and Richmond, effectively trapping the Army of Northern Virginia inside. Sheridan was running wild in the Shenandoah Valley, burning farms, killing livestock, hanging partisans, and threatening to burn entire towns, threats that the weakened Confederate forces in the valley could do little to stop.

Conditions at sea were deteriorating. The CSS *Alabama*, the Confederacy's most successful sea raider, had been sunk off the coast of France in June. Union admiral David Farragut's fleet had run a gauntlet of floating torpedoes and cannon fire from both ironclads and forts to capture control of Mobile Bay in August. Blockade-runners were still making it into ports like Charleston, Wilmington, and Savannah, but more and more Union ships were being added to the blockading squadrons, making it more difficult for blockade-runners to move in and out of ports.

The political situation did not look much better. Despite heavy opposition from people within his own party, the Republicans had renominated Lincoln in early June. At their own convention at the end of August, the Democrats had written a peace plank platform for a former general who rejected it. The Copperheads in Ohio, Illinois, and Indiana who had promised to open a new front in the war had proved to be paper tigers: all talk of revolution but no nerve actually to fight against the Union. The Confederate prisoners in Camp Douglas and Rock Island were still withering away and dying of disease and starvation.

England, France, and all the other European countries were still withholding their support because of the South's ownership of slaves. Canada was reluctantly allowing Thompson, Clay, and the other Confederate agents to operate from within its borders. Only the Vatican had recognized the Confederacy as a separate nation.

Davis in Richmond and Thompson in Canada realized that there was an obvious opportunity coming up with the November elections to strike back at the North someway, somehow. On November 8, the North would choose between Lincoln and McClellan. If that election could somehow be disrupted, the Union might be more willing to look at a settlement with the South.

How to accomplish that disruption was the problem the South faced. The Confederacy did not have armies capable of marching into the North again. But there were loyal Confederate soldiers who still wanted to fight; who still wanted to get even for Sheridan burning out civilians in the Shenandoah; and who still wanted to avenge the death of their commander, General John Hunt Morgan, who had been murdered in Greeneville, Tennessee, on September 4, 1864.

Those men were in Canada.

THE PLAN

Chapter 12

"Organize Only in 'the Territory of the Enemy'"

There was nothing of military value in Franklin County, Vermont, or its county seat, St. Albans, a town of about four thousand resting beside Lake Champlain, unless being one of the largest suppliers of maple syrup in the Union could be considered important to the war effort.

But Franklin County was home to two Union generals: General William "Baldy" Smith, who had organized the First Vermont Brigade, and General George Stannard, who led the Second Vermont Brigade.

Smith had not been a particularly dangerous general to the Confederacy. Just a few months earlier, Smith had inadvertently extended the life of the Confederacy. On June 15, 1864, Smith's division captured the outer trenches of Petersburg, Virginia, a military feat that so surprised the general, he refused to believe that he had accomplished anything. Smith refused to press forward and take the rest of the city out of fear that he was being led into a trap. He was convinced that Robert E. Lee's entire Army of Northern Virginia lurked out of sight, just waiting for his men to begin marching on Petersburg. In fact, most of Lee's men were more than thirty miles to the north around Richmond. Smith had so surprised the Confederacy that Lee himself at first refused to believe that Union troops had made a swift march on his Petersburg defenses.

Smith had a golden opportunity to capture Petersburg, embarrass Lee, make himself a hero, and end the war possibly in the summer of the 1864. Instead, he refused to let his men advance until Lee had rushed in reinforcements to save the city. That blunder of refusing to capture an underdefended city cost Smith his reputation with the Army of the Potomac.

Having Smith, the St. Albans native, in the Union army ranks was an advantage to the Confederacy. Attacking the town on his account made no sense.

But Stannard was another story, and possibly one reason that St. Albans was scouted out and targeted for an attack. The 44-year-old commander of the Second Vermont Brigade was literally the first man to volunteer for service from the state and was one of those generals who often made good battlefield decisions on his own without waiting for orders from his superiors. One of Stannard's decisions cost the South dearly.

Stannard had been just another Union general for the first two years of the war until July 3, 1863. Most of Stannard's men were inexperienced garrison troops detailed to guard Washington City. Most had signed up for ninety-day enlistments, clearly not expecting to see real combat until they were rushed north to join the Third Division of the First Corps at Gettysburg. The brigade arrived too late to participate in the first and second days' fighting. They were put into line on the Union's far left on Cemetery Ridge.

At 1:30 p.m. on July 3, the green boys from Vermont, most of whom had never been under fire before, were shocked to see upward of fifteen thousand gray-clad Confederates emerge from a treed ridgeline one mile to the west of Cemetery Ridge. With the military precision that came from two years of hard fighting, the Confederates started marching straight through cannon fire directly at the Vermonters. Midway across the field, the Confederate line seemingly disappeared as the soldiers dropped into a swale on the battlefield. For a few minutes, the Confederates rested and then up they came over the rise, pushing forward ever closer to the Union line.

On the Confederates came, closing ranks with each swath of men cut down by artillery fire coming from the Round Top hills to the left of the Vermonters. As the Confederates grew closer, the Vermonters could distinguish more of the line coming toward them; the gray ranks became individual men carrying muskets.

As the Confederates crossed the Emmitsburg Turnpike, their ranks made a slight turn to the left, away from the direct front of the Vermonters. If the Vermonters breathed any sigh of relief that they were no longer the targets at whom the Confederates were aiming, it was only briefly.

Stannard saw an advantage in the Confederate movement away from his troops. As the Confederates swung their line to the left some forty-five degrees to concentrate their fire on the Union center, Stannard swung two regiments, the Thirteenth Vermont (which had also been raised from Franklin County) and the Sixteenth Vermont, out ninety degrees from behind their defensive line.

The Confederate brigade commanded by General James Kemper, now to the Vermonters' front, did not notice this threat. Stannard opened a devastating, unanswered fire on Kemper's men, shattering the Virginians and spoiling the Confederate plan to concentrate Kemper's men with the rest of the Confederate attack to punch through on a single point of the Union line.

Not long after this attack, Stannard saw a supporting force of Confederates under General Cadmus Wilcox approaching from the west. Yet again, he swung two regiments out from his defensive line in order to pour flanking fire into the Confederates. Just as Kemper's line had been demolished by the Vermonters, so too was Wilcox's supporting force of Floridians and Alabamians.

The bold movements of Stannard to pull out of a defensive line and to move exposed onto the battlefield had been unordered and not approved by his superiors. Second Corps commander general Winfield Scott Hancock initially rode up to Stannard and shouted that the Vermonter had "gone to hell" by creating a hole in the Union's defensive line. Stannard replied, "To hell it is then, as it is the only thing that can possibly save the day." Seconds later, Hancock was shot in the thigh and Stannard handed his commander a handkerchief to staunch the blood. After the battle, Stannard was praised by his superior generals for his initiative in pulling his regiments out of line and into open combat.

In September 1864, Stannard suffered his fifth and most serious wound of the war. His right arm was shattered by a ball, resulting in its amputation. He was at home recuperating, just ten miles outside of St. Albans, when the war he thought he had left in Virginia came visiting on October 19, 1864.

The Confederate cabinet certainly knew who Stannard was, probably knew where he was from, and definitely knew what his Vermonters had done to Southern hopes of winning a major battle on Northern soil. They must have had some sense of seeking revenge when a coded message was sent on August 20 to the Confederate agents in Canada.

Sent by Secretary of War Seddon to a young lieutenant he had just ordered to Canada in July, the message read: "It is right that the people of New England and Vermont especially, some of whose officers have approved of their course, should have brought home to them some of the horrors of such warfare." That cryptic message certainly applied to Stannard, the first man to volunteer from Vermont.

The October 19 attack on St. Albans was planned to take place between two other much larger attempts to disrupt normal life in the North: former Morgan raider Hines's attempts to release the Confederate prisoners of war in Illinois before the Democratic Party Convention in late August and the still-to-come attempts to disrupt the national election in other major cities on November 8.

Leading the raid on St. Albans was another former member of Morgan's command, 20-year-old Lieutenant Bennett H. Young. A native Kentuckian, Young had been destined to follow in his father's footsteps as a Presbyterian minister when the start of the war brought him home from the seminary. Judging from a wartime photograph showing a smooth-faced young man with thick hair combed back over his head, Young was apparently too young to grow a proper mustache and beard like his comrades. When Young joined the Eighth Kentucky Cavalry, he set aside his seminary teaching of turning the other cheek and became a hot-blooded young man looking for adventure.

He was also looking for revenge. According to a story Young

would later tell a newspaper reporter, he joined the Confederate army after a Union soldier raped a young woman he intended to marry.

Despite his deep-seated anger at what had happened, Young kept a keen sense of humor. While crossing the Cumberland River in Kentucky at the start of Morgan's June 1863 raid, some of the men had taken off everything—including their uniforms and underwear—when a Union patrol came up. Seeing men in the water, the Federals began to fire, unaware that some of Morgan's men were already about to rush at them from the riverbank.

"Those who swam with horses, unwilling to be laggard, not halting to dress, seized their cartridges boxes and guns and dashed upon the enemy. The strange sight of naked men engaging in combat amazed the enemy. The Union pickets did not know what to think of soldiers fighting naked as jaybirds," said Young.

When Morgan and his men invaded Indiana and Ohio on that same raid, Young was amused at how much fear they struck in the hearts of the people.

"[To them we were] real sure enough devils, horns, hoofs and all. Every rhyme was put under conscription to help tell how awful Morgan's men were," said Young. Young's battlefield career ended not long after that comment when he was captured and taken to Camp Douglas on the south side of Chicago.

Camp Douglas was described by one prisoner as "80 acres of hell," housing more than eight thousand Confederates in rude clapboard houses that did little to keep out the rain in the summer or the winds in the winter. When an inspector for the U.S. Sanitary Commission visited the camp when it was still relatively new in 1862, he reported to its commander:

Sir, the amount of standing water, unpoliced grounds, of foul sinks, of unventilated and crowded barracks, of general disorder, of soil reeking miasmatic accretions, of rotten bones and emptying of camp kettles, is enough to drive a sanitarian to despair. I hope that no thought will be entertained of mending matters. The absolute abandonment of the spot seems to be the only judicious course; I do not believe that any amount of drainage would purge that soil loaded with accumulated filth or those barracks fetid with two stories of vermin and animal exhalations. Nothing but fire can cleanse them.

Conditions had not improved by the summer of 1863 when Young and other members of Morgan's Raiders arrived. Their reputation as raiders of Northern soil preceded them, making the Kentuckians and Tennesseans objects of wrath from the guards. When the righteous Young protested to the camp commander about the guards' indiscriminately firing into some of the huts, killing and wounding men who were lying in their bunks, he was thrown into a dungeon. A few weeks later, Young escaped and made his way first to Toronto and then to Halifax, a known staging point for escaped Confederates wanting to make their way south by boarding a ship and then running the blockade back into a Southern port.

It was in Halifax while waiting for his ship south that Young met Confederate commissioner Clay, who was impressed with the young man's desire to seek revenge against the North. Clay wrote out a letter of introduction to Secretary of War Seddon, recommending Young for an important mission back in Canada should he make it safely to Richmond.

Young was a lucky and probably charming young man. He had avoided being shot in combat, survived a Union prison camp, made a successful escape from that same camp into Canada, and then met a high-ranking Confederate commissioner who took a liking to him. It also explains how a lowly private was able to get an audience with the Confederate secretary of war and wrangle a lieutenant's commission that came right from the War Department rather than through normal military channels. Young would have had a better chance of seeking blood revenge had he rejoined Morgan's command, which the general was desperately trying to reform, but Clay's offer of clandestine activities in a foreign country must have appealed to Young's sense of adventure.

At about the same time Hines was receiving orders from the Confederate secretary of war to proceed to Canada and report to Thompson, Young was given orders independent of Hines to return to Canada and report to Clay. Hines's orders were specific in terms of finding ways and means of working with the Copperheads in Illinois, Indiana, and Ohio to create the Northwest Confederacy and to free the Confederate prisoners in the prison camps.

Young's orders were more general. Seddon's orders, dated June 16, 1864, the same date that Young was promoted from private to lieutenant, were no more specific than to report to "C. C. Clay, Jun., for orders. You will collect together such Confederate soldiers who have escaped from the enemy, not exceeding twenty in number, that you may seem suitable for the purpose, and execute such enterprises as may be indicated to you." The order went on to warn Young not to violate Canada's neutrality laws and to organize only in "the territory of the enemy."

Curiously, Young's orders said he and his 20 men would be under the command of the War Department itself and "liable to be disbanded at its pleasure," an unusual arrangement for any military command. But perhaps this plan was necessary for a band of soldiers who would not be wearing uniforms and who would be operating in a foreign country without that country's leaders' knowledge.

Another mystery is why Seddon essentially set up parallel operations in Canada by having Young report to Clay in St. Catherines and not to Thompson in Toronto. Thompson was the overall commander of the Confederate operations in Canada, but Seddon did not even have Young go to meet him.

Seddon may have been trying to play Clay and Thompson against each other to see which one would yield results first. If that is true, Seddon was risking losing control of operations that he would only learn details about in the days, weeks, or months after they had been launched. Tensions had always been present between Clay and Thompson, and it appears that the addition of George Sanders to the mix of Confederate agents operating in Canada only added to the discord.

Young scouted several likely towns as targets for raids across the border, and he quickly settled on St. Albans. For whatever reason St. Albans was targeted, whether because it was the home of Stannard or because it was one of the closest targets to the Canadian border, allowing for a quick escape, the town became something of a symbol for a larger strategy.

Sanders, the mysterious third wheel of the Confederate Secret Service, saw any attack mounted by Young's band as the start of a major campaign to open a new war front in New England.

"St. Albans will merely be the starting point, the inauguration of a system of warfare which will carry desolation all along the frontier. There will be war to the knife and to the hilt. They will be made to think 20,000 men wait in Canada, across the border, eager and prepared. The towns will burn and be pillaged," said Sanders.

Sanders' use of the term "war to the knife and to the hilt" was a chilling phrase that dated back to the Kansas and Missouri border wars of the late 1850s. In those days, guerrillas on both sides indiscriminately raided civilian homes. In 1856, abolitionist John Brown and his sons, using long knives, had hacked several men they suspected of being slave owners to death.

Sanders, of course, was only the cheerleader for the raid. He would be sending younger men across the Canadian border, but he would stay safely behind in his nice, warm, safe hotel room.

There was another reason for attacking St. Albans that would later raise some questions among the Confederacy's defenders. Three banks were in the town, all of them on the town square. With enough men, Young would be able to pick all of them clean before the residents even knew what had happened.

The military mission of striking at the very far reaches of the Union on the Canadian border now had a mercenary element mixed into it. Young was asking his soldiers also to become bank robbers, common thieves who would have been shot down in their own Southern hometowns. Young told his volunteers not to worry about taking the money. All of it would be immediately transferred to the Confederacy where it would be used to help the war effort. None of them would keep any of the money they would steal.

Young began assembling his little band of raiders whom he intended to keep to thirty. Some of them may have been former Morgan men. All had escaped from prison camps and were waiting in Canada for ship rides home. All of them were young, brave, impetuous, and eager to do something for the war effort that was more exciting than sitting around a hotel room.

The twenty-one men who eventually became part of the raid began arriving in St. Albans during the second week of October. They came by train and horseback, traveling in twos or threes so as not to attract attention as to why draft-age young men in such a large group were traveling together. All of them came with cover stories that they freely shared with the clerks at the three hotels in town. Their cover stories were that they came for the good fishing in Lake Champlain, to buy horses, to hunt, and to enjoy the small town's hospitality.

Young claimed that he was a divinity student from St. Johns, Canada. He elaborated on his cover story by reading scripture aloud and carrying a Bible. The men passing themselves off as horse traders likewise knew what they were doing. All of them were from Kentucky, had supplied their own horses when they rode with the cavalry, and were already familiar with the stocky, strong breed of horse that was native to Vermont. Ironically, that breed of horse was called the Morgan, after the last name of the family that developed it. The Morgan was the favorite of Vermont's artillery units since it was a strong horse easily capable of pulling cannons and limbers (two-wheel carts) loaded with heavy ammunition.

Some of the undercover agents got a little too informal in talking with the locals; one boasted that he was "Jefferson Davis," which drew laughs from all those who heard the joke, but maybe a few curious stares at someone who would say such an odd thing so far north in Vermont.

Apparently, hearing the soft Southern accent coming from twenty-one young men who had suddenly appeared in their community did not raise any eyebrows among the Vermonters.

For several days the Confederates cased St. Albans, establishing that no companies of soldiers were home on leave with their muskets; that most young men like themselves were far away serving in the army; that no armory filled with weapons could be turned against them; and that no Union agents were watching them. The town appeared to be just what it was, a quiet farming and fishing community for which the war was a distant distraction.

Young had made one mistake in his planning. He wanted the raid to start on Tuesday, October 18, but that was also the day most farmers came into town to sell produce. With crowds of fighting-age men in town, Young quietly got word to his little army that they would wait a day. After thinking about it, Wednesday would be better anyway. All that money that would change hands on Tuesday would find its way into the banks and would be waiting for them the next day.

The next afternoon, all twenty-one of those nice, young, soft-spoken men made their way onto St. Albans' streets. This time they wore pairs of .36 caliber Navy Colts on their hips. That sight was finally enough to attract the attention of the townspeople. No one in town had any need to wear pistols on their hips. The war was far away. There was no danger in St. Albans that created the need for pistols.

Then Young fired a single shot from his pistol and declared that they were Confederate soldiers. Young ordered the townspeople into the town square where several of the men would be guarding them.

Four-man units moved on the three banks while other units gathered horses. It was in one of the banks that a soldier explained to a customer he was robbing why he was doing it: "We're Confederate soldiers detailed from General Early's army to come north, and to rob and plunder as your soldiers are doing in the Shenandoah Valley."

While the last part of the sentence may have been the motive the raiders claimed in their later defense, the first part made no sense. None of the Confederates on the raid were in Early's army. Early was at that very moment planning an attack for the next morning on General Philip Sheridan's Union army at Cedar Creek, Virginia, just south of the town of Winchester. Either the witness who heard Early's name mentioned got it wrong or the raiders were enhancing their revenge motive by claiming ties to a Confederate army that was indeed operating in the Shenandoah Valley at that time.

The first bank, the St. Albans Bank, lost more than $80,000; the second bank lost $75,000; and the third bank, the First National, lost $55,000. It was in the First National that one of the robbers boomed out a second motive, that the Confederates were in St. Albans in retaliation for what General William T. Sherman was doing to Georgia. By mid-October, Sherman was burning a swath of homes and farmsteads some sixty miles wide on either side of a line from Atlanta to Savannah.

Here and there unaware townspeople wandered into the streets, only to be met with stern looks and drawn Colts by strangers who herded the new captives into the town square. On occasion, a few shots would be fired to show the captives that the Confederates meant business. Some townspeople were wounded when they tried to stop their horses from being taken, but for the most part, displaying a cocked pistol was enough for most citizens to do the bidding of Young's men. Finally, one man, a laborer, was hit by a stray bullet. Mortally wounded, he was carried to one of the hotels.

With all his men now accounted for, Young ordered them to fire the town. The men began reaching into satchels they had with them and throwing small glass bottles of liquid against the buildings. The action puzzled the townspeople for a few seconds, but then they watched as small fires spontaneously erupted as the greenish liquid rolled down the wooden walls.

The bottles were Greek fire, a volatile chemical compound that the raiders must have brought with them from Canada. Once exposed to air, the Greek fire burst into flames, but more than a month of heavy rain had left the walls of all the buildings in St. Albans wet. The fires sputtered out without catching.

As Young and the raiders rode north, he had to be both elated and disappointed. He had collected more than $150,000 in cash that could be given to the Confederate cause, but he had not destroyed St. Albans as he had planned. The town still stood, defying the threat that Sanders had made to create terror in the northeastern states.

Young's force had not gotten away unscathed. Three of his men had been wounded by townspeople who had not been cowed into moving into the town square. One was bleeding heavily, whereas the other two were less serious.

All but one of Young's raiders made it back across the Canadian border with the severely wounded man hiding in a Vermont home. A St. Albans posse illegally crossed the border and found some of Young's men, including Young himself, but the posse itself was accosted by Canadian soldiers who gently but firmly reminded the

Vermonters that they were in Canada and had violated international treaties by coming across the border in search of Young and his men. The posse reluctantly gave up their prisoners on the promise that they would be taken to a Canadian jail to await trial.

All but one of the raiders were found by Canadian authorities and were put in jails while the government authorities pondered what to do with them. Some Union authorities, including General John Dix in New York City, thought for a while about crossing the border to steal away the captives, but cooler heads in Washington prevailed out of fear of creating an international incident. Explaining how a local posse had crossed the border in hot pursuit had been easy, but explaining why a full-scale invasion of Canada had been conducted by regular U.S. troops was another matter.

The reaction in Vermont and all of New England had been as Sanders had hoped and predicted. People who had thought the war was far away in the South now purchased pistols and looked at strangers in a different way. Militia units were called up and drilled in the event another raid would come rushing across the border.

Thompson would later say that he had no prior knowledge of the St. Albans raid. Curiously, Clement Clay also expressed surprise at the attack, as if he had never heard of its planning. When pressed, Clay said that Secretary of War Seddon must have proposed it to Young, even though Clay and Sanders had both attended meetings where the attack on St. Albans had been planned.

On November 1, the St. Albans raiders were brought before a Canadian court to determine if they should be extradited to the United States. Reading about the trial, maybe even attending it, were still more expatriate Confederates who were themselves planning to cross the Canadian border with the intention of harming a Northern city. That city had more than two hundred times the population of St. Albans.

And if these other prospective raiders learned something from the men who had tried to burn St. Albans, it was that Greek fire did not work well on outside, wet, wooden walls. These new raiders determined that they would set fires inside where the chemicals would have a better chance of catching.

Chapter 13

"New York Is Worth Twenty Richmonds"

After the August failure to rally the Copperheads in Illinois to free the Confederate prisoners at Camp Douglas and the October failure on the part of twenty-one Confederates to burn down St. Albans, Vermont, and create a panic in New England, Thompson, Clay, and Sanders were desperate for some kind of success. Every mission the Confederate Secret Service commissioners approved and launched, big or small, had failed. Nothing had worked since the Confederate commissioners had arrived in Canada.

In July 1864, they had tried simple subterfuge to trick the United States into ending its war against the Confederacy. Clay and Sanders, without authorization from anyone in power in Richmond or even Thompson in Toronto, held a series of peace talks in Niagara Falls, New York, with Union representatives, including newspaper editor Horace Greeley and Lincoln's personal secretary John Hay. A suspicious but willing Lincoln sent letters along with Hay laying out his terms that the South had to return to the Union and free its slaves before there would be peace. Clay and Sanders insisted that the Confederacy must remain independent.

The talks ended almost as soon as they had begun with Greeley looking like a foolish tool of Canadian Confederates who had no power to speak for the government in Richmond. Clay and Sanders had intended to trick Lincoln into talking about a forced peace treaty right before his election, but instead, Lincoln successfully portrayed the supposed peace talks as an example of how the Confederates were trying to manipulate Union opinion by using well-known public figures like Greeley.

"Greeley is like an old shoe, good for nothing new, whatever he has been. Like an old shoe, he is so rotten that nothing can be done with him. He is not truthful; the stitches all tear out," said Lincoln in a cabinet meeting.

Then the Confederates tried to open up a second war front by freeing thousands of Confederate soldiers behind Union lines. The often-delayed summer plot led by Thomas Hines to free the Confederate prisoners held in Northern prison camps near Chicago and Alton, Illinois, had not advanced beyond the Confederates waiting in a Chicago hotel room for a Copperhead army that never materialized.

When Hines's plan to free the prisoners by a land attack did not work, thought turned to freeing them with a water attack. Among the first Confederates to listen to these waterborne attack plans were two experienced Confederate scouts who had been sent north to get something moving.

Lieutenant Colonel Robert Martin was twenty-four years old, six feet tall, and 160 pounds. He had been "straight as an Indian" before a Union rifle ball struck him in April 1863, leaving him to walk with a stoop. With clear blue eyes, thick wavy hair, and a Van Dyke–style beard and mustache, the officer who had been a Louisville merchant before the war immediately left behind that mundane existence when he joined the Confederate army in April 1861. Martin was a true believer in the Confederacy, volunteering for its army weeks before Kentucky discussed leaving the Union.

Martin was selected to serve as a cavalry scout by Colonel (later General) Nathan Bedford Forrest. Forrest was so impressed by Martin's leadership skills that he suggested Martin raise his own regiment. Martin, who had mostly operated alone or with small units, did not want that kind of responsibility for other men, so he declined the colonelcy in favor of his fellow scout, Adam Johnson. With Johnson in command, Martin agreed to be lieutenant colonel of the

Tenth Kentucky Cavalry, which was attached to Morgan's brigade in December 1862.

During one short raid over the Ohio River into Indiana, Martin and Johnson showed their ingenuity by fabricating what looked like two cannons from discarded wheels, a stovepipe, and a log. Placing the fake artillery pieces on a hill overlooking the town of Newburgh, Indiana, the two officers rode into the town and convinced its small Union garrison to surrender lest they be shelled into submission. From that moment on, Johnson acquired the nickname "Stovepipe" Johnson. The more modest Martin allowed his colonel to take all the credit for the ruse.

Martin managed to escape capture on Morgan's July 1863 raid by swimming across the Ohio River into Kentucky. He rejoined Morgan's command when it was reformed in the spring of 1864. But just as Morgan discovered, the flower of Kentucky chivalry was mostly dead by this point of the war. The brave, enthusiastic, young men with whom Martin had ridden under Morgan's command were all gone.

During a raid in June 1864, some of Morgan's men robbed a bank in Mount Sterling, Kentucky. The robbery deeply troubled Martin. He sought a transfer out of Morgan's command.

After the war, Martin recalled that through the negligence or indisposition of Gen'l Morgan, the guilty parties were never brought to justice. After this disreputable affair, reflecting odium upon all in the eyes of the Southern public, I decided that if I could honorably do so, I would terminate my connection with the command. Having information that a few young officers of our army were operating in the Northern States in connection with a secret military organization having in view the success of our cause, and having a fondness for adventure and a partiality for secret service, I at once felt that this duty would afford me an opportunity to follow a career suited to my inclinations.

A second man eager to do something constructive with his time in Canada was Lieutenant John William Headley, a baby-faced,

clean-shaven, 24-year-old lieutenant who had most recently served
with the First Kentucky Cavalry under Morgan. Like Martin, Headley had started his Confederate career with the cavalry of Nathan
Bedford Forrest. When the infantry commanders of Fort Donelson,
Tennessee, abandoned their men and fled in February 1862, Forrest's
cavalry refused to surrender. Led by their fiery commander, the men
rode their horses through freezing water toward a narrow notch of
land that was not controlled by the Federals. They escaped to fight
again another day.

Such adrenaline-producing adventure invigorated Headley. He
was soon scouting behind Union lines. It was on one scouting mission
that he met and fell in love with a woman whom he would eventually
marry.

When Headley heard about the February 1864 Dahlgren raid on
Richmond and read the newspaper accounts of how the young Union
lieutenant had planned to assassinate President Jefferson Davis, he
thought of revenge.

> Many a man would express his hope that the day would come
> when there would be a chance to retaliate. It seemed to aggra-
> vate everyone that the public sentiment of the North gloried
> in the persecution of noncombatants, the total devastation of
> homes and all personal property; and especially the subjugation
> and degradation of the Southern people. This Northern spirit
> seemed to be intensified by the conviction that the South could
> only be conquered by ruin and starvation.

Headley eventually transferred to Morgan's command, where he
was elevated to sergeant. At some point, Captain Martin of the Tenth
Kentucky took note of Sergeant Headley of the First Kentucky. When
Martin joined the Confederate Secret Service, he requested that
Headley also receive similar orders and a promotion to lieutenant.
Without asking for any transfer or even knowing that Martin was
acting on his behalf, Headley received orders relieving him of duty in
the cavalry. He was reunited with Martin, and both were ordered to
Canada on September 1, 1864.

While commissioners Thompson and Clay had taken blockade-runners north, Martin and Headley made their way by land passing through Chicago and Detroit. Sending Martin and Headley north by the more dangerous land route rather than sending them by the relatively safe method of taking a blockade-runner was a strange choice made by Confederate officials trying to get capable men in place in Canada. It may have been an attempt by Confederate authorities in Richmond to allow Martin and Headley to maintain cover stories that they were escaped Confederate prisoners heading north should they be arrested before reaching Canada.

Within a few weeks, Martin and Headley were in Toronto posing as escaped Confederate prisoners, a lie to the one hundred real escaped prisoners who must have been forced on the two officers by Richmond in order to mask their true identities as two of the Confederacy's most experienced and successful scouts. Richmond must have correctly guessed that Toronto was swarming with Union detectives who would have focused on any men telling their supposed comrades that they had been ordered to Canada to assist the Confederate Secret Service.

Martin and Headley joined the only two other Confederate soldiers sent specifically to Canada by the Confederate government, Captain Thomas Hines of the Ninth Kentucky Cavalry and Major John Castleman of the Second Kentucky Cavalry. It was probably planned on Richmond's part that all four of the professional soldiers now turned Confederate agents had all served in Morgan's command. They had known each other for at least three years, had fought together, and knew that each was a loyal Confederate officer. There was no chance that anyone at the planning and leadership level could turn out to be a Union detective or double agent.

But even though scouts Martin and Headley had been ordered to Canada, Thompson did not have an immediate job for them. It was during this time that they sat in on informal talks about attacking Northern cities using captured Union warships sailing on the Great Lakes.

Thompson introduced Martin and Headley to Captain Charles

H. Cole, who claimed to have ridden with Nathan Bedford Forrest and John Hunt Morgan. Cole was a somewhat shadowy character.

Headley wrote a postwar book on his war experiences called *Confederate Operations in Canada and New York*. In the book, Headley details the meetings he attended with Cole, but does not specifically say that he recognized Cole as a former Morgan or Forrest officer, even though both he and Martin had served in the commands of both Morgan and Forrest.

In that first meeting with Martin and Headley, Cole talked casually about hijacking ships and steam tugs and using them to attack Chicago, Detroit, Milwaukee, Sheboygan, and Buffalo. Cole made himself out to be a master spy by filing a detailed report on the defenses of each city he thought was vulnerable.

"Buffalo is poorly protected. . . . There is little difficulty in bringing vessels to bear against Camp Douglas [in Chicago]. . . . Milwaukee is an easy place to take possession of. . . . Port Washington [near Sheboygan] is a small settlement with little of advantage, but its people are strong friends and determined in their resistance to the draft. . . . Lake Erie furnishes a splendid field for operations," wrote Cole in a detailed report that seemed to indicate that he had visited each city looking for defense weaknesses.

Of all the vulnerable cities Cole examined, he seemed to be most fascinated with Chicago. To reach Camp Douglas, he suggested capturing local steam tugs, mounting them with cannons, and then moving to within cannon range of Camp Douglas. After the prisoners were freed, the ambitious Cole planned on destroying Chicago's drawbridges so his barges could sail up and down the Chicago River shelling buildings.

Cole did not specify where he would get the cannons he wanted to mount on those tugs. Nor did he explain where he would get crews to man his private navy. All the men imprisoned at Camp Douglas were soldiers captured deep in the interior of the South. It seems unlikely many of them would have known much about operating steam-powered boats on narrow inland waters like canals.

Such grandiose talk from Cole about how easy it would be to attack cities from the water should have raised suspicions in Martin and Headley, two experienced Confederate scouts who were used to lying to enemies deep behind the lines of battle. The cities Cole mentioned attacking were separated by hundreds of miles. To have reached all of them would have required sailing on three of the five Great Lakes: Lake Erie, Lake Huron, and Lake Michigan. Such a trip would have taken weeks. If Cole had made such a scouting trip by ship himself, he did not mention it in the meeting, or at least Headley did not record it.

There was only one Union warship operating on the Great Lakes, the fourteen-gun USS *Michigan*, a paddle wheeler also equipped with sails that was based on Lake Erie. Even if the *Michigan* were captured, it would have taken weeks of sailing to reach even Sheboygan from Buffalo, but Cole talked as if the targeted cities were virtually neighbors of each other.

Still, Cole's ambitious plan sounded good to Thompson. Though Martin and Headley had sat in on the talks with Cole, Thompson held them back for other missions. They were lucky.

Thompson assigned Cole and an experienced sailor and privateer from Virginia named John Yates Beall to hijack two ships, the unarmed passenger steamer *Philo Parsons* and the warship *Michigan*. Both ships would sail to Johnson's Island off Sandusky, Ohio, where more than three thousand Confederate officers were being held in a prison camp on the island. The plan was that the *Michigan*'s fourteen cannons would intimidate the Union garrison into releasing the officers. The highest-ranking officers, including several generals, would board the *Michigan*, the *Philo Parsons*, and any other vessels that could be captured for a quick trip across Lake Erie to Canada and freedom. The rest of the officers would try to make their way to Canada or back to the South on their own.

Once the senior officers were safely in Canada, Beall would then presumably use the *Michigan* to raid the coastal cities of Ohio, Michigan, and Wisconsin just as Cole had suggested. It was an ambitious, complex plan that seems to have been poorly thought out.

Beall, who had commanded nothing more than two small wooden raiding ships on the Chesapeake Bay, would have been in heaven with the 163-foot *Michigan*. It was the Navy's first iron-hulled sailing ship, built more than twenty years before the more heavily armored ironclads CSS *Virginia* and USS *Monitor*. It had a top speed of more than ten knots. Among its guns were one thirty-pounder Parrott rifle with a range of up to five miles and five twenty-pounder Parrott rifles with ranges of two miles. If Beall could follow up his capture of the ship with the capture of coal supplies to keep the *Michigan*'s engines stoked, he would indeed command the Great Lakes' coastal cities as Captain Cole had suggested.

Beall started his mission on September 18, 1864, by capturing the *Philo Parsons* with the help of nineteen other men, who have never been identified, and who were presumably escaped Confederates living in Canada. Beall waited several miles off Sandusky Bay, out of sight of Johnson's Island, for a rocket signal from the *Michigan* telling him that Cole had successfully taken over the ship by drugging the officers and men during a late-night dinner.

No rockets were fired at the appointed time. Beall could see the *Michigan* lying at anchor. Figuring that Cole had forgotten the signal but that the Union warship's crew was indeed drugged, which would explain why they were not sailing out to identify the *Philo Parsons*, Beall decided to press on with the attack without waiting for the signal. As he was preparing to sail toward the *Michigan*, seventeen of Beall's nineteen men told him that the lack of a word from Cole was ominous. Instead of pressing on, they wanted to call off the attack. Beall, who the Federals considered a pirate, was facing a mutiny of his own. Reluctantly, Beall sailed for the safety of Canada where he scuttled the *Philo Parsons*.

Beall's crew had been correct. The captain of the *Michigan* had been alerted to the plot. Had Beall and the *Philo Parsons* approached, they would have been blown out of the water.

Cole would later claim that all had been going well on his end during the weeks prior to the planned hijacking. He had gained the confidence of the captain and his officers by hosting parties for them on shore. They had even taken him aboard the *Michigan* for tours. He had arranged for the officers to drink plenty of wine on the night of September 19, which he hinted would be drugged enough to incapacitate them before any attack by Beall on the twentieth.

Curiously, Cole did not attend the dinner party at which he intended to drug the officers. His story was that the drugs were in the champagne bottles, so he did not need to be at the party to make sure the officers drank it.

That night Cole was arrested in his hotel room on the charge of being a spy. He then revealed the plans for Beall and his men to hijack the *Michigan*.

Though Cole remained in Union custody for many months, he might not have been a Confederate at all. He seems to have been born in Pennsylvania, and there is no hard evidence that he actually served as a captain with Forrest's cavalry or in any Confederate unit.

There were three alternatives to Cole's identity:

First, Cole may have just been what he claimed to be, a loyal Confederate who developed a plan to attack Union waterside cities. Or he could have been a double agent, a Union spy who infiltrated the Confederate Secret Service in Canada in order to disrupt its missions. If that were the case, his arrest would have been part of his cover story in order to root out other Confederate agents.

A third alternative was that Cole could have been lying to both the Confederates and the Federals. He could have been a man whose taste for adventure outran his good sense, resulting in his arrest for being a spy when he was really just playing a game for his own amusement and excitement.

Military adventures such as freeing the prisoners at Camp Douglas and Johnson's Island had not worked. Neither had the St. Albans raid. Thompson decided to try something more subversive and peaceful that did not involve shooting anyone.

Thinking again of something that could undermine the candidacy of Lincoln, the Confederate commissioners developed a last-minute idea of taking over at least one Northern state by honest electoral means. It was a long shot since state elections in 1863 in Pennsylvania, Ohio, and Indiana had all gone for the Republicans, but Thompson still believed stories that Copperheads were anxiously waiting to help the Confederacy.

Once again and inexplicably, Illinois was the focus of the plan. For incomprehensible reasons, Thompson still believed that the Sons of Liberty, the same supposed pro-Confederacy group that had failed to turn out to help free Confederate prisoners of war over the summer, would turn out in Illinois on November 8, Election Day.

Early in October 1864, Congressman James C. Robinson of Illinois, a Peace Democrat, sent word to Thompson that if he was elected governor, he would put more than 60,000 stands of arms in state armories into the hands of the Sons of Liberty. Acting on nothing more than a politician's word, Thompson sent more than $50,000 in Confederate funds to Robinson's campaign. Thompson did not even bother asking what Robinson expected to do with the money since there was only two weeks until Election Day.

The genesis of the plan has been lost to history. But at the same time Thompson was trying to take over Illinois's governorship peacefully, he wanted to disrupt the presidential elections in several states.

Starting around mid-October 1864, Thompson put in motion the most dangerous and ambitious plan the Canadian Confederates had ever conceived—creating chaos in the North on Election Day.

On October 15, 1864, an unusual editorial appeared in the *Richmond Whig* that seemed to be more than the usual article by a newspaper editor expressing frustrations at the destruction suffered in the Shenandoah Valley. This editorial suggested specific actions be taken against the North that could only be accomplished by men who were not already on the front line fighting the Federal armies. The message seemed to be directed at the approximately one hundred escaped soldiers scattered around Canada plus the four officers who were awaiting specific orders.

The editorial began with reports that Sheridan had told Grant he had burned more than two thousand barns and over seventy grain-processing mills in the Shenandoah Valley. The editor commented on the destructive figures with a journalist's calm detachment, but he then followed with a suggestion:

Now it is an idle waste of words to denounce this sort of war. We have simply to regard it as a practical matter, and ask ourselves how it is to be met. There is one effectual way, and only one that we know of, to arrest and prevent this and every other sort of atrocity—and that is to burn one of the chief cities of the enemy, say Boston, Philadelphia, or Cincinnati, and let its fate hang over the others as a warning of what may be done to them, if the present system of war on the part of the enemy is continued. If we are asked how such a thing can be done—we answer, nothing would be easier. *A million dollars would lay the proudest city of the enemy in ashes* [emphasis added]. The men to execute the work are already there. There would be no difficulty in finding here, or in Canada, suitable persons to take charge of the enterprise and arrange its details. Twenty men with plans all preconcerted, and means provided, selecting some dry, windy night, might fire Boston in a hundred places and wrap it in flames from center to suburb. They might retaliate on Richmond, Charleston. Let them do so if they dare. It is a game at which we can beat them. *New York is worth twenty Richmonds* [emphasis added]. They have a dozen towns to our one, and in their towns is centered nearly all of their wealth. It would not be immoral and barbarous. It is not immoral or barbarous to defend yourself by any means, or with any weapon the enemy may employ for your destruction. *They choose to substitute the torch for the sword. We may so use their own weapon to make them repent, literally in sackcloth and ashes, that they ever adopted it* [emphasis added].

The October 18, 1864, *New York Times* reprinted the *Whig* commentary word for word, but made no comment in that issue or in follow-up issues on the thinly veiled Southern threats to burn down Northern cities. Even if the *Whig* was not delivered to Torontó, Headley and Martin would have read the same editorial in the *Times* as Headley noted that all the major Northern newspapers were readily available in Canada.

No one involved ever said how the idea came about. The editorial may have been a coded message to Thompson to put in motion a long-standing order. Or Thompson may have developed the idea after reading the editorial.

But however the idea came about, by the middle of October, the

Canadian agents' plans had shifted from attacking the prison camps to disrupting the November 8 election by setting fire to the North's largest cities.

Though no plan Thompson or his agents tried had yet worked, they can at least be given credit for thinking big. While Hines was obviously the most experienced of the agents from which to choose to put in charge of coordination of such an ambitious plan, Thompson seems to have taken on the planning role himself by assigning individual agents to targeted cities.

The two men he chose to fire New York City had only just arrived in Canada. These were two men who were originally sent there because of their proven skill at scouting behind enemy lines. Now it was time for the big show—Tuesday, November 8, Election Day for the United States of America.

Chapter 14

"Set Fire to Cities on Election Day"

It was an ambitious plan that Confederate Secret Service commissioner Jacob Thompson outlined to Martin and Headley in the Queens Hotel in downtown Toronto. In his postwar book, Headley described a plan to take over both Chicago and New York City simultaneously.

As described by Thompson, on Tuesday, November 8, 1864, an "uprising" would occur in both Chicago and New York City with the ever-ready Sons of Liberty Copperhead group lending muscle in both cities to the Confederate military leadership coming out of Canada. The plan to take over Chicago was essentially the same plan that had failed to materialize during the Democratic convention.

According to Thompson, Hines, Grenfell, "and all available Confederates" would travel to Chicago and Rock Island, Illinois, to organize Copperheads to free the Confederate prisoners at Illinois's Camp Douglas and Rock Island Prison camp. The plan then entailed for the two forces of freed prisoners to combine to a force numbering around eighteen thousand men, almost the size of two divisions.

In Headley's presence, Thompson did not address the fact that the Copperheads had failed to show up every other time Hines had tried to rally them. Nor did Thompson discuss how he expected the tiny force of armed Confederates to commandeer the Chicago Rock

Island Railroad to transport eight thousand weak, sickly prisoners the two hundred miles from Rock Island to Chicago.

According to the plan, the Camp Douglas prisoners would take over the city of Chicago while waiting for the prisoners from Rock Island to join them. Once Chicago was under Confederate control, James Robinson, the Illinois gubernatorial candidate Thompson was secretly bankrolling, would then make that Northern city eight hundred miles northwest of Richmond the capital of the Northwest Confederacy. Once he was in office as governor, Robinson would turn over all the arms in the state armories to this new Confederate army in Illinois.

Thompson was making a great many assumptions: that Camp Douglas and Rock Island could be overrun, that the prisoners would be in shape and willing to fight, that they could capture the railroad to combine the two forces, and, just as remotely, that a Peace Democrat doubling as a secret Confederate sympathizer could win the governor's election in the home state of the president of the United States.

What should have disturbed Martin and Headley was that Thompson was describing a plan that had already been decided before the two of them arrived in Toronto.

While Hines and Grenfell would return to Chicago to carry out a plan that had failed at least twice in the past several months, Martin and Headley would lead an attack on New York. The two experienced scouts were not being asked to scout and find the weaknesses of New York and then report back with a workable plan. They were being told that they would attack the most populous city in the nation, which they had never even visited. No one gave them a plan detailing how they would coordinate such a complex undertaking, or at least Headley did not remember any such details when he wrote his postwar book.

Thompson did offer some thoughts on the mission. He correctly reasoned that if takeovers of Chicago and New York were to succeed, diversions would have to draw the attention of the potentially intervening Federal troops away from the true targets of New York and Chicago. Headley matter-of-factly reported in his book what

Thompson had told him: "Detachments under Captain Churchill in Cincinnati and Dr. Luke Blackburn in Boston would set fire to those cities on election day."

Little is known about Churchill other than Thompson considered him to be "true." Likewise, Thompson did not share with Headley any details about how Dr. Blackburn, a civilian, would be able to command men to set fires in Boston.

After outlining the plans for Chicago, Cincinnati, and Boston, Thompson turned to discuss New York City. After hearing Hines complain that past missions to Illinois to command Copperhead armies had always failed because the Copperheads never materialized, Martin and Headley must have squirmed in their seats when Thompson confidently told the two Confederate officers that "20,000 men were enlisted in New York under a complete organization; that arms had been provided already for the forces in the city; and we would be expected to take military supervision of the forces at the vital moment."

Thompson went on to explain that enlisters would start fires in several locations in New York on the afternoon of Election Day "in order to deter opposition." Once the fires were burning, the hidden army of twenty thousand New Yorkers (equivalent to a corps in Robert E. Lee's Army of Northern Virginia) would capture all federal government offices, including the hordes of gold and silver in the United States Sub-Treasury Building. Finally, the Confederate prisoners at Fort Lafayette would be freed so that they could "unite with our forces." Compared with the twenty regiments of Confederates cooped up at Camp Douglas, the 135 Confederates held in the dungeons of Fort Lafayette would hardly have filled out a Confederate company.

If Martin and Headley were skeptical about the ambitiousness of the plan or the New York Copperheads helping, Headley did not say so in his memoirs. What may have given them confidence was Thompson's assurances that he had already lined up support for the operation, including sending a "Captain Longmire" ahead to the city to attend to details.

That man was probably Emile Longuemare, who claimed in his

postwar papers that he convinced Jefferson Davis in 1862 that a Northwest Confederacy could be created by mobilizing the Sons of Liberty to agitate for rebellion.

Records do indicate that Longuemare did have some contact with Davis. He may well have been the first person to plant the idea in Davis's head that a Northwest Confederacy could be created. Records show that Davis authorized Longuemare early in the war to travel to Democratic strongholds like Indiana and New York to gauge the mood of the people in resisting the war. Why Davis trusted Longuemare with such a sensitive mission is unclear.

Despite Headley's belief that Longuemare was a captain from Missouri, no one by that name's spelling shows up in the current muster rolls of any state. There are dozens of Longmires, including three from Missouri, but no captains and no one named Emile. Neither was Longuemare a politician who Davis would have known from his days in the U.S. Congress. Before the war, Longuemare was a St. Louis, Missouri, wholesaler of wines. That was hardly the type of job that trained him to be a Confederate soldier or a spy.

Headley said only two men in Toronto knew about the mission he and Martin were about to lead. One was Godfrey J. Hyams, an Englishman, and New York City native William Lawrence "Larry" McDonald, who was skilled at manufacturing hand grenades in a hidden basement workshop of his rented Toronto home.

McDonald would have been a valuable addition to the team heading for New York City, as they would be handling a type of explosive with which they were not familiar. But McDonald stayed in Toronto and apparently did not participate in any of the attacks across the border, though he did hook the conspirators up with his brother in Manhattan. If McDonald offered any advice to Martin and Headley before they left Toronto about how to handle explosives, Headley did not record it.

Thompson had some contacts other than Longuemare in place in New York City waiting for the Confederates. The names of two of those New York City contacts are startling: congressman and former mayor Fernando Wood and *Freeman's Journal and Catholic Digest* editor James McMaster (which Headley misspelled as McMasters).

Thompson had met Congressman Fernando Wood at least once in Niagara Falls in the company of former New York State governor Washington Hunt. According to Hines, who also attended that meeting, the two New York politicians told Thompson that efforts to talk peace would go nowhere because the arms manufacturers of the Northeast were making too much money supplying the Union army with cannons and muskets. Hines also claimed to have met with Congressman Benjamin Wood, Fernando's brother, and to have paid him tens of thousands of dollars in exchange for writing articles and editorials in Wood's *New York Daily News*. If Hines's story of the meeting is true, the Wood brothers, both United States congressmen, were consorting with known secret agents of an enemy of the United States.

How Thompson came to know or recruit McMaster is not known. McMaster was a fiery, white-haired, white-bearded convert to Catholicism who had founded the *Freeman's Journal* in 1848, not long after switching his religion from Anglican. He built it into a newspaper that was widely distributed around the United States at a time when New York's nondenominational newspapers were mostly circulated only in that city.

McMaster knew how to court readers. He had been born MacMaster, but changed it to McMaster, which he thought would make his newspaper more palatable to Irish readers who might reject reading a newspaper written by someone of obvious Scots descent. When the Irish became an object of Northern recruitment, McMaster editorialized that they were "being rushed into a fight at which no interest of theirs was at stake."

Staunchly against the war, McMaster was imprisoned for months in 1861 without being formally charged or tried with any crime other than editing a newspaper that did not support the Lincoln administration. He took the oath of allegiance at the behest of his wife to get back to making money for the family, but he never changed his opinion of the Lincoln administration. He feared that once the South was defeated, the United States would begin attacking Catholicism since Catholics are pledged to follow the Pope's instructions rather than the government's. Though he was more careful in writing his opinions, McMaster's newspaper continued to call for peace with the South.

Other than being headed by Martin and Headley, two experienced Confederate scouts, the rest of the sabotage team chosen to attack New York appears to have been chosen at random from among the Confederate escapees then in Toronto.

None of the other six men chosen for the mission were more unusual, or volatile, than Captain Robert Cobb Kennedy of the First Louisiana Infantry.

Kennedy, 29, was born in Alabama into a doctor's family, which moved to Louisiana in his youth. Kennedy entered the United States Military Academy in 1854 at 18 years of age. In his plebe class were Joseph Wheeler of Alabama and Edwin Stoughton of Vermont, two generals for opposite sides who would win fame and infamy after graduating in the lackluster class of 1859, which produced only three Civil War generals. Kennedy himself would be thrown out of West Point after just two years because of too many demerits and too many failing grades in courses as important as mathematics. The final straw came when he and another cadet were caught drunk off the grounds. Kennedy was saddled with a review-board opinion that he had "very little aptitude" for a military life. By 1858, he was on his way back to Louisiana.

When the war started, Kennedy joined the First Louisiana Brigade where he was given the rank of lieutenant. He received a wound at the Battle of Shiloh, Tennessee, in April 1862 that would leave him with a pronounced limp. Seeking out his old friend Joe Wheeler, Kennedy wrangled an assistant's job. During one trip in October 1863 while carrying dispatches from Wheeler to headquarters, Kennedy was captured. He was sent north to Johnson's Island, which he entered on November 14, 1863. Nearly a year later on October 4, 1864, Kennedy propped a homemade ladder on the wooden wall around the prison camp and escaped. He used a skiff he found floating outside the fort to row to the mainland. Instead of making his way south, Kennedy headed north, and within a couple of weeks he had made it to Canada.

Kennedy, the hard-drinking son of a wealthy family who had

flunked out of West Point due to his own negligence and the officer who had been in only one real battle, was now in Canada. The young man who had continually argued with his father and who was considered the family disgrace now wanted to do something to prove his value to both his family and to the military establishment that had rejected him as a fighting man.

Few details survive of the remaining five men who would attack New York City. According to Headley, they were Lieutenant John T. Ashbrook, who had ridden with the Second Kentucky Cavalry, Lieutenant James T. Harrington of Kentucky (whose name does not show up on Kentucky's rosters of soldiers), Lieutenant John M. Price of Maryland (who may have ridden with the Second Battalion of Maryland Cavalry, part of a partisan ranger unit commanded by Harry Gilmor), Lieutenant James Chenault of Kentucky (who does not show up on Kentucky rosters), and a man whose name Headley did not remember when he wrote his book in 1905.

Headley may have forgotten or confused some of the personal details of his compatriots on this mission. He was writing from memory more than forty years after he had participated in the New York attack, and other than Martin and Ashbrook, he had never before met the men who Thompson had assigned to be part of the mission.

Martin and Headley, both 24 years of age, commanded the operation. Kennedy, at 29 years of age, may have been the oldest of the raiders. The ages of the other men are unknown, but they were probably young. After three years of combat, they all knew how to handle themselves in battle wielding .36- or .44-caliber revolvers. They were resourceful: all of them having faced Federal forces at one time or another with presumably six of them (excluding Martin and Headley) having escaped from Union prison camps.

All of them were motivated by a sense of duty toward the Confederacy and by a need for revenge. The Southern and Northern newspapers available in Canada had been detailing Sheridan's actions in burning the Shenandoah Valley all through October. The newspapers were also concerned as to what Sherman would do to Atlanta, which he had captured in September.

On another level, Martin and Headley had also read newspaper accounts of how their beloved, unarmed commander, General Morgan, had been shot dead just two months earlier. They may have wanted to do something to avenge his death. Some of the men were known to have personal reasons for wanting to get back at the Union. Martin walked stooped over from a wound to the chest. Kennedy still limped from a wounded foot.

The motivations of why these men living safely in Canada might return to the fray and risk capture and execution as spies was explained in a postwar article by Edward A. Jackson, a 22-year-old cavalryman from Mississippi. Jackson roomed with Kennedy for the few weeks between the time Kennedy arrived in Toronto and then left for New York City. According to Jackson, the Confederates in Canada, almost all of whom had left farms to join the army, were deeply angered by the destruction of the Shenandoah. When they read of the fired barns and destroyed stacks of wheat, they imagined the loss of their own farms.

We were commanded by John Y. Beall, and were employed by the Confederate government to annoy the Federals in as many ways as possible. It seemed to us that if our fifty [number commanded by Beall] could detain some fifteen or twenty thousand Federal troops on the Northern frontier, troops that otherwise would have helped in crashing our comrades down South, we were doing as much for the cause as any fifty men in the ranks.

We did things that one regrets being obliged to do, but we were responsible for our obedience, not our orders. We did what was commanded by our lawful superiors, and our actions were all legitimate under the horrible usages of war. The Federals fought us with fire and we fought them with fire, but it was a weapon that we did not love as did Sherman, Sheridan, Butler and others, and we in no way inconvenienced the crows, as they did. [The reference to crows relates to Sheridan's boast to Grant after his six-week campaign to destroy the farms of the Shenandoah Valley that a crow would have to pack his lunch if he flew over the region.]

For all their experience in the field, none of the Confederates in Canada had ever trained as an undercover operative. They had always been soldiers wearing Confederate uniforms, though Martin and Headley would sometimes put on civilian uniforms when heading behind Union lines. Headley makes no mention of the team conducting any training in Toronto for any urban attack. He does not say that anyone practiced with the hand grenades or chemical weapons that Larry McDonald was manufacturing in the basement of his house. Headley just recalled that he, Martin, and six others "were assigned with us to operate in New York."

The party of eight men, traveling in pairs but not acknowledging each other, rode the same New York Central Railroad train from Niagara Falls to New York City. They likely wore simple civilian clothes and may or may not have been armed with revolvers that had been smuggled out of New York City by earlier missions and other agents. They did not carry any explosives with them. They had been told that New Yorkers would supply those kinds of weapons of mass destruction.

The eight men arrived in New York City on Thursday, October 27, 1864. Had they picked up a newspaper from a street vendor, their determination to make New York City suffer for what had been happening in the Confederacy could only have been increased. On the same day the team arrived in the city, the *New York Times* published a letter from Lincoln to General Philip Sheridan reading: "With great pleasure I tender to you and your brave army the thanks of a nation and my own personal admiration and gratitude for the month's operations in the Shenandoah Valley, and especially for the splendid work on Oct. 19."

The "month's operations" referred to Sheridan's two-week campaign burning Shenandoah Valley farms. October 19 referred to Sheridan's defeat of Jubal Early at the Battle of Cedar Creek, Virginia, just south of Winchester. With that loss, there was hardly any Confederate resistance now left in the Valley.

Martin and Headley arrived in the Emerald City and checked into the St. Denis Hotel at the corner of Broadway and 11th Street, registering as Robert Maxwell and John Williams, aliases created from using their middle names as their last names. Headley did not say why they used aliases, unless it was a way to try to mask their appearance in the city if some detective had recorded their real names in Toronto. Ashbrook and Harrington checked in at the Metropolitan Hotel at Broadway and Prince Street. Headley did not remember where the other four registered.

Demonstrating at least a rudimentary sense of spy craft, the eight would occasionally change hotels over the coming days so that they would not attract attention by staying so long but without seeming to have a purpose to be in the city.

Robert Cobb Kennedy thought better of using his middle name as an alias. One of his distant relatives was Howell Cobb, a former United States congressman from Alabama who was well known in the North as he had served as Speaker of the House. Howell's younger brother, Thomas, had been a Confederate general killed at Fredericksburg, Virginia, in December 1862. Since using Cobb would only call attention to his name, Kennedy signed the hotel register as Stanton, a subtle swipe at Secretary of War Stanton.

The clerk did not look twice at Mr. Stanton. Neither did he question what must have been Kennedy's pronounced Alabama-born and Louisiana-raised accent. Despite the war, New York still attracted Southerners of both sexes and all ages. Just hearing someone dropping a *g* at the end of a word would not have aroused the suspicions of a desk clerk.

Martin and Headley did not waste any time. The next day, Friday, they called on editor McMaster at the offices of the *Freeman's Journal* at 5 Tryon Row, a block east of City Hall Park, to deliver a letter of introduction from Jacob Thompson. McMaster seemed not at all perturbed that Confederate spies were visiting him in his office. He had already received a letter from Thompson alerting him to their imminent arrival.

Though Headley said that it seemed McMaster was at ease, they all agreed to meet at another less public place than the editorial offices of one of the city's largest newspapers that was edited by a well-known, anti-Lincoln Copperhead. They met at some other unknown

place on Saturday with Longuemare. That led to a Sunday meeting
at McMaster's home at West 50th Street, between Eighth and Ninth
avenues.

McMaster may have felt more comfortable meeting Confederates
at his home because that part of town was practically on the edge
of the city. There would be little reason for Union army or police
detectives to be in the neighborhood compared with the teeming areas around the city's hotels. And if any detectives would start walking the streets in front of McMaster's house, they would be easily
spotted.

Curiously, Headley did not describe any of his six other Confederate conspirators, but he left a vivid and accurate image of
McMaster:

We found Mr. McMasters (sic) to be a determined and very
able man and a true friend. He was a strong character in all
respects. Physically he was of strong proportions without much
flesh. I would say he was at least 6 feet 3 inches in height with a
large frame, hands and feet. . . . Everything about him denoted
strength of intellect as well as body.

At a dinner at McMaster's house, the Confederates and the newspaper editor discussed what would happen on Election Day. Headley
called McMaster "the practical head of the operations in New York,"
and "chief manager of leaders." McMaster said that he wanted the
Confederates to start the fires around the city "which would bring
the population into the streets and prevent any sort of resistance to
our movement." Once the city was in a state of confusion, the army
of Copperheads McMaster led "would not only take possession of
the city and all approaches, but furnish the strength to support the
military authorities." McMaster then claimed that New York governor Horatio Seymour would pledge the state's neutrality in the attack, meaning that he would not call out any militia forces in the city
or the state.

"We were also told that upon the success of the revolution here
a convention of delegates . . . would be held in New York City to

form a Confederacy which would cooperate with the Confederate States and the Northwest Confederacy," Headley wrote in his post-war memoir.

On the following Thursday, McMaster risked inviting the Confederates back to his newspaper office, the second time that the closely watched editor risked detection. Once locked into McMaster's office, the Confederates were introduced to the private secretary of Governor Seymour. The unnamed secretary assured them again that the governor would not call out the state militia in response to the attack. The governor's secretary could make no assurances that Federal troops would be called.

If Headley is to be believed, the Democratic governor, an ardent foe of the war and the Republican administration, knew about the attack plan. Like Congressmen Fernando and Benjamin Wood, Governor Seymour was consorting with the enemy.

The city's Democratic mayor was apparently not aware of any impending attack, intentionally kept out of the loop by McMaster.

New York City's mayor Charles Godfrey Gunther, 42, a fur merchant and volunteer firefighter born to German immigrants to the city, had gone into politics as a loyal foot soldier of Tammany Hall. Defeated in the mayor's race in 1861 by Republican George Opdyke in a three-way race that included former mayor Fernando Wood, Gunther ran for mayor again in 1863 and won after the city soured on Opdyke in the wake of the July 1863 Draft Riots.

One reason McMaster likely did not bring the mayor in on the attack plans is that Gunther had strayed from predictable behavior since first running for mayor in 1861. In the 1861 election, Tammany Hall–backed Gunther had spoiled the re-election bid of Mayor Fernando Wood, who had left Tammany Hall to form his own coalition called Mozart Hall. The three-way race split the vote, which resulted in the election of antislavery Republican Opdyke to take office in a city that was still strongly pro-South.

When Gunther ran again in 1863, he was the one who ran as an outsider from Tammany Hall. He joined forces with a reform-minded businessman who put together a coalition of anti-Fernando Wood voters, other businessmen, and Irish immigrants who resented being blamed by the Republican mayor for the July 1863 Draft Riots. Gunther still labeled himself as a Peace Democrat, but McMaster looked at his bucking of Tammany Hall control of his political career as indicating unpredictability.

McMaster may have been correct in leaving Mayor Gunther off the list of people to be introduced to the Confederates. Too many others also knew that secret agents were either in the city or on their way.

The most important man among them was Union general John Dix, commander of the military district that included New York. On the day after the eight Confederates climbed down from their train, Dix published his suspicions that an attack on the city of New York was imminent.

Chapter 15

"Rebel Agents in Canada"

Union general John Dix, commander of the Department of the East, which covered New York, New Jersey, and all the New England states, had seen combat—just not since he was 14. That was fifty-two years ago when he was an inexperienced teenager at the Battle of Lundy's Lane, a particularly bloody War of 1812 battle just over the Canadian border. Though Dix spent the next ten years in the army, he got out while still a young man to study law.

By 30, Dix was deeply rooted in New York State politics, which led him to national politics. He served as secretary of the treasury under President James Buchanan, a position from which he watched the gathering storm clouds of war. When he heard from a nervous Treasury manager at the New Orleans Mint, Dix replied with an answer that left no doubt about where his loyalties lay: "If anyone attempts to haul down the American flag, shoot him on the spot!"

At 66 with no true professional soldiering under his belt other than his stint more than forty years in the past, Dix was passed over for appointment to active military command when the war started. Still, Lincoln could not afford to brush off such a powerful Democratic politician who seemingly supported his war efforts. Not many New Yorkers liked Lincoln. Since he needed all the friends he could find, Lincoln appointed Dix major general of volunteers on May 16, 1861.

That early commission made Dix the first volunteer major general of the war, though it did not mean much when it came to getting plum battlefield assignments. He was still an old man who had never really held a combat command. There were dozens of professional army officers who were Mexican War veterans, so Lincoln wisely appointed them to the field commands that would actually fight the battles.

Though Dix would never see a battlefield, he would have a major impact on the war. It was Dix, under orders from Lincoln, who rounded up the Democrat members of the Maryland legislature to prevent them from voting to secede from the United States. Lincoln deeply appreciated the actions of a member of the opposition party arresting his fellow Democrats at the insistence of a Republican.

Some months later, Dix entered into negotiations with the Confederate general in his district to arrange for the exchange of prisoners. Those formal contracts between the United States and Confederate States did not sit as well with President Lincoln because it implied a formal recognition of the Confederacy as a combatant rather than a collection of rebelling citizens, which was the way Lincoln preferred to view the citizens to fulfill his view that the Union remained unbroken. Still, Lincoln let Dix's meetings with the Confederates pass as a necessary part of war to get rid of their prisoners and get back those captured Union soldiers.

Aside from overseeing deploying the troops to put down the previous summer's draft riots, Dix had seen no action in the first three years of the war and did not expect to see any for the rest of the war.

Then came the October 19, 1864, raid on St. Albans, Vermont, some 330 miles north of New York City, the same day as the Battle of Cedar Creek, Virginia, some 300 miles to the southwest. On the very same day, two Confederate forces had attacked Union troops within two weeks' marching time to New York City.

Dix no longer saw his command as a backwater of the war, a region too far north to interest Confederates. He saw threats.

On the day after the Confederates climbed down from the train to get their first look at their target, the *New York Times* printed Dix's General Orders 80 which read in part:

> Satisfactory information has been received by the Major-General that rebel agents in Canada design to send into the United States, and to colonize, at different points, large numbers of refugees, deserters, and enemies of the Government, with a view to vote at the approaching Presidential election; and it is not unlikely, when this service to the rebel cause has been performed, that they may be organized for the purpose of shooting down peaceable citizens and plundering private property, as in the recent predatory incursions at the Detroit River and St. Albans. Against these mediated outrages of the purity of elective franchise and these nefarious acts of robbery, incendiarism and murder, it is the determination of the Major-General commanding to guard by every possible precaution, and to visit on the perpetrators, if they shall be detected, the most signal and summary punishment.

Dix went on to order that "all persons from the insurgent States" were required to report themselves to his headquarters so that they could be added to a registry maintained at the headquarters at 37 Bleecker Street. The people would register, and then descriptions of them would be recorded, as would their places of residency.

"Those who fail to comply with this requirement will be regarded as spies or emissaries of the insurgent authorities at Richmond and will be treated accordingly," read the order.

Dix may have been reacting to the St. Albans raid and guessing at the rest, or he could have been hearing from some of the Union spies operating in Toronto. He overreacted to the idea that there were enough Confederate "refugees" in Canada to "colonize" the state and throw the election. He was also wrong that the Confederacy was planning "murders," though one man had died in the St. Albans Raid.

But he was entirely right that Confederate agents had crossed the border. Already they were within blocks of his headquarters.

While it may have amused the most adventurous of the eight

Confederate raiders to have done so, none of them took the time to sign their names to Dix's registry of Southerners. Instead, they did what all other visitors to the nation's largest city do—they became tourists.

They attended the lecture of Artemus Ward, whose real name was Charles Farrar Browne. Browne was one of the nation's premier writers and humorists, a precursor to the stand-up comedian. In the fall of 1862, Lincoln read one of Artemus Ward's *Vanity Fair* articles to his cabinet to get them in a good mood before springing the first draft of the Emancipation Proclamation on them. Among the war-related knee-slappers to which Artemus Ward is credited is, "I have given two cousins to war and I stand ready to sacrifice my wife's brother."

Martin and Headley took the ferry to Brooklyn to hear abolitionist minister Henry Ward Beecher, the brother to Harriet Beecher Stowe, the author of *Uncle Tom's Cabin*. Beecher always drew standing-room crowds at his sermons and lectures.

The Confederates also took in some Democratic Party meetings at Tammany Hall and participated in a huge march down Broadway to promote the campaign of General George McClellan for president. If they had wanted to assassinate anyone, it would have been simple with the way in which Headley described how he and Martin easily worked their way through a throng of politicians who he did not name. The two Confederates, apparently being bipartisan in their politics also attended rallies for "Mr. Lincoln," finding them "equally enthusiastic."

The highlight of that evening was crowding into Madison Square where the two of them sidled up to the speaker's rostrum to hear James T. Brady, a prominent Democrat. That night Headley reported that there were "hisses and groans" whenever Lincoln's name was mentioned, and the "President was caricatured in many ludicrous and ungainly pictures. Indeed there was a vicious sentiment voiced all along the line of the procession against the draft and everyone connected with the management of the war. The spirit of revolt was manifest and it only needed a start and a leadership."

While Headley might have been expressing the dreams of the eight conspirators that what they were about to do would succeed, he still had not met any other Copperheads other than McMaster and Henry "Gus" McDonald, the brother of Larry McDonald.

Gus McDonald allowed the Confederates to keep their trunks at his piano store at 358 Broadway. Headley never said what was in the trunks, but it seems likely they contained the group's revolvers. The trunks apparently did not contain any incendiary explosives because arrangements had been made to pick those up in New York City closer to the time of the attack.

Headley did not express any concern in his postwar book that he had not met any armed New Yorkers willing to stand by his side in street-fighting combat for control of Manhattan once the distracting fires were set. McMaster had assured Martin and Headley on their arrival that twenty thousand New Yorkers were ready to help the Confederates capture the city, but the two Confederates had yet to meet any leaders of this corps-size hidden force.

That must have made experienced soldiers like Martin and Headley nervous. Meeting the leaders of these twenty thousand would be necessary before the attack to develop a command structure, inventory arms, and talk tactics about how these civilian volunteer soldiers would defend themselves against any trained Federal troops who would surely be called to New York City, once it was attacked and set ablaze.

What the Confederates did not know was that more Federals than just Dix had their suspicions about an impending attack. In fact, a Union official stationed in Canada had already revealed the Canadian Confederates' plans to the War Department in Washington.

On Wednesday, November 2, six days before Election Day, New York mayor Gunther received a telegram from Secretary of State Seward.

The telegram was short: "This department has received information from the British Provinces to the effect that there is a conspiracy on foot to set fire to the principal cities in the Northern States on the day of the Presidential election. It is my duty to communicate this information to you. W. E. Seward."

Seward as the source of the telegram seems odd at first, considering that his office normally had little to do with war planning and espionage. That was the job of Secretary of War Stanton. Seward sent the same telegram to the mayors of several northeastern cities as well as the mayors of Chicago and Boston, the other supposed firestorm targets. The mayor of Cleveland received it, but the mayor of Cincinnati (the real target as suggested by Thompson in Toronto) did not.

The next day, Thursday, November 3, 1864, the *New York Times* ran the text of the November 1 telegram at the same time that it was delivered to the mayor of Buffalo under the headline: ANTICIPATED RAIDS FROM CANADA. DISPATCH FROM THE SECRETARY OF STATE TO THE MAYOR OF BUFFALO—REBEL CONSPIRACY TO BURN NORTHERN CITIES. The text of the telegram read: "It is secretly asserted by secessionists here that plans have been formed and will be carried into execution by the rebels and their allies, for setting fire to the principal cities in the Northern States on the day of the Presidential election."

Curiously, the *Times* did not mention that New York City was also a potential target. Either the editors of the *Times* never thought to ask Mayor Gunther if he had received a similar telegram before publishing the story about Buffalo or he lied to them to keep the threat to the city a secret.

The original source of the warning was M. M. Jackson, the United States Consul stationed in Halifax, Nova Scotia, a popular port for Confederates trying to run the blockade. Jackson being the source explains why the warning telegram originated with Seward rather than Stanton. Jackson reported to Seward, so Seward would have wanted to take credit for issuing the warning to the Northern cities rather than let Stanton get the credit since Stanton's own spies had not yet stumbled onto the plot.

When the Confederates read the newspapers, they were stunned. There was their plot laid out for any citizen and, more importantly, any police detective or hotel clerk suspicious of a Southern accent to read.

Not all newspapers believed Seward's rumors. The *New York Daily News*, a Democratic newspaper, claimed that the telegram was simply a Republican administration trick to try to hold down the voter turnout in a major city like New York, which was heavily Democratic and antiadministration.

If the conspirators thought that the War Department had somehow overlooked the threat to New York City, they learned differently on November 4. It was on that day, four days before the election, that Major General Benjamin Butler arrived in the city. Following him were 3,500 Union soldiers.

The ordering of some Union army forces to the city by Stanton may have been in the works before Seward sent the telegram to the cities. Certainly, Stanton would have been aware of some danger to the election process in the North's largest cities. For months, Northern newspapers had been buzzing with rumors that Southerners were heading to Northern states to register falsely as voters to throw the election to McClellan and the Democrats.

Stanton's selection of Butler to head the forces in New York City was both a political ploy as well as a risk to the image of the administration. Butler was a political general from Massachusetts, an odd-looking, bald-headed, unpredictable political maverick with crossed eyes who had nominated Jefferson Davis for president of the United States at the 1860 Democratic convention. General Grant hated him, so Stanton's assignment of Butler to temporary duty to New York City was as much a favor to Grant as it was a legitimate assignment.

Butler wasted no time in informing the city's residents who was in charge. On November 5, he issued an order that explained why he and his troops were there "to meet existing emergencies."

To correct misapprehension, to soothe the fears of the weak and timid, to allay the nervousness of the ill advised; to silence all false rumors circulated by bad men for wicked purposes; and to contradict once and for all, false statements adapted to injure the Government in the respect and confidence of the people, the commanding general takes occasion to declare that troops have been detailed for duty in this district sufficient to preserve the peace of the United States; to protect public property, to prevent and punish incursions into our borders, and to insure calm and quiet.

If it were not within the information of the Government that raids, like in quality and object to that made at Saint Albans, were in contemplation, there would have been no necessity for precautionary preparations.

Butler went on to explain that his army's occupation of the city really was not an example of martial law because "the armies of the United States are 'ministers of good and not of evil': they are safe-guards of constitutional liberty, which is freedom to do right, not wrong. They can be a terror to evildoers only, and those who fear them are accused by their own consciences."

The general then ended his order with a thinly veiled threat to Southerners in the city who might practice "fraudulent voting," which he called "a deadly sin and heinous crime." He cautioned such men that it "would not be well" for them to interfere in the election.

Butler obviously did not know any conspirator names when he first checked into the Fifth Avenue Hotel, the same hotel where Martin was staying. Martin was nervous at first, but Butler soon moved to the Hoffman Hotel.

Even before Butler's arrival, all of the Metropolitan Police were ordered to be on duty on Election Day "to preserve order and prevent disorderly conduct." The *New York Times* said it would be "a dangerous proceeding to attempt a riot," harkening back to the July 1863 riots when the police were caught flat-footed by the huge crowds. The newspaper assured its readers that the "police will be on the alert, and are competent to protect the metropolis, for, after all, the proportion of disorderly-disposed persons will be very small compared with the great mass of order-loving, law-abiding citizens."

Even though he knew nothing about the plot and did nothing to prevent it, Butler's mere presence with his 3,500 troops (overesti-mated at 15,000 by Headley, which may reflect on his skills at scout-ing) spooked the city's Copperheads who had earlier agreed to help the Confederate agents.

According to Headley, writing after the war, two days before the election, "The leaders in our conspiracy were at once demoralized by this sudden advent of General Butler and his troops." Among the few who wanted to go ahead with the attack was a "Mr. Horton of the *Day Book*." That was probably Rushmore Horton, partner in the New York City publishing company Van Evrie & Company. This company published the periodical *New York Day-Book*, which was self-described as a "radical Democratic newspaper" based on the idea that "all white men are created equal."

Another man who wanted to go ahead with the attack was "Mr. Brooks," one of two brothers, either Erastus or James Brooks, founders of the *Express*, a pro-peace, Democratic New York City newspaper that the *New York Times* once admitted "had the reputation of getting all the news possible."

If "Mr. Brooks" was James, he was a current United States congressman, joining Governor Seymour, and Congressmen Fernando and Benjamin Wood in a plot against the United States.

After holding a meeting with "the leaders of the conspiracy" who Martin and Headley still had not met in person, McMaster brought the two Confederate leaders into a meeting at his office on Monday, November 7, the day before the election. McMaster told them that the other leaders had "decided to postpone action" as "we could not afford to make a failure."

Martin and Headley were irritated that they and six other Confederate agents were now in a city filled with what they thought were fifteen thousand Union troops, but the men who had invited them had now backed out of their commitment to help.

"We could do nothing but acquiesce in the views of the New York management," said Headley, who took heart that McMaster promised him that "the delay was only temporary," and the attack would happen once all of the Union troops had left the city.

While the Confederates were upset that the still-hidden army of Copperheads had decided to stay that way, the New Yorkers were probably right to choose caution over action. Too many rumors were floating around the city that something was about to happen, and the rumors floating about in some of the newspapers were entirely accurate.

On November 7, the day before the election, the *New York Times* published an article saying that Butler had been sent to the city because the government

. . . has information that raids on our frontier, like that at St. Albans, are in contemplation by Confederate emissaries; but that he has force sufficient to preserve the public peace, and to prevent and punish incursions upon our borders . . . [Butler's presence] will give the public confidence that the designs of the rebels upon our frontiers and in our large cities will be thwarted. . . . JEFF. DAVIS' organs [newspapers] in Richmond have been lately urging rebels stationed in Canada and in the North to give a helping hand to the sinking Confederacy; and the *Richmond Whig has developed and pressed a grand scheme for firing the cities of the North. This last must not be taken as an idle threat. . . . It would be insane not to be vigilant—not to be amply prepared to promptly crush any disorderly attempts of rebel incendiaries and marauders at the first moment they are discovered* [emphasis added].

Election Day, November 8, went off without a hitch in New York City with thousands of Union troops stationed at all of the polling places. Just as he had lost New York City in 1860, Lincoln lost again in 1864, drawing 36,687 votes to George McClellan's 73,716. Lincoln carried the state by a narrow margin. Nationally, Lincoln won by a landslide, garnering 212 electoral votes to McClellan's 21, which came from the only three states that he carried, Kentucky, New Jersey, and Delaware.

Now that the threat to New York City was over, the editors of the *New York Times* decided to have a little fun, both with Butler's reputation and his legion of critics.

Well, Gen. Butler has been in active command of the city and State of New York for forty-eight hours. So far as we have heard, he has not yet erected a single gallows or hung anybody; he has shot nobody; he has knouted [whipped] nobody; he has hamstrung nobody; he has crucified nobody; he has impaled nobody on a poker . . . he has suppressed no newspapers, and insulted no women. But he took the most active and admirable measures

to secure the peace of the city and State during the election yes-
terday; and the peace has been undisturbed.

Martin and Headley must have been amused themselves when
they read that article. Then they would have noticed another article
about the arrests of some men in Chicago.

Starting with large headlines: THE NEW CHICAGO CONSPIRACY;
COPPERHEADS AND REBELS IN COUNSEL. INFAMOUS PLOT TO BURN
THE CITY AND LIBERATE THE REBEL PRISONERS, the November 9
newspaper articles gave details that must have made the eight Confederates in New York City shiver.

Among the men arrested in Chicago whose names the New York
Confederates recognized were former Morgan raiders George St.
Ledger Grenfell and Captain George Cantrell. Cantrell had originally
been selected to be one of the raiders on St. Albans, but who did not
go on that particular mission.

One paragraph jumped out of the article: "Some of those arrested
are reported to have made confession that their intention was to fire
the city tonight, and release the prisoners at Camp Douglas." Another paragraph mentioned that more than two hundred stands of
arms and a "cart" of loaded and capped revolvers had been found in
one of the conspirators' houses.

Had Martin and Headley read the most detailed of the newspaper
accounts of the foiled plot, they might have become suspicious that a
double agent had set up Hines, Grenfell, and the others.

One newspaper account mentioned that a supply of .44-caliber
Joslyn revolvers had been captured before they could be distributed
to the Confederate prisoners. Only three thousand Joslyn revolvers
had been manufactured during the war as it proved to be unpopular
with Union soldiers. A small number of Joslyns had been sold to the
state of Illinois. Only someone with access to an arsenal in Illinois
could have provided the Confederates with this type of weapon.

Surely, Hines and Grenfell must have had their suspicions if they
inspected the boxes of pistols. Any self-respecting soldier wanting a
reliable weapon would have expected to be given a Colt or Remington
revolver. The Joslyns may well have malfunctioned in any skirmishes

between prisoners and prison guards. The Joslyns may have been given to the Confederates by a double agent with the knowledge that they would have malfunctioned.

Over the next several days, more articles appeared with more news of arrests. According to the newspapers, more than 250 men were arrested with some of them being Copperheads and some suspected "butternuts," Southerners who had come north to vote in the election. The articles described how Colonel Vincent Marmaduke of Missouri was supposed to have commanded the men to march on Chicago once the prisoners were freed. That name was probably unfamiliar to the Confederate raiders, other than he was the brother of Confederate general John S. Marmaduke.

Grenfell, the most prominent of the Confederates captured, would be convicted of spying and sentenced to Fort Jefferson in the Dry Tortugas, a fort located in the Gulf of Mexico some seventy miles west of Key West, Florida. He left the pages of history just as magnificently as he entered them. In March 1868, he climbed the walls of the prison with some comrades, stole a boat, and was last seen sailing into a fierce rainsquall. His body was never found.

What was important to Martin and Headley in November 1864 was that the name of Thomas Hines was not among the men captured. Hines would eventually tell the tale of how he escaped capture in Chicago by hiding in a mattress below a woman who was writhing in anguish as she lay dying. The Union soldiers searched in vain for Hines in the house that night. They finally guessed he had escaped through a window when they did not find him. The next day, Hines walked out of the house during a heavy rainstorm under an umbrella that hid his face. He simply posed as one of the mourners leaving the house who had come to comfort the husband of the now-dead woman.

Once again, Captain Thomas Hines had proved himself a resourceful man, always ready to use any situation that presented itself.

For several days after the election, the Confederates contented themselves by taking turns keeping a watch on Butler at his headquarters, waiting for any sign that he was ready to head back to Virginia and his command of the Army of the James.

With the passing of each day, McMaster became less confident that the operation could work. Finally, he told the Confederates that he was backing out.

"This left us practically at sea," Headley remembered.

Martin and Headley insisted that they still wanted to go through with the attack to "give the people a scare if nothing else, and let the Government at Washington understand that burning homes in the South might find a counterpart in the North."

Even Captain Longuemare, the advance man who had been in New York for weeks, lost his nerve and told the Confederates that he was going to leave the country if they insisted on continuing the attack.

They insisted. Before he left, Longuemare agreed to introduce the Confederates to the most important New Yorker they would ever meet. That man was not the governor, the governor's secretary, any of the three United States congressmen from New York City who had earlier agreed to help them, or any of the three newspaper editors who had promised them twenty thousand foot soldiers to take over the city.

The most important man the Confederates would meet in New York City was the chemist who would provide them with the Greek fire that they would use to set all of the fires. He lived in one of the oldest parts of New York City—Greenwich Village.

BURN NEW YORK

Chapter 16

"Something Dead in That Valise"

Butler left the city a week after Election Day. Following him over the coming days would be the 3,500 troops. All those soldiers' eyes, trained to look for enemies, would soon be on their way back to the battlefields of Virginia. The only forces left in the city were a few hundred garrison troops at Forts Lafayette and Hamilton.

Even though the planned Election Day attack had been canceled due to Butler and his troops, Martin and Headley were determined to do something since "we had told Colonel Thompson he could expect to hear from us in New York City, no matter what might be done in the other cities."

They had given up hope on convincing McMaster and his cohorts to change their minds and turn out once the fires started. The Copperheads had been spooked by the arrival of the troops. Even though the army forces in New York City were now back to a size that could be easily overpowered by the twenty thousand men they claimed to have, the Copperheads were afraid that the details of the plan had been betrayed to the War Department in Washington. They may have been right.

On November 16, the day after Butler left, the *New York Times* published a story thanking Butler for protecting the city since the secretary of war had discovered "a secret organization . . . whose avowed object was to accomplish the defeat of the Union ticket by force." The newspaper compared the organization to " 'the hordes of Lee and the murdering mob of Mosby [John Singleton Mosby, a partisan ranger colonel operating in Northern Virginia].' "

The newspaper then made a fantastic claim that New York contained "fifteen thousand Southern rebels, too slothful or cowardly to brave the dangers and fatigue of the battlefield, but vindictive and vengeful enough to pay the hire of incendiaries and assassins."

The Copperheads must have started breathing hard when they read that article. The newspaper mentioned "incendiaries," which the eight Confederates were, and it mentioned a "secret organization" that had control of over 15,000 men, a number close to the 20,000 McMaster claimed were ready to fight. The newspaper was only wrong in calling that private army "Southern rebels." According to McMaster, they were all New Yorkers who did not like the war or the Republican administration.

The reluctance of McMaster, Horton, Brooks, and the other unknown and unnamed Copperhead leaders to go through with the plan once Butler had left the city should not have surprised Martin and Headley. Hines had experienced and reported back in Toronto the same bravado without backup offered by the Copperheads in Illinois when planning the raid on Camp Douglas. Hines himself had scouted southern Indiana in July 1863 prior to Morgan's raid and discovered that the Southern-sympathizing farmers he was told would join Morgan's command did not exist.

What the New York Copperheads were experiencing was fear of action. It had been easy for them to talk among themselves about how brave they would be when facing Union troops when trying to retake New York once the Confederate flag was flying over City Hall. Now that they had seen 3,500 battle-hardened Union soldiers walking the streets carrying .58-caliber Springfields and sixty rounds of ammunition, they had experienced a change of heart.

Instead of thinking about the glory of taking New York out of the Union, the civilian Copperheads were now thinking about getting shot or captured, tried, and hanged as traitors to the United States. Confederate and Union soldiers were used to taking those kinds of risks, but civilians who went to sleep each night in nice, comfortable beds were not. Whatever nerve the civilian Copperheads had earlier was now gone. They might not have had much to start with because they were still living in the city rather than serving in the army on Southern battlefields.

Martin and Headley had no such fears. They had joined the army three years ago to seek adventure and to repel an army invading their homeland. They had fought and killed men in close combat. Martin had taken a Federal round to the chest, survived it, and came back again to fight. Now that the eight Confederates were here in the largest city of the United States, they were going to make the best of the opportunity they had.

Life seemingly returned to normal for New Yorkers. With the election over, their thoughts turned to the new, upcoming holiday of Thanksgiving.

Newspapers published notices that residents wishing to send Thanksgiving "turkies" to the Army of the Potomac needed to cook them, wrap them in white paper, pack them in straw, and put them in boxes or barrels marked: "Our Defenders, City Point." The birds would then be placed aboard ships heading to City Point, Virginia, a huge Union supply depot east of Petersburg at the confluence of the James and Appomattox rivers.

Lincoln prepared a Thanksgiving Day address for the nation that would be inserted in all the nation's newspapers.

It was Thursday, November 24, 1864, Thanksgiving Day, when Headley started out in search of the Greek fire that the Confederates would need to start the fires. Following Longuemare's directions to the address of the chemist operating out of a room on Washington Place, Headley found the shop in the first block west of Washington Square, a ten-acre park found at the foot of Fifth Avenue and on the eastern edge of Greenwich Village. At one time, the land around the park had been an indigent cemetery and a homestead for free blacks. It had been converted into a park in 1850, and fashionable homes had grown up around it.

The wealthy New Yorkers living around Washington Square had no idea that one of their own neighbors was about to hand over weapons of mass destruction that could burn the city down in one night.

After stepping down a few steps to a basement-level door, Headley knocked and a man with a beard "all over his face" answered. Headley said Longuemare had sent him for a valise. Without saying a word, the old man reached behind a counter and pulled up a satchel. Neither man said another word to each other.

Immediately, Headley realized he had made a number of mistakes, all of which would call attention to him on the street. The two-and-a-half-foot-long valise was much heavier than he had expected it to be. He had to change hands every ten feet, an action that could have drawn the attention of a police officer wondering what in the world could be so heavy in such a small bag.

Headley had not hired a cab to take him to the chemist on Washington Place, and now none of the cabs were to be found on the street. Instead of waiting for a cab or moving east over to Broadway or some other major street where there would be plenty of cabs, Headley started walking south. He struggled with the clanking valise, frequently changing hands as he walked all the way to City Hall Square, nearly one-and-a-half miles south of Greenwich Village. From there he found a horse-drawn streetcar that took him north up Bowery Street, the same direction from which he had come.

Some time after an exhausted and arm-sore Headley plopped himself down on the streetcar's wooden seat, he noticed an odor of rotten eggs, which the other passengers also noted. He assumed that one of the bottles was leaking, but he dared not open the valise to check. Either Headley had been told never to expose the Greek fire to air or he was afraid to be seen by the passengers looking inside his own valise to find the source of the bad smell. Either way, he was lucky that the leaking bottle did not catch fire. Had that happened, the entire streetcar could have gone up instantly when the damaged bottle set off the rest of the contents of the valise.

When Headley finally arrived at his destination of Central Park in one piece, he overheard one of the passengers comment as he exited the streetcar, "There must be something dead in that valise." That comment alone could have attracted the attention of a passing police officer, or a suspicious passenger could have pointed Headley out as he struggled up the street with his heavy bag.

When McMaster backed out of supporting the mission, the Confederates were forced to find another meeting place. All of them realized that meeting in a hotel room or a rooming house was inherently risky. Too many police detectives and employees would wonder why eight men who had seemingly been strangers were now meeting in a single room.

One of them found a cottage near Central Park that was far enough north of the city's major population center that they could count on a reasonable amount of privacy. And if any detectives came around, they too would be easier to spot.

At last, in the safety of the cottage, Headley carefully opened the valise in front of the other seven Confederates in the main room. Inside were 144 four-ounce bottles containing a liquid that resembled water. He did not mention finding any leaking bottles that would account for the bad odor on the streetcar.

What the chemist had prepared was a chemical compound commonly called Greek fire. The original Greek fire was an ancient weapon dating back at least to the seventh century when written reports told of how ships of the Byzantine Empire were equipped with hoses and nozzles from which streams of liquid fire would pour on their enemies from a distance. The Byzantines never recorded the formula for their fearsome weapon that was used to save Constantinople in at least two wars.

By the 1860s, several chemical compounds had some of the properties of the original Greek fire. These were mixtures of sulfur, pitch, dissolved niter, naphtha, and petroleum able to spontaneously combust if the mixture was mixed properly and exposed to a good supply of oxygen.

In 1862, the Federal navy was even experimenting with one inventor who could pump a liquid through a pipe that would ignite once the stream was two feet from the end of the pipe. The liquid fire could stream more than thirty yards, would burn on the surface of the water, and was impossible to put out once it was ignited. That description sounded much like the formula used by the ancient Byzantines.

The inventor refused to reveal his chemical compound so the navy never went beyond conducting the experiments.

During the war, some artillerists such as Union general Quincy Gilmore experimented with shells containing chemicals that would mix on impact and erupt into flames. Until this experiment, most incendiary shells had been heated in ovens and then put down cannon barrels with the obvious danger that the heat itself could set the shells off before they even left the cannon barrels.

In August 1862, Gilmore used some experimental Greek fire shells against the city of Charleston, South Carolina, a practice Confederate General P. G. T. Beauregard called barbaric. Beauregard demanded that Gilmore call a truce in order for the Confederates to evacuate the city if the Federals were going to use Greek fire shells. Gilmore refused.

This would be the second time that Confederates had experimented with Greek fire. The first time had been just a month earlier at St. Albans where the chemical compound did not ignite when Bennett Young's men threw bottles of it against wooden buildings that were soaking wet from days of rain in that part of Vermont. Reports do not indicate who had made Young's chemical weapons, but those bottles were likely made by Larry McDonald, the self-styled hand-grenade expert working in his Toronto basement lab.

McDonald had not made any of the Greek fire for the attack on New York. Transporting the volatile chemical bottles all the way from Toronto to New York would have been dangerous on two fronts. The Confederates might have been subjected to a random police search at any time through any of the states through which they were traveling. And breaking a bottle could have resulted in an unplanned fire.

In his postwar book, Headley inadvertently noted the last of the mistakes he had made that day regarding picking up the bottles that the Confederates planned to use against the city of New York. "None of the party knew anything about Greek fire, except that the moment it was exposed to the air it would blaze and burn everything it touched."

Martin, Headley, and the other six Confederates had spent the last three and a half years of the war becoming proficient with the weapons of the day. They could fieldstrip and load both Colt and Remington revolvers in the dark with their eyes closed. They could look at a musket and tell if it fired .54- or .577-caliber Minié balls. They knew the difference between Spencer and Sharps carbines and the kind of very different ammunition both weapons required. They knew how to use knives and sabers. Although they had come from the cavalry, all of them were skilled enough in soldiering to load, aim, and fire an artillery piece.

These eight men were probably the most highly trained soldiers and the most dangerous men in the city of New York on Thanksgiving Day, 1864. But they did not know anything about Greek fire, the primary weapon they intended to use against that same city of New York.

Remarkably, the eight men who intended to set fire to the city did not find a deserted spot to experiment with the delicate chemical compound that was in each four-ounce bottle. They did not test the difference between pouring the liquid out and smashing it against a hard surface to see which would result in a quicker flame. They did not time how long it would take from the initial flame of spontaneous combustion until a real fire was burning. They did not test how much quicker the initial flame would blaze up if given an even more generous supply of oxygen.

Most important of all, the Confederates did not test what would happen if the Greek fire was used indoors, which was the way they intended to use it. They did not test what would happen if the Greek fire had a limited supply of oxygen such as inside a hotel room.

Eight Confederates who were brave enough to walk into a city of 814,000 people were too excited about finally having the chance to act than they were about testing themselves and their weapons to see if both were actually ready to attack New York City. Martin, Headley, and the others were confident in their abilities. "We are now ready to create a sensation in New York."

Chapter 17

"Do the Greatest Damage in the Business District"

Headley never explained in detail why commercial hotels were chosen as targets other than his postwar memoir assertion that doing so would "do the greatest damage in the business district on Broadway."

There were more than 125 major commercial hotels in New York City in 1864. Most of them were located below 30th Street, with the most famous and desirable locations being along Broadway. City Hall Park, which was seven blocks north of Wall Street, the city's financial heart, had hotels surrounding it.

Hotel living was common in the city. Many upper-class New Yorkers, perhaps as many as three quarters, lived full-time in a hotel. Even commercial hotels usually had some arrangements for individuals or families wishing to live full-time. Perhaps half of the Astor House's residents in 1864 were full-time residents as other newer hotels were attracting the business traveler to the city. With residential discounts some guests could get by on $2-a-day rent, which included cleaning services. That compared to an average yearly rental cost of a house at $500 where the wife of the family was responsible for cleaning. If they could afford it, many middle- and upper-class New York women insisted on hotel living.

Only one of the nineteen hotel targets the Confederates selected was a purely residential hotel where many New York City families lived on a permanent basis either because they could not afford a single-family residence or because they preferred the convenience of having someone else cook and clean. It was also the only hotel frequented by the poor and was better known in the city as being a flophouse for drunks and drug addicts and unsuitable for families.

While city and federal officials would later call the plot "fiendish," the Confederates never intended targeting the lives of civilians. They only wanted to target the property of the hotels. Headley wrote that the time for starting the fires was set at 8:00 p.m. "so that the guests of hotels might all escape, as we did not want to destroy any lives."

The targeted hotels were familiar to the Confederates. Ever since the eight men had arrived in New York City, they had been moving from one boardinghouse or commercial hotel to another. At each hotel, they would use another alias so as not to arouse suspicions with desk clerks or police detectives about stays suddenly extended after November 8.

When the Election Day attack was postponed because of the appearance of Federal troops, the Confederates were suddenly at a disadvantage in keeping a low profile. They had left Canada with no plan other than to attack New York with firebombs on Election Day and then return to Canada on the evening train. Now, they had to stay in the city indefinitely until those Federal troops left. That turned out to be an extra two weeks, but that time frame was unknown to them on November 8.

The necessary change in the attack plans demonstrated just how unskilled at espionage the Confederates were. Morgan's officers had been excellent scouts behind enemy lines, skilled at finding the enemy's weaknesses and developing plans to hit and run if the Federals had the advantage or to bring the Federals to open battle if it was to the Confederates' advantage. They knew and loved that kind of warfare.

Operating in the nation's largest city on foot from hotel rooms was something that was unfamiliar to all of them. Now that the original plan for an in-and-out raid had been ruined, the Confederates were unprepared for a long-term stay in New York City. They had not developed any cover stories that any one of them was visiting the city for business purposes. They had told the hotel clerks who registered them that they would be in town for only a few days. Now they were faced with an indeterminate stay in the city. They had to keep moving to avoid suspicion.

Even the most basic tenets of spying such as hiding in plain sight eluded the Confederates. They could have easily met each other in the lobbies of their hotels to exchange news or better plan their attack by posing as one or two out-of-town businessmen meeting at a common hotel. All they would have had to do is take a quiet table in the hotel lobby, pull some business documents from a briefcase, and start talking to each other as they looked over the documents. No desk clerk or police officer would have been the wiser because New Yorkers conducted business in that fashion every day.

Instead, the Confederates continued to meet as the same group of eight men at the Central Park cottage. That might not have been suspicious on its face, but a group of eight military-age men, all with funny accents, meeting in a house on the edge of the city could have attracted the attention of wandering police detectives who had been repeatedly alerted about Southern agents in the city.

All the Confederates made another mistake when they checked in to their various hotels. They did not carry enough luggage to pose successfully as visiting businessmen. After their last cottage meeting when they distributed the Greek fire vials, they all left carrying virtually identical valises each now filled with more than a dozen four-ounce bottles of the clear-as-water but foul-smelling Greek fire. Then they checked into new hotels with nothing but the valises. The Southerners cushioned the bottles inside the valises with clothes and paper, though one hotel clerk would remember that one valise "clinked" when the guest handed it over to him for transport up to the room.

Some clerks and hotel proprietors would later tell police investigators and newspaper reporters that the men stood out from other guests because they were traveling with such light valises. At least one of the Confederates tried to make his valise seem heavier by the addition of a cavalry boot. That was a packing addition instantly labeling him as one of the arsonists when the valise was checked by police investigators. They wondered why anyone traveling would put only one boot into his suitcase.

Whether they intended it or not, the Confederates chose hotels with class, those with average daily rates ranging from $3.50 a day, more than twice the daily wage of an average New York City worker, to an astonishing $5 a day. They likely chose high-class hotels because these were establishments the loss of which would help emphasize the vast disparity of war losses between the burning of humble Confederate farms in the Shenandoah Valley of Virginia and the opulent businesses palaces in New York City.

St. James: The hotel farthest north that would be attacked was the St. James Hotel on the west side of Broadway and 26th Street. Built in 1859, the St. James was a six-story hotel described in an 1892 travel directory of New York City as "a resort of the better class of sporting men, especially those interested in the turf [meaning horse racing]." It featured a restaurant that was popular with actors since the region had many theaters.

Hoffman House: The Hoffman House at Broadway and covering the whole block from 24th to 25th streets overlooking Madison Square had just opened in 1864. It was the newest of the targeted hotels. The conspirators likely also took a slight pleasure in targeting it since General Butler had made it his headquarters during his stay. Known for its huge banquet hall and in-house art gallery, it attracted a wealthy clientele.

Fifth Avenue Hotel: One block south of the Hoffman House at 23rd Street and Broadway was the Fifth Avenue Hotel, described in an 1869 book on the city of New York as "the great fashionable hotel of New York, and is the haunt and home of stock operators and gold speculators . . . interspersed with really elegant people, one encounters there some absurd specimens of parvenuism [someone who has gained sudden wealth, but who is still inferior] . . . no one talks about anything but the closing rate of gold."

Opened in 1859, the five-story brick-and-white-marble Fifth Avenue Hotel was the first hotel in the nation to install an elevator, or vertical railway as it was first called. When the Fifth Avenue Hotel opened, detractors called it Eno's Folly because its owner Amos Eno had built so far north of most of the businesses in the city. Bankers were so sure that the hotel was so far away from where most guests would want to stay that they refused to finance it. Eno's financing for the $2 million building came from Boston bankers who may not have known how far uptown Eno was planning his establishment.

The critics and bankers were quickly proved wrong as the hotel was an instant success. Lincoln stayed there while visiting the city to give his famed Cooper Union speech. It took more than four hundred employees to run it. One London correspondent, noting that each room had a private bathroom, crowed that the Fifth Avenue Hotel had the same opulence as Buckingham Palace.

The conspirators were very familiar with the Fifth Avenue Hotel. Presidential candidate War Democrat George McClellan had addressed his supporters from one of its balconies while the Confederates listened to his campaign promises to continue the war just as Lincoln was doing.

Everett House: The Everett House at Broadway and 17th Street at Union Square, attracted an arts clientele of actors and writers.

St. Denis Hotel: The St. Denis Hotel at Broadway and 11th Street was built in 1848 and was one of those hotels that attracted celebrities such as General Grant. It looked out onto Grace Church, one of the city's best-known churches with its spire knifing into the sky.

LaFarge House: The LaFarge House on Broadway at Bond Street was a hotel housing five hundred guests. It was popular with out-of-towners as it was adjacent to the Winter Garden, one of the city's most popular theaters. According to the *New York Times,* its owner was also a staunch Democrat, which led to many of his guests being "mostly of Southern stripe."

When the *Times* noted that a Republican rally walked past the hotel, it commented, "The hotel bore the infliction with patience, and behaved throughout with the utmost decorum, as became the dignity of its marble front."

If the Confederates knew that the owner was a Southern sympathizer, it made no difference to them. The hotel was a target.

Metropolitan Hotel: The Metropolitan Hotel at Broadway and Prince Street, a large brownstone that could accommodate six hundred people, was popular with westerners. The hotel had one of the largest dining rooms in the city, and it featured an entrance to Niblo's Theater, another of the city's more popular theaters with a seating capacity of more than two thousand.

St. Nicholas Hotel: The St. Nicolas, occupying a full block at Broadway and Spring Street, was just one block south of the Metropolitan. The St. Nicholas was one of the first hotels to cost more than $1 million in construction costs. Opened in 1854, it featured more than six hundred rooms and more than one thousand guests a week were accommodated. Visiting author Charles Dickens called it: "The lordliest caravanserai in the world." Room rates ranged from a high of $5 a night (at a time when soldiers were making $11 a month) to a low of $1. In the more expensive rooms were gold brocaded curtains and beveled mirrors.

The Confederates might have had an extra motive for torching this hotel. It was also the headquarters of General Dix, the man who had issued orders for all Southerners living in the city to register their names and addresses. They planned to leave more than their calling cards at the hotel.

The Astor House: The most famous of the targeted hotels, and the second oldest, was the Astor House, found on the west side of Broadway, just at the southern tip of City Hall Park between Vesey and Barclay streets. When the Astor House opened in 1836 after four years of construction, one newspaper reporter wrote that New Yorkers could now feel what the Romans must have experienced when they looked at the Colosseum. Among the amenities that so wowed the newspaper reporter was the bathing and toilet facilities that were found on each floor. Medicinal baths were available with an attending physician keeping track of what sorts of chemicals went into the water.

Some of the newfangled technology in the Astor House was dangerous to infrequent hotel guests in the 1830s. Each room had gaslights when most homes still used candles. When guests unfamiliar with how gaslights worked blew the flame out rather than turn off the gas jets, they were asphyxiated in their sleep. Savvier hotel guests recognized what had happened to previous guests when they found some room doors marked with gouges where hotel staff had jimmied the door locks to recover the bodies of the dead guests.

The Astor House's architect was also unaware that when he picked blue marble for the façade that a nearby prison also featured the same color façade, leading to some jokes that Astor's new hotel was just a better class of prison.

Tennessee congressman David Crockett stopped off to see the 390-room hotel while it was still under construction just before leaving for Texas where he would lose his life at the Alamo in March 1836. Knowing that hotel developer John Jacob Astor had made his money buying animal pelts, Crockett said, "Lord help the poor b'ars and beavers. They must be used to being skun by now!"

In 1864, the quarter-century-old hotel was still considered among the city's finest, even though newer hotels had surpassed it in opulence and amenities. Still, in the words of well-known poet and art critic Walt Whitman, the Astor House was "a specimen of exquisite design and proportion."

City Hotel: The City Hotel was across the street from the Astor House.

Lovejoy's Hotel: Opposite the Astor House on the southeast corner of City Hall Park was Lovejoy's Hotel, another old hotel dating from the 1830s. Lovejoy's featured 250 rooms and a dining room where travelers interested in finding good food at bargain prices could eat a plate of meats for six cents and a plate of vegetables for three cents.

One critic did not like the type of people who stayed at hotels like Lovejoy's: "The class of persons you meet there are not apt to be as cultivated and agreeable as at the Broadway houses. You must pay something for your company as well as your accommodations; and most persons in this country are willing to do so, if they have the money, or can borrow it."

The writer went on to explain: "New York generally is a very expensive place, but you can live cheaply if you are willing to go where your fastidiousness is not consulted, and cleanliness is not ranked second to godliness. Thousands of persons keep up a certain respectability of appearance here on a slender income; but they suffer more from their false pride than they would be willing to do in a worthier cause."

Tammany Hotel: The Tammany Hotel was a block northeast of Lovejoy's on Park Avenue. The Tammany was the headquarters of the Democratic Party, the place to see and be seen if one was a visiting Democrat from out of town. But because it was so steeped in politics, the average business traveler often chose other accommodations.

Belmont Hotel: Located on Fulton Street, between Nassau Street and Broadway, the Belmont was one of the few of the targeted hotels that broke from the flat-roofed, rectangular look of the others. The Belmont had a six-story tower on one end that rose above the other four stories. On top of the tower flew an American flag.

Brandreth's Hotel: Benjamin Brandreth, born in England, made a fortune selling Brandreth's Pills, a laxative that cleaned the bowels within minutes of taking the pill. A pioneer at mass advertising the product that he claimed purged the body of just about everything bad in it, Brandreth needed a way to convert and conserve his fortune in cash. One way was to build his hotel in 1857 at Broadway and Canal Street.

Howard Hotel: The Howard Hotel was the southernmost hotel targeted on Broadway. It was located at the intersection of Broadway and Maiden Lane, four blocks north of Wall Street.

Several of the hotels were located off Broadway:

Gramercy Park Hotel: Gramercy Park Hotel was located beside the private one-acre park between 20th and 21st streets and Third and Fourth avenues that was used for a camp for the soldiers guarding the city. Southerners preferred staying in the hotel. Diarist George Templeton Strong lived in the neighborhood.

The United States Hotel: The United States Hotel at Fulton, Water, and Pearl streets, just two blocks west of the East River, was the oldest hotel targeted, having been finished in 1833. Designed by its owner, Stephen Holt, who named it Holt's Hotel, the hotel had a marble façade that made it the most elegant hotel of its day until the Astor House was finished a few years later. When its owner set the room rate at $1.50 a day for its 220 rooms, New Yorkers were aghast that someone would even attempt to charge visitors to the city so much money when the same man also sold meals at the extravagant price of twenty-five cents.

Holt also knew how to save money. During the two years it took to build the hotel, Mrs. Holt handmade 1,500 towels, 400 pairs of sheets, and 250 quilts to go in all the rooms.

Noting the hard work of Mrs. Holt, one newspaper report observed: "A man with such a wife may well build his house of marble and fill it with luxuries."

The outstanding feature of the United States, renamed when Holt's Hotel was sold soon after opening because of his inability to keep up with maintenance expenses, was the cupola on its roof. At 125 feet above the ground, the cupola gave visitors a fantastic view of the city and the East River. Because of its proximity to the East River, the hotel was a favorite of guests arriving by ship from all over the East Coast.

The New England Hotel: For reasons unknown, the Confederates targeted only one residential hotel, a flophouse called The New England at 38 Bowery Street. Songwriter Stephen Foster was living there for 25-cents-a-day rent when he fell and gashed his neck in January 1864. Foster was one of the nation's most popular composers. He wrote *My Old Kentucky Home,* which would have been popular with the Kentucky-born raiders. He made little money from his song writing. He died with thirty-eight cents in his change purse. It is likely pure coincidence that the Kentucky-born Confederates would have targeted the hotel where Foster died.

The Hanford Hotel: Located at the east end of Grand Street, was a five-story hotel. Its proximity to the East River likely meant it was the favorite of ship captains and other seafarers.

The only target that was not a hotel was the one that all the conspirators should have chosen—the docks along the Hudson River. The docks were an excellent target since the prevailing winds blew from the west toward the city. Any fires started on the eastern bank of the Hudson would have naturally blown toward the city's structures.

For decades, New York City had been a port of entry for international trade. The number of ships docking in the city doubled in just fourteen years from 1835 to 1849 with more than three thousand ships from 150 foreign ports docking in the city in 1849. Those ships carried half the nation's imports and nearly a third of its exports. In the following decade, the amount of goods increased another 60 percent.

With the increase in shipping came an increase in the need for docks. By the time of the war, there must have been one hundred docks each on both the Hudson and the East rivers. Even then, ships had to anchor in the rivers and wait their turns for loading and unloading. To accommodate all of that loading and unloading, hundreds of warehouses sprang up on Manhattan Island along both rivers.

Growth along the waterfront came so quickly and profits were so high that no one had time to maintain and renovate the docks or the warehouses because they were unwilling to take them out of service for any time at all. By 1860, the waterfront on both rivers was decaying and dilapidated but just as crowded with products such as lumber, hay, turpentine, gunpowder, fuel oil, cotton, military uniforms, and a hundred other types of cargo that all shared something in common: they were highly flammable.

The East River was also home to important iron foundries that had played a major role in building Union ironclads. By 1863, ten different military contractors operating along the East River employed at least 7,500 ironworkers. By 1864, most of the Union navy's ironclads had been built and deployed to Southern rivers and coastal waters, but the facilities that had mass-produced them were still operating, making tempting targets.

By November 24, 1864, the nation's second official Thanksgiving, everything was ready. The targets had been selected. The Greek fire had been distributed. The Union troops that had been on every street corner had left for the battlefield.

Some newspapers printed Lincoln's Thanksgiving Proclamation, which included the lines: "Order has been maintained, the laws have been respected and obeyed, and harmony has prevailed everywhere except in the theatre of military conduct."

On Friday evening, November 25, 1864, six of the eight Confederates held their last meeting at the Central Park cottage. Price and the man whose name Headley could not remember in his book failed to report, apparently having lost their nerve. As the six Confederates left the cottage, Robert Cobb Kennedy said to Headley, "We'll make a spoon or spoil a horn [a saying dating back to Colonial days when spoons were carved from cow horns meaning the Confederates would have either total success or total failure]."

Chapter 18

"It Blazed Up Instantly"

The attack on New York City could have been prevented on the same morning it occurred had only those leaders in civilian and military authority listened to intelligence coming from men who worked for them. For weeks, ever since the *Richmond Whig* had published an editorial calling for the destruction of Northern cities with the embedded line that "New York is worth twenty Richmonds," rumors had been flying around the city that Confederates would try to burn it.

Federal and city leaders may have had at least two chances to intervene in the plot. The first chance was at the end of October when U.S. consul M. M. Jackson in Halifax reported to Secretary of State Seward that he had uncovered the plot. This was the source of the telegram sent to New York's Mayor Gunther warning of a potential attack.

The second chance was a few days after Jackson filed his report when a double agent, who the Confederates thought was working for them, but who was really working for the Union, reported the same or similar plot to his boss, Secretary of War Stanton, in Washington City. That man, whose name was not mentioned in War Department reports, was probably Richard Montgomery who also went by the alias James Thomson.

According to Assistant Secretary of War Charles Dana writing in a postwar memoir, a young Union War Department clerk (the unidentified Montgomery) approached Dana in 1864, offering to play the role of a Confederate agent. The clerk's plan called for him to ingratiate himself with Confederate Secret Service officials in Canada and then volunteer for the dangerous job of carrying dispatches back and forth between Canada and Richmond. Then, as the agent, he offered to stop in Washington on each trip to share all dispatches he was carrying. Dana said he liked the idea proposed by the young man he described as "well dressed and patriotic."

The young man, whom Dana never names, but who is identified as Montgomery/Thomson by the biographer of another double agent, convinced Clement Clay in St. Catherines, Ontario, that he would make a good courier. The letters, reports, and orders Montgomery was supposed to carry from Thompson in Toronto and Clay in St. Catherines to the Confederate cabinet in Richmond made their first stop at the War Department in Washington. The envelopes were opened, the dispatches were read and copied, and the items were put back into a similar envelope of English manufacture and sealed. Montgomery was then sent on his way to Richmond. The original dispatches were always delivered and never substituted, though the envelopes were sometimes substituted if they were damaged while being opened. Dana said obtaining the right kind of paper envelope and an imitation seal that looked like the real one originally sealed in St. Catherines took some time to acquire. Still, according to Dana, the months-long ruse worked, and the Confederates in Richmond never noticed any differences in handwriting, envelopes, or seals.

One day, on a date Dana did not record, but which was after the November 8 election and some days after Jackson in Halifax had issued his warning, Montgomery, the double agent, arrived in Washington with a dispatch he said was particularly important:

It was found to contain an account of a scheme for setting fire to New York and Chicago by means of clock-work machines that were to be placed in several of the large hotels and places of amusement—particularly in Barnum's of New York—and to be set off simultaneously, so that the fire department in each place would be unable to attend to the great number of calls that would be made upon it on account of these Confederate conflagrations in so many quarters, and thus these cities might be greatly damaged, or even destroyed.

David Homer Bates, a military telegrapher in the U.S. War Department in Washington, who wrote his own postwar book on his experiences, independently confirmed Dana's postwar account of the startling dispatch. Bates wrote that one of his bosses, Major Thomas Eckerd, was dispatched to New York to warn General Dix and Superintendent John Kennedy of the New York Metropolitan Police of the impending attack. Bates never gives a date for Eckerd's trip, but subsequent events would have made it Thanksgiving Day, November 24, with Eckerd arriving in New York City on Friday, November 25, the day of the attack.

Both Bates' and Dana's postwar accounts agree that Eckerd had a seemingly unlikely encounter in which he recognized the spy (Montgomery) in a horse-drawn taxi on his arrival in New York City. Eckerd claimed that Montgomery told him all the details of the upcoming plot, including naming the hotels that would be fired and the names of the Confederate conspirators.

Bates' and Dana's accounts differ completely on the reaction of army and city officials in New York when told the city would be attacked that night.

Bates said that Dix and Kennedy both believed the story of the impending attack and that police detectives were dispatched around the city to look for the suspicious men and to prevent fires in the named hotels. Dana said neither Dix nor Kennedy believed that such an attack was imminent, and they did little planning to stop it.

Whether the New York City police superintendent and the Union general in command of the city did try to stop the attack by looking for the Confederates or ignored the warnings has never been proved one way or the other. What is known is that the attack went as planned—though the results the Confederates expected did not occur.

Friday night, November 25, 1864, would have been a day of celebration for New Yorkers. The calls for piety and sacrifice from President Lincoln were meant only for Thanksgiving Day. The rain that had fallen earlier in the week had washed the horse-manure dust from the streets. That meant the smell was washed away. The piles of horse manure that could have clung to men's shoes and women's dresses were gone. It was time to go out on the town.

It was a big night for those who enjoyed cultural activities. The Academy of Music, at the corner of 14th Street and Irving Place, was sure to have its four thousand seats filled with patrons watching Donizetti's five-act opera *Don Sebastiano*.

At Niblo's Theater at Broadway and Prince Street, *The Corsican Brothers,* a play adapted from a book by Frenchman Alexander Dumas, was continuing. While many American-born playwrights might grumble that they could produce works of art as entertaining as any Europeans, New Yorkers at the highest social strata thought otherwise. They liked their operas and plays to come from Europe.

Over at the Winter Garden Theatre at 624 Broadway, just south of Bond Street, three brothers who had never before performed together on one stage were preparing to put on Shakespeare's *Julius Caesar* as a fund-raiser to erect a statue to the playwright in Central Park. Those were the Booth brothers, Junius Brutus Booth playing Cassius, Edwin Booth playing Brutus, and the youngest brother, John Wilkes Booth, playing Mark Antony. According to the November 25, 1864, *New York Times,* the Booth brothers were "worthy sons of a worthy sire." Still, there was entertainment for the masses who had no interest in French and British plays and Italian operas.

Directly across the street from the Academy of Music was the Hippotheatron, where New Yorkers without hard-to-get tickets or cultural interests could watch ladies on horseback perform backflips and other gymnasts complete amazing feats such as leaping over as many as fifteen horses lined up shank to shank.

Van Amburgh & Company's Menagerie at 536 and 541 Broadway had just opened two weeks earlier with an elephant called Tippoo Saib, supported by other acts the *New York Times* described as "highly-educated ponies, monkeys and mules [that] will amuse and astonish visitors with practical evidences of their sagacity and superior training."

If that entertainment seemed too highbrow, the curious could walk up to Barnum's American Museum at Broadway and Ann Street to see what Phineas T. Barnum's own advertisement described as "Three Mammoth Fat Girls, Weighing One Ton! Three Giants, Two Dwarfs, Indian Warriors, French Automatons." The automatons were intricately engineered human-looking figures that could perform multiple tasks such as moving their arms, legs, and heads as if they were alive.

If the previous day's weather was any indication, the temperature would steadily but slowly fall until Saturday's dawn temperature would record just below freezing. Just like Thanksgiving Day, the weather promised to be clear. That meant carriages would be heading up to the construction site of the seven hundred acres of Central Park above 59th Street and stretching all the way north to 106th Street. Trumpeted by its designers as the first large urban park in the nation, New Yorkers were actually growing impatient to use the space that had already been under construction for seven years. Even with the excuse that there was a war on, jaded and skeptical New Yorkers wondered if the park would ever be finished as the need for it had been debated for more than a decade before the land was acquired in 1857.

The streets were crowded and alive with people. That is just how the Confederates wanted it: people on the streets at an early hour so they would not be caught in their rooms during the ensuing fires.

While Headley did not mention time coordination of setting the fires in his account, that seems to have been part of the plan. Headley said he entered his Astor House sixth floor room at 7:20 p.m. He built a pile of flammables on the bed, including furniture, the drawers of the bureau, and the washstand, adding newspapers and turpentine for good measure. He carefully opened one of the bottles of Greek fire and spread it "on the pile of rubbish. It blazed up instantly and the whole bed seemed to be in flames before I could get out."

Headley then targeted the City Hotel and the Everett House. After leaving the City Hotel, he looked up from Broadway to his room at the Astor House and saw a bright light, indicating that his fire was still burning, but that no alarm had yet come from any of the guests. When he set his fire at the United States Hotel and left his key at the front desk, Headley thought the clerk looked at him with a funny expression. He wondered why, fearing that the clerk might have looked into his valise and found it empty. (All the Confederates were now carrying the bottles of Greek fire in the pockets of their coats.)

All the fires set that night were discovered by either guests leaving their rooms or hotel staff working on the floor, indicating that the Confederate plan to set the fires when people were awake in order to minimize the chance of lives lost was flawed.

Had the Confederates delayed their attack by seven hours from 8:00 p.m., Friday night, to 3:00 a.m., Saturday morning, the Confederate mission to burn New York might have been accomplished. Instead, they struck at 8:00 p.m., a time when citizens, hotel guests, hotel staff, police, and firefighters were wide-awake and ready to react to clanging fire bells.

An exact time line of the attack is impossible to determine because the men were working independently and had varying degrees of success at starting their fires. Some of the fires were discovered almost immediately, whereas other fires smoldered for hours before being discovered. The fires are better tracked by looking at the reports of the hotels fired, starting from the most northern one. All the following descriptions are taken from an in-depth *New York Times* article on November 27, 1864.

The *St. James* was probably targeted by Martin, who had registered at the hotel under "John School, Md." at 5:30 that same afternoon. A fire in a room was discovered at 8:43 p.m. when a guest in an adjoining room leaving for the evening noticed smoke coming from under the door. The hotel staff broke down the locked door, and it was empty except for a black valise, a single, still-filled bottle of Greek fire, and some matches. A strong odor of phosphorous was in the room.

The *LaFarge House* was a target of Ashbrook. A fire was discovered at 9:30 p.m. by guests and staff. The fire set on bedding and furniture was extinguished so quickly that the newspaper reports said the hotel owner estimated the damage to be no more than $256. The room had been rented to a J. B. Richardson of Camden, New Jersey. The clerk must not have listened carefully enough to accents. Ashbrook was a native of Kentucky, with an accent that probably did not sound much like someone from New Jersey.

The *Metropolitan Hotel*, a target of Harrington, had one room set on fire with damage estimated at $1,500. Its fire was discovered at 10:00 p.m. with the fire being "speedily extinguished by the servants of the house" before the fire department arrived. In the room, investigators found a valise, an empty bottle, and a pair of boots. The valise contained a pair of pantaloons and a pair of "prunella" gaiters (leather or canvas leggings that buckled over a soldier's ankle to protect his lower pants legs from ripping when walking through underbrush), which seemed an odd clothing choice for downtown Manhattan.

The *St. Nicholas Hotel*, a target of Ashbrook, had three rooms torched all in a row, plus a fourth room on the opposite side of the hall. The fires were discovered at 8:55 p.m. Three of the rooms were completely "burned out," at a damage estimate of $3,000. The fire department of the hotel kept the fires from spreading. According to the *New York Times*: "Had it not been for the admirable arrangements for taking care of fires at this house, it would have entirely burned down."

A boarder at the hotel noticed two suspicious men in the hallway just before the alarm was given. According to the boarder, one man said to the other, "It will be alright," just as they left the lobby.

Guests staying at the *Astor House*, Headley's first target, congratulated themselves early Saturday morning for having escaped the Confederate attack. Just to play it safe, however, the hotel manager conducted a room-to-room check. When he reached the top sixth floor and opened room number 204, which seems to match Headley's description of where he stayed, smoke billowed out.

Curiously, Headley's description of setting the fire at the Astor House and the official version filed by a police detective named Devoe, who pushed his way past the smoke to see the fire, do not match. Headley said he piled furniture and bedclothes on the bed and set them ablaze. Devoe said a portion of the floor had been raised, a fire built in the hole, and then the bed pulled over the burning hole. Headley and the detective agreed that he had poured some turpentine on the pile to help it burn. Damages were estimated at $500.

Lovejoy's Hotel, a target of Kennedy, seems to have had two rooms fired. One fire was discovered at 10:30 p.m. when an unknown person discovered a fire of piled bedclothes in a fourth floor room. At midnight, another fire was discovered on the same floor inside a carpetbag, which had been placed inside a mattress. The newspaper accounts say the damage was limited to the loss of the bedclothes.

Tammany Hotel, which was supposed to be a target of Kennedy, had a fire in a third floor room registered to a man from Rochester, New York, named C. E. Morse. The newspaper accounts list the damages as being limited to the bedclothes. The newspaper said Mr. Morse's signature in the guest book looked similar to the signature of a suspect who signed the guest register at the St. Nicholas Hotel. That suspect should have been Ashbrook. Either Ashbrook took over Kennedy's assigned hotel or the police detectives were wrong in their handwriting analysis.

The *Belmont Hotel*, a target of Martin, experienced a fire on the third floor of a room occupied by a supposed Union officer who had signed himself in as "Lieutenant Lewis, USA." Six unused bottles of Greek fire (described as phosphorous by the newspaper) were found in the room. Martin was known to have brought a Union officer's uniform with him from Canada as a disguise. He intended to wear the uniform on Saturday morning, anticipating that police detectives would be looking for men in civilian clothes, not men in Union blue. Apparently, Martin was the only one of the eight conspirators who intended disguising himself.

The *Howard Hotel*'s fire apparently started by Chenault smoldered until 3:30 a.m. Sunday morning before it was discovered by a night watchman. The fourth floor room was registered to an S. M. Harner of Philadelphia. Like the others, bedclothes and furniture had been piled on the bed and saturated with the Greek fire.

The *United States Hotel* fire, supposedly set by Headley, was discovered at 8:45 p.m. on the top or fifth floor. The desk clerk had rented that room to a young man with a valise who wanted a ground floor room, but who reluctantly took one of the few available on the top floor. The desk clerk claimed that the young man was wearing a wig and false whiskers, which aroused his suspicions though not enough to report the strange man to the owner of the hotel. Headley does not mention attempting a disguise in his postwar book, and no hotel clerks reported anyone checking into their establishments that afternoon attempting a disguise.

The *New York Times*, believing the clerk's assertion that the young man wore a disguise, speculated that if all the "villains who have taken part in this nefarious business" also wore disguises, identifying suspects would have been difficult.

The *New England Hotel*, a target of Kennedy's, was apparently the last hotel targeted because a man giving his name as George Morse (a variation of the alias used at the *Tammany Hotel*) checked in at 11:00 p.m. Morse left almost immediately, saying he would soon return. The fire broke out within a few minutes of Morse leaving. Morse was described as 35 years old, florid complected, and fair haired, and he wore a gray coat. Kennedy was actually 29 years of age in November 1864, bearded, and walked with a pronounced limp, which the clerk failed to mention if he noticed. He did wear a long, gray coat.

Only one of the hotels targeted seemed to have been one that the conspirators had given some thought to as far as what types of structures surrounded it.

The *Hanford Hotel*, which does not appear on Headley's list of targets in his book, apparently forgotten by him as he wrote about his experiences some forty years after they occurred, was close to the East River on Grand Street. According to the newspaper reports, detectives speculated that this hotel, isolated from all the others, was targeted because it was near a lumber planing mill and a lumberyard.

"It is believed that the desperadoes intended that by setting fire to the hotel that flames would extend to the mill and lumberyard, and thus a general conflagration throughout the east side of town would be effected," wrote a reporter for the *New York Times*.

Perhaps half of the targets never even ignited. The *Fifth Avenue*

Hotel, the *St. Denis*, and the *Hoffman House*, all supposed to be set by Martin, were never mentioned by newspaper accounts as having been fired. The *Everett House* and the *City Hotel*, set by Headley, apparently never caught fire either. Whoever tried to fire the *Brandeth House* and the *Gramercy Park Hotel* also failed.

Kennedy tried to set fire to one target of opportunity that likely would have drawn the ire of Martin and Headley had they known about it in advance. Kennedy and Chenault ducked into Barnum's museum for a few minutes thinking that the streets would soon be filled with panicked hotel guests fleeing flames. As they were leaving, Kennedy smashed a bottle of Greek fire on a set of stairs. The fire was quickly noticed and doused.

Headley wrote that he was astonished when he noticed the people rushing out of Barnum's as "I did not suppose there was a fire in the Museum."

Headley said that panicked people were climbing out of second and third floor windows, and the manager was calling out for people to help him evacuate his animals.

The only intended target that was not a hotel other than Barnum's museum was what all the targets should have been—the docks on the Hudson River. Headley reported that he walked over to the Hudson, which he called by its common New York name of North River, and threw six bottles of Greek fire at "places." He identified only one target, a barge filled with bales of hay that was ablaze when he started walking back toward Broadway to check on the progress of the other fires.

When Headley was on Broadway (which he misidentifies as the Bowery Street) in front of the Metropolitan, he saw Kennedy limping along in front of him. Headley, in a fit of youthful exuberance, sneaked up behind the other Confederate and firmly clasped his hand on Kennedy's shoulder. Kennedy spun around and almost drew his revolver, thinking a police officer was collaring him. Kennedy laughed when he recognized Headley, then said aloud, "I ought to have shot you for giving me such a scare."

There the two Confederate conspirators stood on the busiest street in New York City with fire bells clanging all around them loudly laughing and talking in their Kentucky and Alabama accents about drawing revolvers and shooting each other.

Once again, the Confederates' lack of training in espionage was showing. Real spies would have signaled to each other without being obvious. These two were cavorting on a public street filled with panicked civilians, frantic firefighters, and suspicious police officers. Headley's and Kennedy's unthinking actions called attention to themselves. They could have been arrested that same night had anyone overheard their conversation.

As Headley and Kennedy walked up and down Broadway to survey their work, they were disappointed that none of the targets were enveloped in flames. What they heard, however, did give them pause. All the conversations they could overhear were about "hanging the rebels to lamp posts or burning them at the stake."

The average New Yorker had already reached the same conclusion that city and army officials would reach the next morning. The newspaper rumors that Confederates might attack the city were true.

Headley speculated while still in the street that the Greek fire had not performed as promised. In fact, he now believed that their supposed friend in the city, Longuemare, and the Washington Square chemist who had prepared the Greek fire "had put up a job on us after it was found that we could not be dissuaded from our purpose."

What Headley did not speculate on, but which newspaper reports in the following days would decide, was that the Confederates had not properly used the Greek fire. The chemist had said nothing to Headley at all about how to use the bottles he gave him. The Confederates had not practiced with it at all in Toronto when they had access to explosives expert Larry McDonald. The only practice the Confederates had taken with the substance was throwing a few bottles at some boards outside their Central Park cottage, where it seemed to work fine.

The Confederates' mistake was not practicing with the Greek fire under the same conditions they would have inside an enclosed hotel room. Had they poured the bottles out on their piles of furniture and clothes and then opened the hotel room window to give the fledgling flames a steady supply of oxygen, the fires likely would have grown in intensity.

Headley himself had noted that the Greek fire seemed to work fine when he first poured it out on his room in the Astor House. He said it flamed up right away. But he did not say in his detailed description of how he piled the bedding and furniture that he had left the window open to feed the flames with fresh, near-freezing air coming from a small but steady wind from the west.

Frustrated that their month-long stay in New York City had left them without a victory, the Confederates did the only thing they could do. They checked into still more hotels and went to bed.

Chapter 19

"A Vast and Fiendish Plot"

The Confederates slept late on Saturday, not arising until 10:00 a.m. Headley and Martin sat down for breakfast at a restaurant at Broadway and 12th Street but suddenly lost their appetites when they started reading the *New York Herald, New York World, New York Tribune*, and *New York Times*. All the newspapers branded the attack a "rebel plot." What drew their attention most was a headline in the *Times*: PROMPT ARREST OF REBEL EMISSARIES and THE POLICE ON TRACK OF OTHERS.

Headley misremembered the newspaper accounts, or he embellished his memories when writing his book. He claimed:

All our fictitious names registered at the different hotels were given and interviews with the clerks described us all. The clerk of the United States Hotel especially gave a minute description of my personal appearance, clothing, manners, and actions. He said I did not eat a meal at the hotel, though I had been there two days as a guest, and had nothing in my black satchel.

In fact, none of the newspapers printed the aliases of the Confederates and no detailed descriptions were given.

Shaken from reading the newspapers that all accurately speculated that the Confederates had perpetrated the attack, the two got up from their table without ordering. They and the other four conspirators spent the rest of the day hiding out in the Central Park cottage. They passed the day reading the newspapers, which printed rumors that some people had already been arrested.

Some of the newspaper stories were completely wrong as to who was guilty. Several newspapers told of the arrest of a Baltimore woman who had visited several of the hotels that had been fired. They had not worked with a woman. The woman was later freed when the police finally believed her story that she was looking for someone, and it was a coincidence that she was in many of the hotels that were fired.

At 4:00 p.m., the Confederates left the cottage to go back downtown to eat and find out what the latest editions of the newspapers were saying. Martin suggested they recover the trunks they had left at Henry "Gus" McDonald's piano store at 358 Broadway since they might contain some articles of clothing that could be used as evidence to track them down. As Martin got out of the cab that was going to continue on to a restaurant where Headley would order for both of them, he saw Katie, Gus McDonald's daughter, standing at the window of the store. Katie was fully aware of the plot details, and Martin saw that Katie was holding the palm of her hand out in a stopping motion. She then nodded behind her. Shaken and pale, Martin jumped back into the cab without saying a word. A disturbed Headley stared at Martin, but the captain did not say anything at all out of fear that the cabdriver could overhear their conversation.

Once they were at the restaurant and at a private table, Martin whispered to Headley that behind Katie he had seen a crowd of men inside the piano store. They must have been police detectives.

That detectives were in the piano store was disturbing. As far as Martin and Headley knew, none of the six Confederates had visited the McDonalds since arriving in New York City more than a month ago.

That could mean one of four things: First, New York detectives had tailed the Confederates from the moment they stepped from the train and took their trunks to McDonald's. Second, someone in

Canada had betrayed them to New York authorities. Third, one of the Copperheads who knew about the plans had betrayed them. Or last, one or both of the two men who had backed out of the plot at the last minute had betrayed them and the McDonalds. As would be proved later, this last scenario was the most likely.

Martin and Headley returned to the cottage wondering whether they had been followed and what the fate of the other four men was who had also gone to breakfast. When the other four returned, all expressed mild surprise that none of the six had yet been arrested as the newspapers were reporting arrests were being made all over the city.

They waited until 8:00 p.m. that Saturday night to leave the city by way of the Hudson River Railroad. It was agreed that the two men who had been seen the least around the city, Harrington and Ashbrook, would buy sleeper berth tickets for all of them. While it might seem suspicious that two men would be buying tickets for six men, the Confederates took that chance rather than all of them showing up at the ticket office.

Harrington and Ashbrook were only partially successful. Though their destination was the Canadian side of Niagara Falls, they were able to buy tickets only as far as Albany, 150 miles to the north.

When all six arrived at the train depot at 9:00 p.m. for the scheduled train departure at 10:30 p.m., they somehow recognized their particular sleeper car parked on a siding. Rather than wait with the gathering crowd to board, they used the cover of darkness to slip aboard the sleeper.

Each of the men climbed into his sleeping compartment. Martin then walked down the aisles warning them that if detectives boarded the train to look for them, that each man should be ready to rush out the back of the railroad car and try to get lost in the crowd. Martin said he would cover them. Martin's words were that he would "start the ball" if detectives boarded the train. While Headley did not say so, each of the men must have been armed with one or more loaded revolvers.

Just as the Confederates suspected, detectives were watching the railroad depot. Headley, apparently peeking from a dark window, noted that most passengers walked down the platform with packages and valises, but several men had nothing in their hands. As their sleeper car was hooked to the rest of the train, the incendiaries remained quietly secluded in their sleeper berths with the curtains drawn.

The Confederates waited for an hour after the train pulled out of the station before getting undressed. They had wanted to be fully dressed as they probably carried revolvers in their frock coat pockets. They also stayed dressed because if they had to jump from the train, curious citizens would have noticed men wandering around the countryside in sleeping gowns.

The train pulled into Albany at 6:00 in the morning. No trains were running on Sunday to Niagara Falls, more than three hundred miles to the west. They scattered to different hotels and stayed in their rooms all day. That night they took another sleeper to Niagara Falls where they crossed over into Canada and safety early Tuesday morning, November 28.

Back in New York City, the newspapers were still reporting on the fires, and some New Yorkers had to defend themselves against rumors that they were involved.

Hiram Cranston, owner of the New York Hotel, wrote a letter to the *New York Times* just two days after the attack in response to a question posted in the newspaper by an anonymous person who penned himself as Inquiring Mind. That person had written to the *Times* asking in print as to why the New York Hotel was not burned when so many other similar establishments had been targeted.

"In the first place, the New York Hotel is almost exclusively a family hotel, and kept always full, so that a suspicious character, one who travels only with 'a small black leather bag' cannot obtain a room," wrote Cranston.

In the same short letter, Cranston hinted that he thought Inquiring Mind was the Astor House manager, Charles Stetson. Cranston quoted from the *New York Herald* that police believed the Astor House had been used as a meeting place for the conspirators because the fireplace in the room of one of the suspects (Headley) had been frequently used.

Cranston got in his dig at a competing hotel manager with the ending paragraph of his letter to the editor: "You see the Astor House was the rendezvous point of the conspirators. Yet Stetson is not accused of keeping a house for thieves and incendiaries. I am led to believe that he is only saved by having his house set on fire. Will you oblige me by asking 'Inquiring Mind' if I cannot convince my fellow citizens of my 'loyalty' by some other manner than by setting fire to my hotel."

Some newspapers were brimming with anger, even though the plot had completely failed. Horace Greeley, writing in the *New York Tribune*, wrote:

We waste no words this morning in arguing that the plot to burn New York which failed on Friday night was a Rebel plot. . . . Six weeks ago the Richmond press threatened and foretold just such an attempt, defended it as justifiable warfare, and chuckled in advance over the anticipated success. Their sole chagrin will be to hear that it has been tried and has failed, and they will discover with rage, but without emotion or shame, that it is not so easy as they thought to burn a city that holds a million people, and that is protected by the safeguard of a civilization unknown to their barbarous society.

Greeley went on to hint that an unnamed hotel may have been the headquarters of the conspirators as it was not burned. (Cranston's New York Hotel? Greeley does not say.) He also regretted that Butler and his troops had left the city, hinting that New York City should have remained under martial law. Greeley called for the removal of "traitor immigrants from the South and traitor sympathizers from the North."

Even Democratic newspapers reacted with anger. James Gordon Bennett's *New York Herald* somehow correctly guessed that "Morgan's Guerrillas" were involved. The newspaper called for the "perpetrators to be tried by a court martial and hanged immediately."

The *Herald* discussed the attack this way:

A vast and fiendish plot to burn down our Empire City gave rise to most profound excitement among all classes of our citizens.

There was no panic, no evidence of ridiculous fright or the wild apprehension that might naturally be expected to result from the discovery of a conspiracy, which if successful, would have been accompanied by such unspeakable horrors. They had escaped by a miracle from a dreadful calamity [that] might have left half the city in ashes and consigned thousands of innocent persons—men, women and children—to the most horrible of deaths. . . . The city of New York has undoubtedly enjoyed a most wonderful escape.

Some newspapers kept their sense of humor and the spirit of what being a New Yorker was all about. The *New York World* reported on a conversation between two investigators: "When one of our most conspicuous officers of police was asked by a distinguished federal military man the other day whether he thought the incendiaries were rebels or thieves, he instantly replied with some indignation in his tone: 'Rebels of course! Do you suppose our New York thieves would have bungled the business so stupidly?' "

The *World,* writing more than two weeks after the attack, not only thanked the police and fire department for saving the city but also criticized the police for not having arrested the real culprits since it was obvious that the Confederates had likely fled by train:

With the whole night in which to work up the case, with the telegraphs at their command, with the hotel registers offering the names, and the hotel clerks freshly impressed by the faces of all the persons concerned, it is certainly a most remarkable circumstance that neither the federal authorities or the police have any persons yet arrested and held to answer for this crime.

The *World* also correctly guessed that the Confederates did not target family hotels out of concern for the lives of civilians, and hit on the major reason the fires did not ignite as they should have done: "In their tenderness about grilling their fellow creatures, these extraordinary incendiaries seem to have invariably closed the windows of the rooms in which they lit their fires, thereby making a draft impossible."

The *World* ended that particular story on the attack with a little dry wit referring to the well-known Democratic Party's aversion to the 1863 Conscription Act: "This aversion to a draft may be perhaps interpreted as a Copperhead trait."

In a later edition, the *World* noted that the scene at the Winter Garden Theatre was embarrassing when the people watching the Booth brothers perform *Julius Caesar* heard cries of "Fire!" coming from the LaFarge.

> Men seemed to blanch and lose all self-control, and women, who did not fall into stupor or faint helplessly away, bade momentarily goodbye to modesty and risking skirts and crinolines and to a degree sufficient to free play to their limbs, fairly made over sofas, chairs, and camp stools and even clamored over the edge of the gallery and first circle, eager to jump into the frightened theater of fugitives below. Yet quiet was restored, and the performances produced before audiences reassured and hardly diminished in numbers.

The *World* took the incident to complain that it was a poor safety practice to allow patrons to put chairs in the aisle so exits were blocked.

The New York Daily News, owned by Congressman Benjamin Wood, who had prior knowledge of the Confederate attack, must have aroused ire among New Yorkers when it claimed that officials were rushing to judgment in blaming Confederates. Its editor claimed that Richmond's newspaper editors were angry that Davis had rejected their suggestions of attacking the North.

"It is not permitted by the code of Christian civilization to avenge atrocities wantonly committed on the innocent and non-belligerent by retaliating on other innocent and non-belligerent persons. President Davis did himself honor by persistently rejecting the hell-broth of Richmond editorial cooks."

The *Daily News* then reminded its readers that most New Yorkers were opposed to the war. "Can it be dreamed that the Confederate government wanted to burn up the wives and children of those opposed to the war?"

The *New York Evening Tribune* totally misunderstood the reasons Confederates targeted commercial hotels early on a Friday night: "The fact that the incendiaries last night selected hotels and places of amusement, the places most densely crowded with helpless women and children to begin their diabolical efforts shows their hearts cowardly and wicked enough for any atrocity."

The *New York Sun* reported on the need for excitement by some New Yorkers:

The crowd in front of the hotel (St. Nicholas) having learned that a dozen or more other hotels were burning looked up at the building expecting in every moment to see the flames burn from every story. Some of the disappointed expressing their disgust, avowed a determination of finding a fire somewhere, started off on a journey of discovery. At a later hour they probably went to bed without being gratified, unless the more enthusiastic tried their own vitals with whiskey, guaranteed to burn when it hits bottom.

The *Sun,* in a burst of fire department boosterism that had no basis in reality, claimed that the incendiaries would have failed anyway since the fire department could handle a hundred fires at once.

The *Brooklyn Daily News* could not resist taking a "we told you so" attitude when it repeated a quote from an earlier edition. The newspaper editor reminded readers that weeks earlier it had called for the removal of "thousands of Southern refugees, who eagerly hating the community that supports them in safety, plot nightly in company with their sympathizing Northern friends, how they can most cruelly sting the hand that interposed between them and starvation."

James McMaster, the Copperhead leader who backed out of gathering the twenty thousand disaffected New Yorkers to help the Confederates take over the city, must have been sweating even in November. He had to wonder if the authorities suspected him of helping the Confederates. His opposition to Lincoln was well known. He had to wonder if detectives had trailed the Confederates to those meetings at his home or office.

In his reporting for his newspaper, McMaster rejected the idea that the fires were started by criminals because they would have been "more terribly effective from intimate knowledge robbers would have had on where to strike!"

Without citing any sources, McMaster charged that some people he knew believed that a government conspiracy was behind the attack. McMaster wrote: "There are some firm in the persuasion that it was, altogether a bogus plot, gotten up by some servants of the Government, by way of terrifying the people of this city into desiring and asking for the inauguration of a purely military government for the city."

Later in the editorial, McMaster wrote that the attackers were likely Confederates, but he believed they had an excuse for trying to set fire to New York City. He thought they had been hurt unjustly:

Men whose hearts have been burned to ashes by horrible outrages committed on their mothers, sisters, wives, daughters, perhaps on their own persons! Or, they have seen their own quiet homes in no way the lawful spoil of war burnt, and themselves beggared. . . . Men, in various ways, rendered utterly desperate by a sense, not merely of war being made upon them, but of wrongs forbidden by the modern laws of war.

For reasons only he could answer because doing so drew attention to his already well known Copperhead reputation, McMaster even speculated on the home states of the raiders, specifically naming Virginia and Kentucky, home states to six of the eight original raiders. The only state McMaster did not name as a home of the raiders was Louisiana, where Kennedy's family now lived.

Even if he was under surveillance, McMaster could not resist protesting what he considered the big government policies of the Lincoln administration.

"Debt is slavery. The advocates of a strong government religiously believe in a huge national debt. It enables them to keep the masses at work for the benefit of the few—that is to transfer the contents of the poor man's pockets to the rich," said McMaster.

Harper's Weekly, the only true national newspaper of the 1860s, took the curious editorial opportunity of the failed plot to condemn not only the Confederacy but the whole idea of "State sovereignty" in any form.

"We have, in the attempt of Friday night last, a fair intimation of what we are to expect when New Jersey and Vermont and Pennsylvania are independent powers between which and the independent empire of New York a quarrel chances to arise."

The newspaper then went on to condemn the peace movement and to instruct U.S. leaders to continue the war, which it expected the nation to do anyway, since the "inevitable consequence of the plot will be a firmer purpose and a more unhesitating hand in striking at the heart of the rebellion."

The Richmond newspapers were not sympathetic to the panic of New Yorkers. The *Richmond Sentinel* wrote that New Yorkers were simply addicted to entertainment and the fires were just that: "The Yankee demands his daily sensation as passionately the toper his toddy, the Indian his tobacco, the Chinaman his opium, and a nervous lady her green tea. The numerous fires lately kindled in New York provide the latest entertainment."

Like the theory McMaster floated in *Freeman's Journal* in New York, the *Sentinel* in Richmond speculated that the attempt to burn New York City was an inside job, a federal government plot against the city.

New York gave an immense majority against Abraham Lincoln. He owes it no favors. He owes it the hate of a little soul. If he could have it burned, it would accomplish several purposes. 1. He would glut his vengeance. 2. He would be furnished with the occasion of the Confederates with a crime. 3. He might inspire the people of New York City with the same ferocity which dwells in his own bosom; thus, while punishing them for past opposition, he would convert them to his friends and supporters. . . . The tracks to the lion's den all point one way. They all point to Lincoln as the incendiary, and all forbid such an idea as to Confederate authorities.

One person who was not really a victim of the fire saw an opportunity for self-promotion. On November 27, just two days after the fire, that ever-ready promoter Phineas T. Barnum wrote letters to the editor of all of the city's newspapers. He was concerned that the newspapers had printed accounts that his American Museum had been set on fire. Barnum wrote that he had eleven people on staff roaming the floors of his museum "looking to the comfort of the visitors and ready at a moment's warning to extinguish any fire that might appear.

"As proof of the efficiency against fire, I submit the fact that instead of 'slight damage' being done to the Museum last night, as reported by a morning paper, so speedy was the extinguishment of the flames arising from the liquid ignited on the stairs, that not even a scorch is visible."

Barnum went on to claim that his museum was "as safe a place of amusement as can be found in the world. The Fire Marshal and insurance agents will corroborate this statement."

If Barnum really believed his museum was fireproof, he was mistaken. It would burn to the ground in 1865.

In an editorial written a few days after the plot, Greeley of the *New York Tribune* ruminated on just how close the rebels had come to achieving their goal and how truly lucky the City of New York had been:

Fearful loss of life, the wide-spread nature of the conflagration resulting from the size of the buildings in which it originated, the combustible nature of the contents and the utter powerlessness of the Fire Department, although assisted by the united efforts of the public, to cope with the conflagration starting from so many public points, without feeling convinced that a catastrophe was imminent, without a parallel during late years, and early to be compared with the magnitude of the earthquake in

Lisbon, the great fire of London, the burning of Rome, or the destruction of Pompeii.

Even though Headley blamed the chemical composition of the Greek fire for its failure to burn readily as the reason New York City was not set ablaze, at least two New York newspapers blamed the conspirators' lack of knowledge about basic chemistry.

The *New York Tribune* wrote: "What seems to have escaped them [Confederates] was that for its rapid and complete ignition, phosphorous, like all other combustible articles, requires an abundant supply of oxygen, and this, by closing the doors so carefully, they deprived it of. Here was their grand mistake, and is no doubt owing to this principle that New York is not in flames at this moment."

It was a strange observation. New Yorkers had just avoided being incinerated, but they wanted to tell the Confederates who had botched the job just how New Yorkers would have done it, and how New Yorkers would have been better at it.

THE AFTERMATH

Chapter 20

"If Convicted, They Will Be Executed"

Gideneral Dix seethed with anger at what had happened in New York City. An unknown number of Confederate agents had crossed the Canadian border and ignored his orders to register at his headquarters. Not only had the Confederates ignored his order to register, but they had tried to set the city on fire. Even worse, they tried to burn down his headquarters, the Hoffman House, and with him in it.

Dix responded to the attack as any other general steeped in army bureaucracy would do. He issued two more orders:

On the day after the attack, November 26, 1864, Dix issued General Orders 92, which read in part:

> A nefarious attempt was made last night to set fire to the principal hotels and other places of public resort in this city. If this attempt had been successful, it would have resulted in a frightful sacrifice in property and life. The evidence of extensive combination, and other facts disclosed today, show it to have been the work of Rebel emissaries and agents. All such persons engaged in secret acts of hostility here can only be regarded as spies, subject to martial law, and to the penalty of death. If they are detected, they will be immediately brought before a court-martial

or military commission, and, if convicted, they will be executed without the delay of a single day.

On the same day, Dix issued General Orders 93, which echoed General Orders 80 that had been issued on the day the Confederates arrived in New York. Both Orders 80 and 93 demanded that "all persons from the insurgent states" register at one of Dix's branch headquarters at 37 Bleeker Street. "If any such person fails to comply with this requirement, he will be treated as a spy."

Dix then did an unusual thing in General Orders 93. A major general of the U.S. Army threatened New York civilians with punishment. He did not check with the War Department in Washington to see if he had that kind of authority before issuing the order.

"Keepers of hotels and boarding houses are requested to send to the same headquarters the names of all persons from insurgent States taking lodgings with them immediately on the arrival of such persons. It is not doubted that the danger the city just escaped will insure a compliance with this request. If anyone fails to comply with it he will be held responsible for any evil consequences which may result from the omission."

Dix never explained what would happen if the hotelkeepers did not turn in someone from the South who signed their registers. The new order directed at hotels was worthless. As written, the order would not have prevented the attack. All the Confederates by way of Canada had signed the desk registers as being from loyal Union states such as Maryland, Pennsylvania, and New Jersey. The clerks were in compliance with General Orders 80 even if they thought it odd that someone from New Jersey had a Kentucky accent. If the man with the soft Southern drawl said he was from New Jersey, who were they to question him?

Dix stayed out of the way when police superintendent John Alexander Kennedy began his investigation of the attack. Kennedy, 61, a native of Baltimore, was not a professional policeman. In fact, he had never even walked a beat before being appointed as police commissioner in 1860 as part of the patronage system of Mayor Fernando Wood.

While Kennedy may have been without police training, he was a fearless man. During the draft riots of July 1863, he willingly waded into a crowd of angry protesters to try to disperse them. The crowd turned on him and beat him to the ground resulting in severe injuries. It took weeks for him to recover, but the 61-year-old man went back on the job of protecting the city from criminals.

Kennedy put his chief of detectives on the case, John S. Young, an apparently dogged police officer who was known by fellow officers and criminals alike by the nickname of "Old" Young.

Young had actually begun investigating and trying to stop the attack while it was still underway. Once the first reports of burning hotel rooms came into police headquarters, Young and his detectives visited dozens of commercial hotels to warn the proprietors to have buckets of water standing by in the event of fires.

By Saturday morning, Young was sure that the Seward telegram warning of Confederate incursions across the border was accurate. Young may have suspected, or had been tipped to, the Confederates' presence in the city since his detectives were at Gus McDonald's piano store on the day following the attacks. It was Young's men whom Martin saw through the window and whom Katie McDonald was warning him about. Either someone, such as John Price or the forgotten incendiary, tipped the police to McDonald's involvement or New York City detectives had tailed the Confederates to the store on the day they arrived.

If Kennedy and Young did have prior knowledge of the attack other than Seward's warning telegram, they buried the evidence. They did not want to run the risk of having the newspapers and the city's Common Council accuse them of being negligent in their duties of tracking down tips that could have led to a prevention of the attack before it was launched.

After gathering all the evidence they could in New York City by looking at the burned rooms and checking the signatures on the hotel registers, Young and a group of his detectives set off for Toronto. They made straight for Toronto's Queens Hotel, the unofficial headquarters of the Confederate Secret Service.

The New Yorkers initially blew their cover by asking for Martin,

Headley, and Kennedy by name. Hearing of the strange men asking for them, the Confederates secluded themselves in houses around the city, and successfully avoided any confrontations with Young.

With the detectives so closely on their heels and in possession of their names, Headley convinced himself and others that Godfrey J. Hyams, the Englishman, was a double agent. In addition to accusing Hyams of alerting New York authorities to the impending attack, Headley accused him of telling the Federals in advance of the planned takeover of the passenger steamer *Philo Parsons*, the plans to free the prisoners at Chicago and Rock Island, and the plans to fire Boston and Cincinnati.

Headley offered no proof against Hyams other than that the Englishman knew of the plans, and he was absent from Toronto when they returned from New York City. When Hyams discovered he was suspected of being a spy, he left Toronto. No Confederates tried to track him down to get the truth out of him.

Headley never mentions Montgomery by name as a suspect. Reports in Chicago on why the attack on Camp Douglas failed included some vague information that someone in Canada had revealed the plans. That could have been either Montgomery or Hyams or some other double agent who never revealed himself.

On December 5, 1864, Secret Service commissioner Jacob Thompson sent a lengthy report on the previous months' missions to Secretary of State Judah P. Benjamin (he should have addressed it to the man who created the Secret Service, Secretary of War James Seddon, but it was apparent that Seddon was on his way out of the cabinet). In the letter, Thompson complains that "detectives, or those ready to give information, stand on every street corner. Two or three cannot interchange ideas without a reporter."

Thompson made little mention of the failed mission to burn New York other than to say that "their reliance on the Greek Fire has proved a misfortune. It cannot be relied upon as an agent in such work. I have no faith whatever in it, and no attempt shall hereafter be made under my general directions with any such material."

Even though Thompson admitted that the attack on New York

City failed, he still maintained that "the attempt on New York has produced a great panic, which will not subside at their bidding."

Thompson, like Headley, had never actually worked with Greek fire. Their opinion of the bottled chemicals as a weapon created a curious juxtaposition with the opinions of people who were on the receiving end of the weapons of mass destruction.

The Confederates, who knew little of Greek fire's chemistry and its need for a healthy supply of oxygen to combust spontaneously and to grow its fire in intensity, decided that it was useless as a weapon. The police detectives who experimented with the bottles of Greek fire that had been left behind by the Confederates thanked the chemical ignorance of the rebels for saving New York from being turned into ashes. When the police opened one of the bottles at their headquarters, it immediately flared up, surprising and frightening them. The Greek fire worked just as it was supposed to do.

Martin and Headley were not yet tired of their behind-the-lines adventures. They joined an expedition with Beall to free several Confederate generals who were being transferred by rail from Johnson's Island Prison in Ohio through upstate New York to an ultimate destination of Fort Warren in Boston Harbor.

While preparing to leave Canada for Buffalo, where they expected to intercept the train, the Confederates in Toronto received a copy of yet another order from Dix, General Orders 97, dated December 14, 1864. Once again, Dix must have issued the order without checking in with the War Department as he clearly overstepped the limits of his authority. Still, the words of the order were sobering.

All military commanders on the frontier are therefore instructed in case further acts of depredation and murder are attempted, whether by marauders, or persons acting under commissions from the Rebel authorities at Richmond, to shoot down the Depredators if possible while in the commission of their crimes; or if it be necessary with a view to their capture to cross the boundary between the United States and Canada, said commanders are directed to pursue them wherever they may take refuge, and if captured, they are under no circumstances, to be surrendered, but are to be sent to these headquarters for trial and punishment by martial law.

Dix had just told what few troops he had in the field in his backwater command over New England and New York that they had permission to invade Canada. Not only could they invade a sovereign nation without asking permission from the president of the United States, but they had Dix's permission to do battle with any Canadians, military or civilian, who got in the way of chasing suspected Confederates.

The meaning of the order was not lost on Headley who wrote: "It therefore appeared that if any of us were caught we were to be shot down and if we escaped to Canada we would be pursued into that country by troops of the United States and brought back for trial by a court martial."

Reading Dix's General Orders 97 must have made Lincoln scream. He would have dropped Dix's order and run to the War Department telegraph office to dash off a blistering telegram to his rogue general. The telegram must have warned Dix not to do something really stupid—like start a foreign war on the northern border while a domestic one was still raging in his own country.

Three days later, on December 17, Dix issued General Orders 100, which revoked permission for Union troops to invade Canada in pursuit of Confederates.

Just as every other attempt by the Canada-based Confederates to do something worthwhile to distract the Union, the plot to free the Confederate generals failed. Beall was trying to wake his sleeping companion in a train depot in Niagara Falls while they waited for the train carrying the Confederate generals when they attracted the attention of some suspicious detectives who initially claimed to be looking for escaped prisoners of war. On questioning, the detectives took Beall and his sleepy buddy into custody. One of the men on the Union's most wanted list had been captured thanks to his friend's unfortunate nap in a train station.

Martin, Headley, and the other Confederates did not learn until later that Beall had been captured, but when he did not show up at the rendezvous, the attempt to free the generals was canceled.

Just as they had ever since setting up shop in Canada six months earlier, the Confederates retreated to Toronto. The last attempt by the Confederacy to score some kind of victory in New York State was spoiled by one of its own sleepy soldiers.

The sleeper would later give evidence against Beall that he was the same man who had tried to hijack the *Philo Parsons* several months earlier. Beall was taken to New York City, given a show trial in front of a military commission, and hanged in March 1865 as a spy.

In December 1864, it was obvious to even the most optimistic Canadian Confederates that the war was over for them. Beall had been captured and was being threatened with execution. The six Confederates who had tried to set fire to New York City could only imagine their fate as the eight hundred thousand residents of that city were already convinced that for a bit of luck on their part they would have been burned alive.

Getting home to the South seemed a dicey proposition at best. Detectives from New York City were swarming over Toronto looking for the few Confederates they were not already watching. While the detectives could not legally arrest them in a neutral country, Dix's previous orders ignoring the territorial rights of Canada made it plain that these civilian police officers might not be above kidnapping and hauling back to New York City the men who had tried to set fire to it.

The New York City detectives sent to ferret out information on the attack proved better spies than the Confederates ever hoped to be. After the initial mistakes made by some detectives of going into Toronto bars and asking for the Confederates by their real names, another set of detectives who would not be as readily recognized came up from the city to continue the investigation.

Led by chief detective Young, this new team of detectives slipped easily into Toronto's small circle of Confederate sympathizers. According to newspaper stories published in February 1865, all the detectives had to do to win over Confederates was pretend that "they were seemingly bitter Secessionists, harboring intense hatred of all things that smacked of Yankeedom." The New Yorkers cursed Ben Butler and every other Union general, "affected Southern manners," and spat on the United States flag—all actions that worked to "hoodwink our resident rebels to gain just the intelligence which they sought."

Detective Young himself convinced Larry McDonald, the Toronto explosives expert, that he was a Southern sympathizer. Meeting on the Canadian side of Niagara Falls, McDonald told Young just about everything the detective wanted to know about the attack on New York City. McDonald even told Young that eight men had come to New York, but two had lost their nerve. In fact, the attacks were carried out by just six men, not the scores or hundreds like some rumors had been saying.

McDonald enjoyed talking to his newfound friend. He trusted him enough to start embellishing his own limited role in the attack. According to the newspaper accounts, McDonald claimed to have been the mastermind behind the plot. McDonald even told Young the real names of the conspirators and what aliases they had used while registering at the hotels. Most damaging of all, McDonald told Young that two of the conspirators, Kennedy and Ashbrook, would soon be leaving Canada for the South.

Detective Young thanked his new bosom buddy and scooted back across the Canadian border with the valuable intelligence he needed to start finding the fiends who had tried to firebomb his city. Once he was back in New York State, Young made sure detectives all along the Canadian border, including those in Michigan, would be on the lookout for a 29-year-old man with a florid complexion, a beard, and a pronounced limp. This man who had called himself Stanton while checking into New York hotels was really Robert Cobb Kennedy.

With no more missions to win the war on tap, and the loss of the Confederacy becoming more obvious with each depressing notice of the movements of Grant and Sherman, the Confederates were getting homesick.

Martin and Headley were willing to sit tight and wait for the heated search for them to cool, but Ashbrook and Kennedy were ready to risk capture for a chance to go home. Rather than head to

Halifax and catch a ship south that would run the blockade, they decided on a faster but more dangerous route. They would ride the trains through Michigan, through Indiana, and then down into Kentucky.

Kennedy had papers drawn up that identified him as Robert Cobb of Illinois, but he also carried with him a Confederate twenty-dollar bill for use when he got back safely to the Confederacy. Once again, the Confederate spies were showing their ignorance of true espionage. Kennedy had not given thought to what would happen if he were questioned and searched in a Northern state. He would not be able to explain away possession of a Confederate bill.

Kennedy and Ashbrook made it as far as Detroit. The two could not find seats together in the same train car, which proved to be Ashbrook's good luck. As he watched, two detectives walked up to Kennedy from behind, grasped him by the arms, and said, "You are Stanton."

Ashbrook watched Kennedy reach for his revolver, but the two detectives already had him in their grasp. With the attention of the two detectives focused on Kennedy, Ashbrook leaped from the moving train into the night. Luckily, he landed in a snowbank and was unhurt. As the train clattered on, he made his way to a nearby farmhouse. The next day he took another train to Cincinnati, and from there, he was able to make his way to Kentucky and safety.

Kennedy, the hard-drinking Louisianan who had survived a gunshot and imprisonment in a cold prisoner-of-war camp, was now on his way back to New York City, the place he had tried to burn. This time, he would not enjoy the luxuries of New York City's finest hotels. This time, he would find himself in one of its prisons. *He would never leave.*

Chapter 21

"Trust to Luck"

Robert Cobb Kennedy had two personality traits that both served and disserved him. He had always been independent and anxious to make a contribution. But he also disliked authority figures in his life.

Before leaving home for the United States Military Academy, he and his father often quarreled about his future. After just two years in the most prestigious military college in the world, West Point, he was released with a heavy collection of demerits and a reputation for ignoring his studies in favor of heavy drinking.

When the war came, Kennedy eagerly joined the army to serve his new country, the Confederacy. After getting wounded in the thigh, he longed for more combat duty, but reluctantly settled for the dull job of staff aide to a general with whom he had been friends while both were cadets at West Point. Captured and imprisoned after having fought in just one big battle, Kennedy had shown initiative by escaping from a prison that was protected on all sides by the waters of Lake Erie. He made his way to freedom in Canada where, instead of taking the time to rest from his imprisonment, he immediately volunteered to get back into the fray.

Kennedy's independence might normally have served him well as an undercover incendiary in New York City. Spies should be self-sufficient, not needing constant instruction from some superior.

But Kennedy also had a flair for the dramatic, a desire to stand out, a trait that good spies do not have or desire. He signed his New York City hotel register with the unusual last name of Stanton, what he must have considered an amusing poke at Secretary of War Stanton. Stanton was such an unusual name that desk clerks might have looked up and taken notice of the man writing it on their registers.

As mentioned earlier, Kennedy naturally had trouble blending into the background, which also hampered his performance as a spy. He had a florid or reddish complexion in his face. At 5 feet 8 inches, he was two inches taller than most men. And because of the wound he received early in the war, he walked with a pronounced limp. He also wore a heavy, ill-fitting, double-breasted gray coat, hardly the type of garment that a man who could afford to check into a fine New York hotel would own. He stood out from most men walking the streets of New York City.

After setting his hotel fires, on a whim Kennedy tried to set fire to Barnum's American Museum by tossing a bottle of Greek fire onto a set of stairs. Had the flames caught, one avenue of escape for the hundreds of people inside on a Friday night would have been blocked. It was a violation of what the Confederates had agreed not to do during their attack—endanger the lives of civilians. That probably was not a mean streak in his character, just the liquor that he had been drinking clouding his judgment.

Later that same evening after firing the hotels, Kennedy had almost pulled his revolver on Headley when his commander had playfully clapped him on the shoulder. The two of them then stood in the middle of Broadway laughing about how they had almost shot each other. Discreet spies they were not.

Now Robert Cobb Kennedy, the man New York police detectives knew as Stanton, was in their custody. Incredibly, one of Kennedy's first acts once in jail was to write letters to several men asking if they would bail him out. Kennedy must have thought himself clever in writing the letters by mentioning in the opening of the letters to each man that they did not know him, but he was asking them the favor of loaning him $1,500 in bail money.

Kennedy did know at least one of the men. That was James Mc-Master, editor of the *Freeman's Journal and Catholic Register*, who had been the Confederates' New York City contact. Another, Congressman Benjamin Wood, had met with Canadian Confederates on at least one occasion and may have taken money in exchange for pro-Confederate editorial policy in his newspaper, the *New York Daily News*. The third man, Hiram Cranston, was the owner of the New York Hotel. Cranston was already having trouble convincing the public that he was not in on the plot since his hotel had been bypassed during the attacks. Now he had one of the incendiaries writing to him and asking for bail money.

In each letter, Kennedy told the men that Confederate Secret Service commissioner Jacob Thompson would be happy to refund any bail money they advanced to get him out of jail.

All the men must have blanched when the letters Kennedy wrote were delivered to them by a New York City jailer named Hays. Hays had been planted in Kennedy's cell by police superintendent Kennedy and General Dix to report on everything Kennedy did, said, or wrote.

All the men who received letters told Hays they did not know Kennedy and would not be advancing any accused Confederate bail money.

The fact that Kennedy even knew their names well enough to ask them for money must have raised suspicions among his jailers. How would a Confederate captured in Detroit, Michigan, know the names of three residents of New York City—unless he had recently been in the city and had met them in person.

Major John Augustus Bolles, the judge advocate general who would try both John Yates Beall and Kennedy before a military commission convinced Kennedy to make a statement. Kennedy admitted in writing that he had been in New York City in November and had used the name Stanton when registering at a hotel.

He then made an incredible claim for an escaped Confederate prisoner of war. Kennedy said he had come to New York City from

Halifax, Canada, to vacation before finding a ship to run the blockade to Wilmington, North Carolina. He made no mention of setting fire to any hotels.

Kennedy was transferred out of a city jail into one maintained by the Federal army at Fort Lafayette when a penknife was found hidden under his mattress. Always one to say whatever was on his mind, Kennedy bluntly told his guards that he had planned to use the knife on them when he got the chance.

The federal government did not waste any time putting Kennedy on trial. The secret trial, which was closed to the city's newspapers, opened on January 31, 1865, barely a month after his arrest. The trial was conducted at Dix's army headquarters on Bleeker Street and opened with Kennedy acting as his own attorney.

Bolles opened the trial by calling Hays, the jailer, who explained to the court that Kennedy had as much as admitted to him that he was one of the incendiaries. Police superintendent Kennedy testified that Hays had told him that Kennedy had admitted to setting the hotel fires.

When Bolles called one witness, Kennedy turned to see who it was. It was a familiar face, one that must have made his blood run cold.

The witness was John M. Price of Virginia, one of the two Confederate incendiaries who had lost his nerve and had not shown up at the Central Park cottage to collect his share of the bottles of Greek fire. The Confederates had never known what had happened to either of the two men. Now here one of them was in a New York City courtroom about to testify against one of the men who had fired the city.

Assuming that Headley's postwar account was accurate and Price was one of the eight members who came to New York to fire the city, the young Virginian lied through his teeth on the witness stand. Price claimed that he had met Kennedy only after Kennedy had returned from the New York expedition. When asked if he had ever been to New York City, Price answered that he had been in New York about a month or six weeks before the fires were set. When asked if he had been involved in the fires, Price answered that he had been asked to go on the mission, but he could not go for an unexplained reason. Price said he did not learn that the objective was to burn the city until after the party had left Toronto.

Price was asked if he knew Kennedy was part of the team selected to set fire to New York City. Price claimed that he thought he heard Kennedy say he was one of the team members when he met him for that supposed first time when Kennedy returned from New York.

When Kennedy got up to cross-examine Price, he decided not to accuse Price of being part of the team. He had realized that if he did that, he was implicating himself as well as Price. Instead, Kennedy tried to find out when, where, and how Price had been arrested, but Price gave him no clues.

After questioning Price, Kennedy realized that acting as a lawyer was no substitute for having a real one defending him. He asked for a postponement of a few days until he could find one. The request was granted.

Kennedy turned to the only person he knew in New York City, an old friend from West Point. How Kennedy knew his former classmate Edwin H. Stoughton (ranked 17th out of 22 in the 1859 West Point class) was a lawyer in New York City is unknown. He never said, and it is just as well that he did not. If Kennedy had visited Stoughton in November, Stoughton might have been accused of being an accessory to the crime for not turning in his old friend who was an escaped Confederate soldier roaming the streets of the city.

Before Stoughton was a lawyer, he was a Union general. His legal skills in 1864 would have had to have been better than his skills at being a general in 1863.

By March 1863, Stoughton had parlayed his limited military skills and contacts into a brigadier generalship, though he was far from the front lines at his garrison headquarters in Fairfax Court House, Virginia, about thirty miles southwest of Washington. Stoughton was deep in sleep one night when Confederate colonel John Singleton Mosby and twenty-nine of his partisan rangers quietly rode into town and captured Stoughton's headquarters guards. Mosby tiptoed into Stoughton's room and tried to wake him. The snoring Stoughton was a heavy sleeper. Finally, drawing his saber and raising up the end of the general's sleeping gown, Mosby slapped Stoughton's bare behind with the flat of his saber.

A startled Stoughton rose up indignantly, thinking he was looking at one of his own scouts, and asked if he had captured Mosby, who had been harassing Stoughton's picket lines.

"No. I am Mosby—he has caught you," Mosby replied. He threw Stoughton's uniform to him and ordered him to dress because he was now going behind Confederate lines.

When an amused Lincoln heard that Mosby had made off with more than fifty horses and a captured Stoughton, Lincoln said, "I can make generals with the stroke of a pen, but I can't make horses. I do regret losing them."

The incident made Stoughton the laughing stock of the Union army and killed his military career. After being exchanged and released from prison, Stoughton lost his commission, and moved to New York City to practice law with his uncle.

Stoughton did not have much time to prepare a legal case for Kennedy. He apparently never even asked his client the most basic question all lawyers at least think of asking their clients, did he try to set fire to the city of New York?

On February 10, 1865, Stoughton took over Kennedy's defense. Stoughton's strategy was weak, but he had to stick with what Kennedy had already said in open court: Kennedy was just an escaped prisoner who had visited New York while waiting for a ship to take him back south. It was merely a coincidence that the hotels had been fired at the same time that Kennedy, using the alias Stanton, had been in the city.

It was a flimsy defense, but the prosecution's case was flimsy too. So far, all Bolles had presented in court was Kennedy's own admission that he had used the name Stanton while registering at a hotel. He had also called as a witness a planted jailer who claimed that Kennedy had talked vaguely about the fires. But, more damaging, he had called an admitted Confederate soldier who claimed that Kennedy had been on the mission to fire the city.

Stoughton was able to persuade McMaster to testify. McMaster probably agreed to appear, because if he did not, it would seem that he was afraid to be in the same room with an accused Confederate spy.

McMaster lied from the minute he got on the stand and said that he had never met Kennedy. If Headley's account was accurate, all the incendiaries had met McMaster in their first meeting in his office and later in a second meeting at his home.

McMaster suggested in court that he had his own theory about who started the fires: "Some half crazy women, or non-combatants" must have started the fires. "No man engaged in fighting, much less a commissioned officer, would have attempted to burn down the City of New York, and attack it in its strongest points instead of the weakest and do so little damage."

His following statements were so muddled that the prosecutor did not even bother cross-examining him. Stoughton, too, could make little out of the editor's testimony. Little good had come from it other than McMaster telling the court he had never met Kennedy. Only McMaster and Kennedy knew that was a lie.

Stoughton summed up his defense of Kennedy on February 23, 1865, by pointing out that the United States had produced only two witnesses, jailer Hays and Hays's boss, police superintendent Kennedy.

The case against Confederate Kennedy was weak on its face. No witnesses had come forward to say that they had seen Kennedy or anyone else setting any fires. The military commission had not even brought in any hotel desk clerks to testify that they recognized Kennedy as a man who had stayed in their hotels. The only person who had testified that Kennedy was anywhere near New York at the time of the fires was Price, and he was relating information (he said) was secondhand to him.

Bolles covered for his lack of evidence against Kennedy by saying that any soldier caught in civilian clothing is by definition a spy and eligible for execution. Kennedy had been caught in civilian clothes in Detroit, and he had been carrying Confederate money. He said that Kennedy had given a confession of sorts to Hays, the jailer, and that should be good enough to convict him.

Though there was no real evidence against him and only Kennedy and Price knew that he was truly guilty of setting fire to the hotel rooms, Kennedy was found guilty by a unanimous vote of the military commission. He learned of his sentence of death by hanging when he was handed a letter from Dix to the commander of Fort Lafayette. The military commission had not even brought the accused into the courtroom to hear the verdict.

Kennedy immediately dashed off a letter to his father telling him of his fate. Thinking of how he would be remembered, he told his father:

> Although I receive an ignominious death, I have been guilty of no act that should cause, you, mother, or any of the children to blush for their son or brother. I am simply in the hands of my enemies and I am to die. I can die but once and the only disgrace in the matter lies on those who condemned me to death merely on the evidence of perjured witnesses. I do not fear death, but would so like to see you all again. May God bless you and may every true Southerner resign his life as cheerfully as I do mine.

Stoughton helped Kennedy compose a letter to Lincoln asking for mercy. Kennedy admitted to being "an enemy of your Government since the outbreak of the present, unhappy war, but I have been an open, and honorable one. I am not a spy, or a guerrilla—holding each character in abhorrence. . . . The nation of which you are Chief Magistrate, is certainly powerful enough to be generous, to protect itself without resorting to unnecessarily severe measures towards those so unfortunate as to fall into the hands of its authorities."

No one but Kennedy himself knew for sure that he had just lied to both his father and the president of the United States.

Dix issued General Orders 24 on March 20 that were printed in all the newspapers on March 21. They listed the charges and guilty findings. The orders said that Kennedy would be hanged at Fort Lafayette on Saturday, March 25.

Dix added his own editorial comments to the order:

> The attempt to set fire to the city of New York is one of the greatest atrocities of the age. There is nothing in the annals

of barbarism which evinces greater vindictiveness. It was not a mere attempt to destroy the city, but to set fire to crowded hotels and places of public resort in order to secure the greatest possible destruction of human life.

He made it clear that there would be no hope of mercy from Lincoln or him when he ended the order with: "Crimes which outrage and shock the moral sense by their atrocity must not only be punished and the perpetrators deprived of the power of repeating them, but the sternest condemnation of the law must be presented to others to deter them from the commission of similar offenses."

The *New York Times* noted after Dix's order that Kennedy had attempted to break out of his cell by using a heated poker to try to pry off the lock. The smell of burning wood gave him away, and he was restrained.

The *Times* then ended its article by noting that P. T. Barnum intended to borrow a photograph of Kennedy that Kennedy himself had commissioned. Barnum said he would make a wax image of Kennedy and display it as a memento of the attack. Barnum never missed any opportunity to grab a little news coverage for himself and his museum.

On the day before his execution, Kennedy wrote a letter to his mother opening with the obvious: "Your eldest son dies tomorrow. . . . Let it be a comfort to you under this grievous affliction that I feel that I can meet that death if not with resignation, at least with calmness. . . . This will be a terrible blow but let us hope that we may soon meet in another and better world." He ended the letter with: "Think not of my faults, think not of my weaknesses but remember me only as your loving and unfortunate son."

With no hope of a reprieve, Kennedy decided at 10:30 p.m. on Friday, March 24, that he no longer had to lie about his involvement. He dictated a long statement where he admitted starting fires in Lovejoy's Hotel, Tammany Hotel, New England House, and Barnum's Museum. He said the fire in Barnum's was only "a joke." He had been drinking and only wanted to scare people.

He ended the confession with:

I wish to say that killing women & children was the last thing thought of. We wanted to let the people of the North understand that there are two sides to this war & that they can't be rolling in wealth and comfort, while we at the South are bearing all of the hardship & privations. In retaliation for Sheridan's atrocities in the Shenandoah Valley we desired to destroy property, not the lives of women & children although that would of course follow in its train.

The next morning, Kennedy wrote a thank-you note of sorts to Detective John "Old" Young who had given him a bottle of whiskey. He told Young he bore him "no malice. You did your duty as detectives."

He also wrote a note saying that Gus McDonald, the brother of Larry McDonald, had nothing to do with the plot. That was a lie. Gus McDonald had stored the luggage of the Confederates from the day they alighted from the train. His daughter had saved Martin and Headley from arrest by signaling to Martin through the front window of the piano store.

As Kennedy was marched to the gallows, an unusual contraption that used weights to jerk a man skyward to break his neck rather than rely on his own weight falling through the gallows floor, he became increasingly agitated. As the noose was placed over his head, Kennedy began singing an old Irish drinking song:

> Trust to luck,
> Trust to luck,
> Stare Fate in the face,
> For your heart will be easy
> If it's in the right place.

At 1:30 p.m., Captain Robert Cobb Kennedy was dead. Though pressed to do so, he did not name the five other men who had participated in the attack. Nor did he name Price, the reluctant incendiary who had testified against him before the military commission. Nor did he tell anyone the names of the Copperheads in New York City who had helped plan the attack. He also exonerated Gus McDonald who had helped the Confederates.

Kennedy may have been a hard-drinking soldier and careless spy in life, but in death he proved himself to be loyal to the friends and strangers who had helped him try to achieve his military objective.

Chapter 22

"A Terror for Our Citizens"

Martin, Headley, Kennedy, Ashbrook, Harrington, and Chenault all failed miserably as incendiaries. Not a single one of the fires they started advanced beyond the hotel room in which they had set it. As at least two newspapers pointed out, all the conspirators had left the windows to their hotel rooms closed. That robbed the room fires of the oxygen they needed to turn into raging infernos, which would have spread to the entire hotel.

Even if a hotel had caught fire, this type of target was so obvious once the first two fires were discovered that police wisely sent officers to all hotel managers. The managers set out buckets of water on each floor and checked all guest rooms for any yet undiscovered fires. Several smoldering, oxygen-deprived fires were discovered this way and easily extinguished.

Before midnight, the police had already determined that the fires were started by Confederates who had crossed the Canadian border. Within a few days, the police had the Confederates' real names, their aliases, and a good idea where to find them in Toronto. Within two weeks, the police had collected virtually all the details of the plot by doing nothing more elaborate than posing as Confederate sympathizers and spitting a few times on the American flag to prove it.

Despite the hyperbole of the newspapers' coverage of the attack (the *New York Times* called it "the terror of our citizens"), New York City was never in any real danger of burning down just from the randomly set hotel room fires. The Confederates had botched the job by their own ignorance of the chemical properties of Greek fire.

But what all the newspaper editors, police chiefs, fire chiefs, city officials, and Confederates themselves failed to take into account was how the incendiaries could have better planned their attack. New York City could have easily burned down the night of November 25, 1864.

Had the Confederates taken into account five factors, they could have accomplished their vaguely formed mission of destroying the Union's largest city.

1. *The Confederates should have acted like true spies by blending into New York City's background so no one would notice them as being out of place.* From the first day they arrived in New York City, the Confederates did nothing related to the mission except meet with the Copperheads and later with each other. Even at this simple task of making contact with supposed friends, they proved themselves careless amateurs.

By meeting with Copperhead leader McMaster at his newspaper office, they risked their own security. McMaster had been jailed for months early in the war for his antiadministration editorials. Even after his release from military prison and restarting the newspaper that had been closed by order of the federal government, McMaster continued to condemn Lincoln's policies. If anyone in New York City was being watched by local police and Union army personnel, it was McMaster.

McMaster's newspaper office was literally just steps away from City Hall, making it easy for Metropolitan policemen to keep their eye on him and his visitors. All the curious police detectives would have had to do was ask one of McMaster's employees about the identities of eight young men meeting with him at one time in his office, and the police could have learned that all the visitors had Southern accents.

Visiting at McMaster's home did not help the Confederates'

security. The editor lived on Fifth Avenue, somewhat removed from the center of the city at that time so that any large group of men approaching a prominent house could have been noticed by neighbors and any strolling policeman.

If meeting with McMaster on multiple occasions was necessary, only Martin and Headley, the two leaders of the plot, should have done it. There was no need for the other six Confederates to tag along and crowd into McMaster's office. It seems doubtful that the other six would have said much of anything of importance. In short, two men meeting with McMaster would not have aroused suspicion, but eight at one time could have roused the curiosity of McMaster employees who could have informed the police of the unusual out-of-town visitors.

What the other six conspirators should have been doing while Martin and Headley were meeting with McMaster was polishing their identities as out-of-town businessmen. Headley does not mention doing any of that in his postwar book, so it seems likely the Confederates just signed into their multiple hotel rooms and waited nearly a month to commence the attack.

Kennedy did develop an identity and reputation for himself while staying in his hotel, but it was the wrong kind. According to one newspaper account written about Kennedy after he was executed, the Alabama native raised in Louisiana got into repeated arguments at the St. Nicholas Hotel about the South's right to secede. He so angered the other pro-Union guests that the hotel manager asked Kennedy to check out and find some other hotel.

Just hearing Kennedy's accent and his arguments could have been enough for a hotel desk clerk to send for a police officer. As proved later when he was arrested in Detroit, Kennedy was a poor liar. He would not have been able to convince any New York City detective that he was a visiting businessman. While he probably would not have revealed any names of other plotters, since he did not turn them in while he was in jail and facing execution, Kennedy still might have revealed enough of the plot to have detectives scouring other hotels looking for other men with Southern accents.

2. *Good spies and saboteurs find the best targets.* Setting fire to

top-floor rooms in swanky hotels on a Friday night of a busy holiday weekend attracted attention from the newspapers, but those targets were not the ones that would have done the most damage to New York City and the Union.

With some 144 bottles of Greek fire collected from the Greenwich Village chemist, the conspirators could have easily started upward of one hundred separate fires in highly flammable locations. Being in town for a month, they could have put in repeated orders with the Greenwich Village chemist for still more bottles of the chemical compound, perhaps acquiring it in larger bottles to start larger initial fires. Even if the New York City chemist had refused them more bottles, there was time to have smuggled in bottles from Larry McDonald's basement weapons manufacturing lab in Toronto.

Had they thought far enough in advance and continued to collect bottles of Greek fire, in one night six Confederate incendiaries could have started at least one hundred, perhaps as many as five hundred separate fires in the city.

The area of town that all the incendiaries should have been scouting for targets most likely to set fire to the rest of the city was the Hudson River shoreline about a mile west of the Broadway hotels.

By 1864, there were more than one hundred piers and wharves each on both the East and the Hudson rivers. The Hudson River's piers attracted smaller schooners and barges coming down the Hudson and Erie Canal from upstate New York. The East River shoreline, closer to the Atlantic Ocean and with newer piers and warehouses, attracted the oceangoing vessels that were key to the city's reputation as the nation's leading port for importing and exporting.

Because the Hudson drew fewer of the oceangoing vessels, its facilities had deteriorated over time. Leading city fathers complained that the piers were rotting away and were underused while clipper ships were waiting in the East River for dock space.

The twenty square blocks on the west side of Manhattan bordering 20th Street on the north, 10th Street on the south, the Hudson River on the west, and Ninth Avenue and Greenwich Avenue on the east (containing what is now the Art Gallery District and the Meatpacking District) was probably the most flammable part of the entire city. Apparently, since this area of the city was already run down and neglected, some of the most dangerous and flammable industries in the city were located there.

At the intersection of Gansevoort and Ninth Avenue at 14th Street, located on blocks facing each other were a camphene distillery and a turpentine distillery. In the mid-nineteenth-century camphene (bicyclic monoterpene) was distilled from alpha-pinene to create a type of cheap fuel for table lamps. The camphene was so volatile that the *New York Times* published an article in July 1852 detailing how sixty-two people had already died that year from camphene lamp explosions. Even a little heat was enough to make it explode because the compound's flash point was just 104 degrees, giving it a current-day danger listing of "highly flammable."

The turpentine distillery on the neighboring block was much larger. While manufactured gas was replacing turpentine as a fuel, it was still used for outdoor lighting in some older parts of the city. Like camphene, turpentine was highly flammable.

Just south of these two refineries on Bethune Street was a lime-processing center. Unslaked (unprocessed) lime can explode when quantities of water are poured on it.

Above the camphene and turpentine distilleries at 18th Street and Ninth Avenue was an unspecified chemical works. Virtually beside the chemical works was what might have been the most flammable, explosive block in the entire city—The Manhattan Gas Works.

By the 1850s, gas manufactured from the processing of bituminous coal had virtually replaced most other forms of public lighting in the major urban areas along the East Coast. New York City was the nation's largest consumer of manufactured gas by the 1850s, burning more than 600 million cubic feet per year compared with Philadelphia's 300 million cubic feet per year.

Cities routinely granted permission for gasworks companies to tear up streets to lay cast-iron pipes carrying gas to businesses and homes. In exchange, those companies provided aboveground public lighting at low or reduced cost to the city. The gas companies made up for the expense of lighting the city streets by regularly raising their residential rates, an irritating fact that made gas companies like Manhattan Gas Works the most universally hated institutions in any city.

Manhattan Gas Works had been embroiled in pricing controversies for more than a decade by 1864 because consumers were constantly complaining to the newspapers and their councilmen that the price of gas kept going up. Customers complained that the meters in their homes were defective, resulting in a false reading on how much gas they were actually using, which, in turn, resulted in their being overcharged.

To combat its bad image, Manhattan Gas Works invited members of the public to stop by their plant and watch how the gas was manufactured. This lack of security, allowing men off the streets to mingle with the company's 150 employees, could have given Confederates the opportunity to look for methods to sabotage the plant. Managers freely discussed the operation of the factory with any interested citizen. A few well-asked questions might have told even inexperienced Confederate spies just how vulnerable to fire and explosion the plant was.

Explosions at gas factories were not uncommon in the mid-nineteenth century, though the worst accident suffered at Manhattan Gas Works during its early history was the collapse of a poorly constructed building in the 1850s, resulting in the crushing deaths of several employees. Most of the municipal gas company explosions that happened in the mid-1850s in Baltimore, Boston, and Middletown, Connecticut, occurred in the purifying houses. In these buildings were huge cast-iron vessels filled with sheet iron plates covered with lime that removed the carbonic acid and hydrogen sulfide as the manufactured gas flowed into the vessels. If something went wrong with the process, the hydrogen sulfide being extremely flammable could be dangerous.

In an 1855 accident in Middletown, a weight fell on a purifying tank. A hole was punched in the tank, resulting in an explosion of the gas inside, which completely demolished the building. In an 1856 accident at the Montreal Gas Works in Canada, a worker carried an "unguarded lamp" into the purifying building looking for a leak, resulting in an explosion that burned three workers.

Another vulnerability of the Manhattan Gas Works was the system of water-filled cast-iron tanks that were used to regulate the gas pressures sent through the cast-iron pipes to the far reaches of the city. At that time, few valves were inserted into the pipes to regulate the gas pressures throughout the entire gas supply system. That resulted in customers closer to the plant complaining about too much gas pressure at their homes and businesses, often resulting in gas leaks, and customers on the eastern end of the city complaining about too little pressure.

The danger in this factory-only regulation of gas pressure meant that should the water levels in these tanks fall for any reason (such as Confederate sabotage), the pressures of the gas leaving the factory and flowing underground all over the city could increase far beyond what would be safe in businesses and homes. If there was an ignition source, such as an explosion or firebomb at the gas plant, the cast-iron pipes, without any system of built-in shutoff valves to prevent a catastrophe, could conceivably transport the exploding, burning gas all over the city.

If the Confederates had started fires at the Manhattan Gas Works, the camphene and turpentine distilleries, or the chemical works, there was plenty of fuel to keep them going. There were maritime warehouses lining the waterfront. There was a planing mill with mounds of highly flammable sawdust on Gansevoort Street where it met Horatio. There were lumberyards on every corner of Tenth Avenue between 19th and 13th streets as well as lumberyards as close to the main part of the city as Seventh Avenue and 15th Street. There were several alcohol distilleries, an oil manufactory, and coal yards in the district. The west side of Manhattan was one huge danger zone that was ripe for a firebomb attack. To have started such a huge fire, the incendiaries would have had to have known what they were doing.

3. *Good spies are familiar with the weapons they choose.* While the original formula of the Byzantines' Greek fire is still a mystery, variations of a spontaneously combustible substance were fairly well known in the 1860s, though everyone had his own version of how it was made.

Larry McDonald, the Toronto bomb maker, probably was the

manufacturer of the Greek fire that the St. Albans raiders used in October 1864. During that raid, the Confederates broke several bottles against buildings, but weeks of rain had left the boards soaked, and the expected conflagrations did not occur. Had they broken their bottles against dry, seasoned wood inside buildings, flames should have erupted.

McDonald apparently did not offer, and the New York City conspirators did not ask him, to show them how the chemical compound worked before they left the relative safety of Toronto. It would have been fairly easy for the Confederates to search out a few abandoned cabins in the Canadian woods around Toronto to test McDonald's version of Greek fire, but Headley makes no mention of any practicing.

The formula used by the Greenwich Village chemist is unknown, but in the only experiment the Confederates tried on a few boards outside their Central Park cottage, the liquid flamed and ignited the wood. This means that Headley's postwar criticism of the chemist's abilities, even accusing him of intentionally sabotaging the formula so it would not burn once the New York Copperheads lost heart, was unwarranted. Had the chemist actually sabotaged the operation, the random bottle the Confederates used in Central Park in their singular attempt at practice would not have flared up.

The name of the long-bearded chemist working from the basement-level room in the 70 block of West Washington Place remains unknown (the city directory of 1864 did not cross-reference professions with names), but he fully understood and planned for the burning of New York City. No one knows what the chemist was thinking. Had the Confederates attacked the west side of Manhattan, his own home in Greenwich Village would have been in the path of advancing flames.

4. *Good saboteurs wait for the right conditions.* The original Confederate plan was to disrupt Election Day, November 8. When General Butler and his 3,500 Union troops arrived to protect the polling places, that plan was put aside, and the Confederates waited for what they thought would be the right opportunity. They picked the day after Thanksgiving for no apparent reason other than they

had grown tired of sitting in their hotel rooms. What should have guided their intentions was the weather.

According to scant newspaper accounts of the weather in 1864, the days leading up to Thanksgiving weekend had been rainy. Friday, November 25, was a beautiful, clear fall day with few clouds in the sky. Still, the ground and the walls of wooden buildings would have been at least damp if not still wet from the previous week's rain.

No one kept detailed weather reports in the city before 1874. But modern-day calculations of wind-speed averages for the date of November 25 show wind speeds on that night likely averaged around 10 miles per hour with winds sweeping across Manhattan Island from the west/northwest. That is a noticeable if slight wind that could have aided the spread of any fires started on the west side of the city toward the rest of Manhattan.

However, had the conspirators stayed poised for action with a few hours' notice and waited for a windy night, nature could have helped them accomplish their mission. If they had waited for a night with a sustained wind speed of at least 15 miles per hour or more, common at the end of November, flames and sparks would have flown much more easily through the air. Closely packed wooden buildings could have caught fire just from the wind pushing the flames into adjoining buildings.

5. *Attacks are more successful when the target is sleeping.*

Kennedy's confession just before he was executed made it clear that the loss of human life was not the Confederates' objective. Headley made the same point in his postwar book. To that end, the Confederates timed their attacks for 8:00 p.m. on a Friday night on a holiday weekend, a time they knew that most hotel guests would be strolling the sidewalks, riding in carriages, attending the theater and operas. Very few people would be sleeping at such an early hour.

What the Confederates did not plan for, however, was that those same people, safe from being caught in their beds during a hotel fire, would be awake to see and smell smoke. The city's four thousand volunteer firefighters were also awake and roaming the streets, ready to rush to their respective station houses to respond to the fire alarms that started that early evening.

Had the Confederates waited for a windy night and struck at 3:00 a.m., instead of a mild night at 8:00 p.m., the New York City Fire Department would not have been able to extinguish all the fires they would have set. *Fire would have consumed New York City.*

Chapter 23

"They Sacrificed Everything"

B y 1864, New York City was no stranger to devastating fires. The city's first urban fire started the night of September 21, 1776. It was probably set in a tavern on Whitehall Street by members of General George Washington's retreating Colonial soldiers to deprive advancing British army troops the luxury of the city's houses during the approaching winter. Spurred by strong winds, the fire easily swept through the rude wooden buildings and burned uncontrolled all through the night. By the next day, around five hundred buildings had been destroyed before British sailors were able to bring the fire under control. The British did little to rebuild the city, and the citizens, now living under martial law, made few efforts on their own, knowing that any new residences could be confiscated for military use.

The city's second major fire came on the night of December 16, 1835. This fire also started at a single source, a dry goods store. Within minutes, strong winds were spreading the fire. Freezing temperatures hampered the firefighting efforts as water moving through the canvas hoses froze. The fire lasted so long and grew so large that fire companies from as far away as Philadelphia, nearly one hundred miles to the southwest, were able to respond.

Before the fire was out on the afternoon of the second day, nearly seven hundred buildings in thirteen acres in the city's nascent financial district had been destroyed, including the Merchant's Exchange (today's equivalent of the New York Stock Exchange). The only thing that stopped the fire was that it burned through all the buildings in the southeast quadrant of the city before reaching the East River. The fire chief even tried blowing up buildings in its path to try to rob the fire of its fuel, but this did not work.

Once the fire was out, instead of praising the fire chief for his innovative thinking, the city's Common Council removed him from office because he had destroyed private property in his effort to stop the fire. Since the fire was mostly in the financial and business district, no lives were lost.

The city's third large fire broke out in a whale oil store on New Street on July 19, 1845. The fire spread rapidly to a saltpeter warehouse on Broad Street. The resulting explosion was said to have been heard in Brooklyn and Jersey City. At least two hundred buildings were destroyed. Four firefighters and at least twenty-six citizens died.

In December 1853, a single carelessly discarded match led to a fire that started at the publisher Harper & Brothers, but soon spread to fifteen other buildings, all of which were destroyed. Four firefighters lost their lives.

On April 25, 1855, the city's volunteer fire department was devastated by the loss of eleven men killed and twenty injured when the Jennings clothing store on Broadway near City Hall burned and then suddenly collapsed on the men inside trying to extinguish the flames. It was the worst fire disaster in terms of loss of firefighters the city had ever experienced.

On October 5, 1858, the Crystal Palace, an exhibition hall that stretched two full blocks from 40th to 42nd streets on Sixth Avenue, burned within thirty minutes. Though built of glass and iron and considered fireproof, the exhibits inside from all over the world were not. They were readily combustible, leading to the melting of the glass and iron.

By 1864, the New York City Fire Department consisted of around 4,000 men divided into 50 engine companies, 56 hose companies, and 17 hook-and-ladder companies. Everyone was a volunteer, driven to service in such a dangerous job by a sense of community and personal pride in serving one's city, a love of competition to prove one's own fire company was faster at getting to fires and better at putting them out, and the knowledge that volunteering with the right company with the right political connections could lead to a paying patronage job.

Fighting fires often went beyond pure competition. Fistfights frequently broke out between companies for the honor of putting out small fires while the fire that drew the firefighters to the site in the first place was ignored until the fight was settled. It was common for fire companies to sabotage each other's efforts, including standing on hoses to reduce water pressure or, in some cases, cutting the hoses of competing companies.

Hose companies, which were supposed to carry and stretch hoses for the engine companies, would sometimes sit idly by waiting for their favorite engine company to arrive at a fire. If a disliked rival company arrived first, the hose company on site would refuse to help unless lives were in danger.

The chief engineer or city fire chief in 1864 was 41-year-old John Decker, a volunteer firefighter since 17 years of age. A large and fit man at 190 pounds, Decker was devoted to the service and to doing what was right. In 1863, when the Colored Orphanage was attacked during the Draft Riots, Decker stepped forward and tried to talk the crowd out of what they were doing. He was beaten for his efforts, but his stalling enabled some firefighters and orphanage staff to evacuate the children before it was set afire.

Decker seemed to be talking about himself as well as all the men under his command when he was quoted about the deaths of several fellow firefighters: "They sacrificed to it [firefighting] health, wealth, strength, wife's society, everything."

While Decker was an honest and conscientious chief, even pushing for fiscal reform within the department to root out waste and corruption in buying and repairing firefighting equipment, he and his fellow firefighters were leery of new technologies. They particularly disliked the steam-powered pumpers that had been in use for more than twenty-five years in some other cities.

Decker, understanding that steam-powered pumpers could replace hundreds of volunteers, sincerely believed that man-powered and man-pulled fire engines were more efficient. He maintained that the man-powered pumpers could start throwing water immediately onto fires while steam-powered engines would still be building pressure. The first steam-powered pumper did not go into service in New York City until 1859.

When first confronted with steam pumpers, the firefighters staged contests where they demonstrated that their hand pumping could throw a stream of water just about as high and as far as steamers could (180 feet high and 230 feet laterally). What the firefighters were more reluctant to acknowledge was that teams of forty men on a hand pumper had to be relieved every five minutes as the rapid, up-and-down pumping motion was exhausting. Once the steam pumper had built up pressure, it could pump all night as long as its firebox was kept supplied with a steady supply of fuel. The firefighters had an answer for that advantage of the steam pumper, pointing out that firefighters were sometimes forced to tear down wooden picket fences and throw them into the firebox at some long-lasting fires. By 1862, the fire department had purchased only sixteen steam pumpers.

Decker and his men did not even like the idea of horses pulling their equipment to the fires. Men still pulled most of the engines, hose wagons, and ladder wagons because they enjoyed the athleticism of running in tandem with other men while rushing to fires.

Even if Decker had accepted steamers and brought his department into line with modern times, the city still had potential firefighting problems. The underground pipes feeding from the twenty-year-old Croton Aqueduct and reservoir (site of today's New York Public Library on Fifth Avenue and 41st Street) that kept the city supplied with water for drinking and firefighting were already leaking. That meant there was reduced water pressure at the fire hydrants.

Even worse, if a fire occurred in the oldest, most southern parts of the city, firefighters had to deal with smaller, older leaking pipes, meaning the available water supply was less than in the parts of the city that were more modern. The lack of water pressure in the older parts of the city so worried Decker that he asked for funding from the

Common Council to modify hand pumpers and purchase more hose so the East and Hudson rivers could be used as sources of water.

In 1864, the water pressure at the hydrants was what gravity and pumping by steam or hand could provide. It would be another forty years before civil engineers would develop a method for installing high-pressure water hydrants.

Two other problems faced by the fire department were the lack of proper equipment at all the fire companies and a complete disregard for building practices that could make evacuation of flammable buildings safer. When a fire broke out in a tenement on Elm Street in the Lower East Side in February 1860, the first responding fire companies had ladders that could reach only the first four floors of the six-story building that was crowded with more than one hundred people. The building was not equipped with fire escapes because no one in the city government had thought to force building owners to build them. Twenty people, including whole families, perished.

Decker, as well as chief engineers before and after him, constantly worried about the fire hazards they did not know about, such as the nature of the contents of warehouses. While the fire insurance companies had published books of maps distinguishing between houses and commercial buildings, the maps did not list the flammable materials that could be found inside the buildings. The area just north of City Hall, near the intersection of Canal and Broadway, now known as the Tribeca neighborhood (which was near the location of many of the targeted hotels), was so crowded with warehouses and garment factories filled with flammable cloth the firefighters dubbed the region Hell's Hundred Acres.

While having enough equipment and water pressure to fight individual fires would have been a constant concern of firefighters in the 1860s who remembered the fires of 1835, 1845, and 1855, learning of fire breakouts was not. A system of fire towers connected by telegraph to most of the fire stations, as well as to a headquarters in the basement of City Hall, was kept manned twenty-four hours a day. If a citizen reported a fire to a neighborhood fire tower, its location was telegraphed to the fire stations, and a coded alarm of fire bells was rung to alert volunteers which fire districts should respond. All the telegraphs were working and the fire bells were rung on the night of the Confederate attack.

Although several fire companies responded to the alarms, none of the fires set by the Confederates were extinguished by the city's fire department. Though no true firefighting occurred, Decker and his lieutenants were active that night ordering hotel managers to put multiple buckets of water on each floor.

Decker and his 4,000-man department were lucky that the Confederates were so lackadaisical in their fire attacks. Even if the Confederates had ignored the flammable targets on the Hudson and had just set fire to their hotel targets, the city could have burned if the Confederates had only practiced with their vials of Greek fire.

Had the Confederates coordinated with each other, all set their bed linen and furniture fires around 3:00 a.m. on Saturday morning, and left their hotel room windows open so a steady supply of oxygen could have fed their fires, the room blazes might have gone undiscovered. The fires could have spread from one room to another, possibly melting and igniting the gas lines in each room. If that had happened, the fires would have quickly spread to the rest of the upper floors where the Confederates had taken rooms.

By the time Decker's department could have responded and arrived, the fires would have already been well engaged. The firefighters might not have been able to keep the blazing hotels from turning into a citywide conflagration.

No published history of the New York City Fire Department or newspaper accounts of the 1860s mentions the department fighting multiple fires at the same time. All three of the city's catastrophic fires in 1776, 1835, and 1845 started from single sources, and the fire department was unable to keep them from spreading to hundreds of other buildings. Even after the department had grown in the number of firefighters and had acquired more and better equipment, memorable single-source fires such as the 1855 Jennings building fire, the 1859 Crystal Palace fire, and the 1860 Elm Street tenement fire all proved uncontrollable. In each case, the best the firefighters could do was to keep the blaze contained to the source building so the fire did not spread to surrounding structures.

The first hotel fire to be discovered that night was at the St. James. One block south of it was the Hoffman House. One more block to the south was the Fifth Avenue Hotel. At that time in the history of New York City, 26th Street and Broadway, site of the St. James, was considered on the north side of the city. Most of the fire companies would have been located to the south. It would have taken a long time for firefighters to gather at their stations and then pull their equipment north through the streams of carriages along a crowded Broadway on a Friday night.

Assuming the Confederates had coordinated their fire bombings to all happen at one time, the city's firefighters would have been faced with an unprecedented situation when they arrived at the St. James fire, the historically known first fire to be reported. Presumably, by their arrival at the St. James, the other two nearby hotels, the Hoffman House and the Fifth Avenue Hotel would have been on fire. The responding fire companies would have encountered three blazes at once within three blocks of each other with the streets crowded with evacuated hotel guests and curious spectators.

The engine companies would have been drawing water from hydrants on the street corners of Broadway and 26th, 25th and 24th streets. The reservoir was just fifteen blocks away, but there are no records to determine if there would have been enough water supply to fight all three fires at once. The firefighters may have resolved to fight one hotel fire at a time to keep up the water supply and pressure, or they may have abandoned all three hotel fires to wet down surrounding buildings in an effort to keep the simultaneous blazes from spreading.

Assuming that many of the city's fire companies would have rushed northward to fight the first three reported hotel fires, they would have been out of position when the fires at the LaFarge, the Metropolitan, and the St. Nicolas would have erupted some twenty blocks to the south of the St. James. Then, within minutes, fire bells would have gone off alerting the city to still more fires another twenty blocks south at the Astor House, Howard Hotel, Lovejoy's Hotel, Tammany Hotel, and the Belmont Hotel.

Assuming that the Barnum museum staff was able to put out the fire Kennedy set in that stairwell, as they did, there still would have been five hotels clustered around City Hall Park that would have been ablaze at the same time.

This fire cluster was deep in one of the oldest parts of the city with the old, smaller, leaking water supply pipes. The winds, blowing at an estimated 10 miles per hour, could have pushed the fire to the east, northeast, and southeast of City Hall. Here were hundreds of poorly constructed wooden tenements just like the one on Elm Street where twenty people had died just four years earlier. Less than a half mile to the east of City Hall were the warehouses along the East River, including one massive building on John Street where highly flammable naval stores (turpentine, pine pitch) were kept prior to export. Tied to the East River docks were hundreds of wooden sailing ships with their flammable canvas sails furled, but still vulnerable to catching fire from flying sparks.

Assuming the Confederates had coordinated their fires to start at 3:00 a.m., by 4:00 a.m. the New York City Fire Department would have been fighting at least a dozen single source fires at one time separated by at least four linear miles. At least seven of those fires would have been in the older section of the city where Decker had warned the Common Council that low water pressure made it difficult to control fires.

The real trouble for the firefighters would have come if the Confederates had spent more time looking for more vulnerable and flammable targets than the hotels.

Had the Confederates targeted the highly flammable targets of the city, they could have started even more massive fires that could have been overwhelming. Had they operated as a team moving between targets on the west side of the city instead of as individuals setting fires to hotels along Broadway, the incendiaries could have started a minimum of one hundred separate fires using just their original supply of 144 bottles of Greek fire. If they had gone back to the Greenwich Village chemist and collected more bottles, they could have started upward of five hundred fires on the west side of the city filled with flammable targets with a westerly wind sweeping sparks and flying debris toward the rest of the city.

The most flammable targets would have been the camphene, turpentine, and varnish refineries; the chemical works; and the dozen or more lumberyards all located near West Street between 12th Street and 20th Street, in what is now Chelsea and the Meatpacking District. Had they been able to control the night-shift staff of the Manhattan Gas Works, learned that the most explosive building on site was the purifying plant, and set a bomb that could have ignited the supply of gas in the pipes buried under the city, the Confederates could have started a true citywide disaster. The disaster could have been even worse had the Confederates stocked up on their supply of Greek fire.

If the conspirators had started a large number of fires on the west side and still had some bottles of Greek fire, they could have set still more fires at their hotels, their original targets. And the nightmare would have been compounded if there were multiple fires on the west side of the city and in the center of the city with westerly winds helping spread the flames.

As brave and as skilled as the city's four thousand volunteer firefighters had proved themselves to be over the previous one hundred years, they would not have been prepared to have fought 12, 100, or 500 simultaneous fires set among highly flammable targets. *New York City would have burned down.*

Epilogue

What Happened to the Principal Characters

Robert Cobb Kennedy was the only Confederate incendiary who was tried and executed for the attack. Executed at Fort Lafayette, which was later destroyed in order to put up pilings for the Verranzano-Narrows Bridge, he was initially buried in a graveyard at Fort Hamilton, New York, a still-existing fort in Brooklyn virtually in the shadow of that same bridge. His remains were removed some years later and reburied somewhere in Brooklyn. His family and friends published some postwar articles detailing how his fate seemed to be predetermined by a military commission anxious to punish someone for the attacks in the North.

Robert M. Martin and John W. Headley both successfully made their way south after the war, even running into Confederate president Jefferson Davis in Salisbury, North Carolina, after Davis and the Confederate cabinet had fled Richmond. Martin made his way back to Kentucky without incident where he was surprised to find out that a warrant had been issued for his arrest. Like Kennedy, Martin was transported to Fort Lafayette to await trial for the attack on New York City.

For unclear reasons the trial never took place. A federal court judge finally released Martin in February 1866 when the prosecution failed to supply the court with papers the New York City police department claimed to have in its possession that the police said Martin had written boasting of the attack. The prosecution claimed that Martin's history of being a Confederate soldier should be enough to convict him of some crime, but the incredulous judge said that the only evidence that Martin had been a soldier had come from his own attorney and that evidence was inadmissible. The judge released Martin and no further charges were brought against him.

Ironically, Martin moved to Brooklyn in 1874 where he lived for fourteen years operating a tobacco warehouse. He later moved back to Kentucky but returned to New York City in late 1900 to try to find a doctor who could treat his festering lung war wound. He died at 61 years of age in January 1901, and was buried in Brooklyn's Greenwood Cemetery.

Headley returned to Kentucky and apparently went unnoticed by Union army authorities because he was not arrested like Martin. He was elected Kentucky's secretary of state in 1891 and served through 1896. He published *Confederate Operations in Canada and New York* in 1906. It remains the only first-person account of the Confederate Secret Service's activities. Headley moved to Los Angeles, California, where he died in 1930 at 90 years of age.

Harrington became a lawyer in Los Angeles, and Ashbrook became an insurance broker in Kentucky. John Price, the Virginian who lost his nerve and did not show up that night, was apparently picked up by the police and held in custody until he could testify at Kennedy's trial. After that his fate is unknown.

Gus McDonald, the piano store owner who allowed the Confederates to stow their luggage at his store, was freed from jail after Kennedy signed a paper saying that he did not know Gus. That was clearly a lie that Gus did not challenge as it saved his life.

Oddly, Larry McDonald, Gus's brother and the bomb maker in Toronto, also apparently escaped execution. How he did this is unclear since it was Larry who personally met chief of detectives John "Old" Young and drunkenly told the story of how the attacks were carried out with his expertise.

Jacob Thompson, the commissioner of the Confederate Secret Service, who could never post a successful mission to his credit, fled to Europe when he heard of Lincoln's assassination out of fear that he would be accused of complicity. There remains some question if Thompson took some hard currency with him that rightfully belonged to the Confederate government, for he seemed to have plenty of money during his expatriate days in Paris. Some historians accuse him of taking between $100,000 and $300,000 in Confederate gold, more than enough to qualify for a fortune in 1865.

Finally ensured that he would not be arrested, Thompson returned to the United States and settled in Memphis, Tennessee, in 1869. Though his prewar fortune had been lost, he did not seem to be hurting for postwar cash. When he died in 1885, he left a fortune of $500,000, including land on Long Island, New York, and stock in the Bell Telephone Company, which Thompson had invested in some time after the company was formed in 1877.

Clement Clay, the second in command of the Confederate Secret Service in Canada, made his way to Richmond the same night that Davis was escaping the city on April 2, 1865. Clay joked with Davis on arrival at the Confederate White House that it seemed odd he was making his way into the city just as everyone else of importance was rushing out of town. Clay rode the train with Davis as far as Danville, Virginia. Realizing that Davis was not really trying to escape, Clay left his boss and made his own way south. Suspected in the Lincoln assassination, he was imprisoned with Davis for a while in Fortress Monroe, Virginia. Like Davis, he was eventually cleared of any involvement in Lincoln's assassination. He died in 1882.

Just as he had mysteriously showed up in Canada supposedly to help the Confederate cause, George N. Sanders, the hanger-on to Clement Clay, also mysteriously disappeared from public notice after the war was over.

There remains one mysterious character from the Confederate Secret Service operating out of Canada: Richard Montgomery, if that was his real name. He was the double agent who carried Jacob Thompson's dispatches to Richmond. Montgomery and two other men claiming to be Union spies in Canada would testify at the Lincoln assassins' trial in May 1865 that Jacob Thompson had planned the president's assassination in Toronto. Montgomery testified that John

Wilkes Booth met with Thompson to discuss how to either kidnap or kill Lincoln.

Prosecutors eventually discounted Montgomery's testimony at the Lincoln assassins' trial in Washington City that Davis himself as well as Thompson had approved in advance of the assassination. The prosecutors set aside the testimony when suspicious newspaper reporters looked into Montgomery's tales and found holes in his stories, such as a confused time line on when Montgomery claimed to have met Thompson. Other captured records indicated that Thompson was not in town when Montgomery claimed to have met him. Fearful that the three double agents had lied about the connection between Davis, Thompson, and John Wilkes Booth, the prosecutors quietly dropped the case against the top Confederates.

The intriguing question remains: If Thompson correctly predicted the attack on New York City using his sources from Canada, why would he make up the connection between Jefferson Davis and Lincoln's assassination?

If Montgomery was right on the vast and fiendish plot to attack New York City, was he wrong on the plot to kill the president of the United States?

Acknowledgments

Thanks to Joe Vallely of Flaming Star Literary Enterprises for representing me. This is our third book Joe has sold after *The Politically Incorrect Guide to the South* and *Pursuit: The Chase, Capture, Persecution and Surprising Release of Confederate President Jefferson Davis.*

Thanks to editor Michaela Hamilton and the rest of the staff at Kensington Publishing for taking on the sobering story of how New York City could have been destroyed in one night.

Thanks to Danny Lafluer, Theodore Edwards IV, and James Davidson III, all of Lafayette, Louisiana, for permission to use the photo of Robert Cobb Kennedy.

Ted O'Reilly in the manuscripts division of the New-York Historical Society found some references to the November 25, 1864, weather. Sue Kriete, reference librarian at the New-York Historical Society, and Jill Slaight of the department of rights and reproductions helped find some photographs for the book.

Thomas Lisanti, manager of photographic services and permissions at the New York Public Library, helped find some photos. I also want to thank all the staff at the New York Public Library for their assistance in finding microfilmed and original newspapers and maps including Saskia Scheffer who prepared a pan and zoom file that allowed me to look at an old fire map.

Dr. Keith C. Heidorn, The Weather Doctor, helped with some details on weather history.

Dr. Bruce Turner, Head of Special Collections at the Edith Garland Dupré Library at the University of Louisiana at Lafayette, found and copied some Kennedy-related material.

Jim Morony at the New York City Fire Department Museum showed me around the great museum and told me about some of the old equipment they have.

My old buddy Bob Williams of Jamestown, North Carolina, who reenacted with me in Florida with The Leon Rifles and who still reenacts with me today in North Carolina with the Twenty-sixth Regiment of North Carolina Troops, researched what troops would have been sent to New York during the election.

Finally, I always acknowledge my wife, Barbara, to whom I have been married for twenty-five years. Her decision for us to move to the mountains of North Carolina has made writing while looking down on the New River and out at Mount Jefferson a pleasure.

Source Notes

~~~~~~~~~~

Prologue: "A Born Gentleman to the Tips of His Fingers"

3 **One man who knew Morgan:** Description of Morgan by James Fry, quoted in Cathryn J. Prince, *Burn the Town and Sack the Banks* (Carroll & Graf, New York, 2006) p. 66.

4 **Morgan was also loquacious:** John Hunt Morgan, proclamation, March 15, 1862.

Chapter 1: "Decayed Is Here"

15 **"Other ruins loom upon the eye":** Charles Dickens, *American Notes for General Circulation* (Chapman & Hall, London, 1842).

Most of the city's 814,000 residents: Eric Holmbeck, *The Historical Atlas of New York City* (Henry Holt, New York, 1994) p. 110.

16 **"Commerce is devouring inch by inch":** William Cullen Bryant, quoted in ibid., 71.

Chapter 2: "A Traffic in Enslaved Africans"

24 **According to census records:** Ira Berlin and Leslie Harris, eds., *Slavery in New York* (New-York Historical Society, New York, 2005) p. 63.

A 1730 law passed in New York: Ibid., 76.

25 **More than seventy were arrested:** Anne Farrow, Joel Lang, and Jenifer Frank, *Complicity: How the North Promoted, Prolonged and Profited from Slavery* (Ballantine, New York, 2005) p. 81.

When the slave owners ignored: Ibid., 81.

26 **Over the next thirty years:** Ibid., 82.

White New Yorkers needed little persuasion: Jill Laporte, *New York Burning* (Alfred A. Knopf, New York, 2005) p. 59.

28 **tremendous profits:** Edgar J. McManus, *A History of Negro Slavery in New York* (Syracuse University Press, New York, 2001) p. 26.

Estimates range as high: Hugh Thomas, *The Slave Trade* (Simon & Schuster, New York, 1999) p. 271.

Since it was a common practice: McManus, *History of Negro Slavery*, p. 25.

29 **That fact indicated to researchers:** National Park Service, *The African Burial Ground: Return to the Past to Build the Future*, Skeletal Biological Final Report, part I, p. 531.

So many New York slavers: *New York Weekly Post Boy*, July 14, 1755, and December 25, 1756, p. 172; quoted in McManus, *History*.

According to the U.S. Census: Ibid., pp. 176–77.

Congress finally passed a law: James Madison, State of the Union Address, December 5, 1810.

Chapter 3: "A Great Distribution Point for Cotton"

32 **Over the next one hundred years:** Stephen Yafa, *Big Cotton . . .* (Viking, New York, 2004) p. 78.

33 **In 1860, right before the war:** Edward Glaeser, *Urban Colossus: Why New York Is America's Largest City*, www.econ.brown.edu/econ/sthesis/IanPapers/tnyc.html, 2006, p. 12.

34 **New York State alone had 150 banks:** Harold Woodman, *King Cotton and His Retainers . . .* (Beard Books, University of Kentucky Press, Lexington, 1968) p. 172.

In the early nineteenth century: Edwin G. Burrows and Mike Wallace, *Gotham . . .* (Oxford University Press, New York, 2000) p. 336.

34 **Just twenty years into the nineteenth century:** Farrow et al., *Complicity*, p. 18.

35 **Giddy New Yorkers:** Ibid., 23.

"Without the intervention of great capital": Samuel Powell, *Notes on Southern Wealth and Northern Profits* (C. Sherman & Sons, Philadelphia, 1861) p. 24.

"The growth in wealth in the cotton states": *Financial Register of the United States*, August 16, 1837, p. 63.

36 **The *Journal of Commerce*:** *The New York Journal of Commerce*, December 12, 1849.

A decade later, another economist: Stephen Colwell, *The Five Cotton States and New York . . .* , (Cornell University Library, Ithaca, N.Y., 1861).

"Every southerner should visit New York": William Caruthers, *The Kentuckian in New York* (Self-published, New York, 1834).

38 **"May you never need a return":** *New Orleans Picayune*, August 23, 1853.

39 **"Or shall we":** Burrows and Wallace, *Gotham*, p. 552.

"We mean, sir, to put you abolitionists down": Samuel J. May, *Some Recollections of the Anti-Slavery Conflict* (Scholarly Publishing Library, Ann Arbor, Mich., pp. 127–28.

40 **"The ships will rot at her docks":** Alfred A. Smith, "A Southern Confederacy," *De Bow's Review*, Article 61, 1859.

Chapter 4: "Money Is Plenty, Business Is Brisk"

41 **"I expressed great dissatisfaction":** Philip Hone, *The Diary of Philip Hone* (Dodd, Mead, New York, 1927) p. 79.

"I am desirous that persons": Ibid., 254.

42 **"with the aid of one or two cotton crops":** Ibid., 264.

"The terrible abolition question": Ibid., 278.

One of the speakers at the meeting: William Goodell, *Slavery and Anti-Slavery: . . .* (Self-published, New York, 1853).

43 **"In my strolls of three days":** *New York Times*, August 29, 1854.

44 **"The bribe was, in fact, $1,500"**: Warren S. Howard, *American Slavers and the Federal Law 1837–1862* (University of California Press, Berkeley, 1963) p. 128.

Of 125 slave traders: Ibid.

45 **Instead of awarding the men:** Abbott Brothers, *Reports of Cases in Admiralty, Argued and Determined in the District Court of United States for the Southern District of New York* (Little, Brown, Boston, 1857) p. 279.

"Our Authorities would do well": *New York Times*, April 22, 1853.

"If they will not do it": *New York Times*, November 24, 1854.

46 **"The price for the clearance":** *New York Daily News*, May 30, 1860.

"It will not thank us": *New York Daily Tribune*, June 5, 1860.

By 1860, on the eve of the war: Farrow et al., *Complicity*, p. 26.

47 **All the ships:** *New York Times*, December 1, 1860.

"The laws against it are": *New York Times*, December 26, 1860.

48 **"If we understand Judge Smalley":** *New York Times*, December 27, 1860.

"Another future mayor": Jerome Mushkat, *Fernando Wood (Kent State University Press*, Kent, Ohio, 1990) p. 11.

51 **"Mayor Wood's secessionist Message":** *New York Sun*, January 8, 1861.

Chapter 5: "The Meetings of These Madmen"

53 **Bennett was reacting:** *New York Tribune*, May 9, 1850.

54 **"The root of the evil":** *New York Post*, August 3, 1858.

"Between January 1859 and August 1860": W.E.B. Du Bois, *The Suppression of the African Slave-Trade* . . . (Longman's Green, London, 1896) p. 123.

55 **"The Government treats the whole matter":** *New York Times*, August 10, 1859.

"[D]owntown merchants of wealth": *Journal of Commerce*, quoted in Ron Soodalter, *Hanging Captain Gordon* (Washington Square Press, New York, 2007) p. 71.

55 "The most successful of the Merchant princes": *New York Tribune*, June 5, 1860.

His first trial ended: Warren S. Howard, *American Slavers and the Federal Law* (University of California Press, Berkeley, 1963) p. 204.

56 "With free trade at the South": Letter of Lamar to Howell Cobb, February 22, 1861, Toombs, Stephens, and Cobb Correspondence, p. 554; quoted in Philip Foner, *Business and Slavery* . . . (University of North Carolina Press, Chapel Hill, 1941) p. 294.

57 "The depreciation of property": Powell, *Southern Wealth*, p. 173.

58 "Why not trade directly with our customers": *Charleston Mercury* (South Carolina), October 14, 1857.

"New York, the prime cause": *New Orleans Crescent*, reprinted in *New York Herald*, December l4, 1857.

60 "The result of this coalition": "Speech of Hon. Robert Tombs on the Crisis Delivered Before the Georgia Legislature", December 7, 1860.

"The people of the South": Edward McPherson, *The Political History of the United States* (Edwards & Solomon, New York, 1865) p. 13.

The *Journal of Commerce*: *Journal of Commerce*, February 1, 1861.

"The passage of the Bill": *New York Herald*, February 8, 1861.

61 "To pass it when a part of them": *Annual Report of the New York Chamber of Commerce for 1861*, pp. 2–4.

Chapter 6: "The City of New York Belongs to the South"

62 "The City of New York belongs almost as much": *New York Post*, February 14, 1860.

63 "New York City, the emporium of trade": *Richmond Enquirer*, reprinted in the *New York Herald*, November 16, 1859.

Other irritated Southerners: *Journal of Commerce*, January 19, 1860.

65 It was not a slave insurrection: Abraham Lincoln, "Cooper Union Speech," February 27, 1860.

"Wrong as we think slavery is": Ibid.

According to the *New York Times*: *New York Times*, February 29, 1860.

66 "No man ever before made": *New York Tribune*, February 28, 1860.

The *New York Evening News*: *New York Evening News*, February 28, 1860.

68 "He represents the most cruel": George Templeton Strong, *The Diary of George Templeton Strong* (September 14, 1860; repr., University of Washington Press, Seattle, 1988).

69 "There is no virtue in Pearl Street": *New York Tribune*, September 17, 1860.

The *Rochester Union*: *Rochester Union*, September 25, 1860.

They were determined to "save the federal Union": John Hardy to Samuel J. Tilden, August 2, 1860, Tilden Letters, as quoted in Foner, *Business and Slavery* . . .

In a speech at Cooper Union: Irving Katz, *August Belmont: A Political Biography* (Columbia University Press, New York, 1968) p. 62.

70 Four days before the election: *Journal of Commerce*, November 3, 1860.

71 "The contest, on the part of the Republicans": *New York Times*, November 7, 1860.

The New York Chamber of Commerce: *Annual Report (1861)*, p. 18.

At the same time as they were pleading: *New York Herald*, January 9, 1861.

"The refusal at Washington": A. T. Stewart to Thurlow Weed, February 20, 1861, Weed Papers.

"We learn that in consequence": *New York Tribune*, April 8, 1861.

"We are either for the country": *New York Tribune*, April 20, 1861.

Chapter 7: "That Which Comes Easy Goes Easy"

76 Clothing merchants like A.T. Stewart: Burrows and Wallace, *Gotham* . . . , p. 875.

78 "Things here at the North": Ibid., 877.

79 "They pull them down": *Harper's New Monthly Magazine* (1864): 230.

"If I could save the Union": Lincoln Letter to Greeley, August 22, 1862, *New York Tribune*.

82 "The rabble was perfectly homogeneous": Strong, *Diary,* pp. 237–38.

84 "Crush the mob!": *New York Times,* July 14, 1863.

   "Some of them": Barnet Schecter, *The Devil's Own Work* . . . (Walker, New York, 2005) p. 230.

85 The *Times further charged*: *New York Times,* July 23, 1863.

86 "We shall see the giant, but hollow bulk": *Richmond Enquirer,* July 18, 1863 reprinted in *New York Times,* July 22, 1863.

   "Our compliments to our Northern 'brethren'": *Richmond Dispatch,* July 18, 1863, reprinted in *New York Times,* July 22, 1863.

Chapter 8: "How Sad Is This Life"

91 "The noise became more deafening": Mary Ann Loughborough, *My Cave Life in Vicksburg* (D. Appleton, New York, 1864) p. 56.

92 "It would appear, sir": Letter from P.G.T. Beauregard to Quincy Gilmore, August 22, 1863 in *The War of the Rebellion.*

93 "I want peace": William T. Sherman to City Council of Atlanta, September 12, 1864, in *Memoirs of General William T. Sherman,* William T. Sherman, D. Appleton & Co, 1875, pp. 600–608.

   "Behind us lay Atlanta": William T. Sherman, *Memoirs of General William T. Sherman* (D. Appleton, New York, 1875) p. 179.

96 "Take all provisions": Robert Scott et al., *The Official Records of the War of the Rebellion,* ser: 2, vol. 43, pt. 2 (GPO, Washington, D.C., 1880) p. 698.

98 "The wholesale devastation of the valley": Robert Tomes, quoted in John Heatwhole, *The Burning* (Rockbridge, Berryville, Virginia, 1998) p. 211.

Chapter 9: "A Fire in the Rear Will Be Opened"

100 The Belleville, Illinois, *Democrat*: Belleville Democrat, November 16, 1860, quoted in Wood Gray, *The Hidden Civil War* (Viking Press, New York, 1942) p. 41.

   [The Founding Fathers]: *Kenosha Democrat,* January 11, 1861, quoted in *The Hidden Civil War,* ibid., 42.

   The *Detroit Free Press*: *Detroit Free Press,* January 29, 1861, quoted in *The Hidden Civil War,* ibid., 47.

101 "What are we to think": *New York Times*, April 10, 1861.

"The specimens had probably been": *Chicago Tribune*, April 17, 1861.

102 With that explanation: George Washington, "Whiskey Rebellion Proclamation," August 11, 1794.

103 "I can be no party": Telegram of John Ellis to Lincoln, April 16, 1861.

104 "It is believed": Abraham Lincoln to Congress, July 1, 1861.

105 On April 27, Lincoln: Abraham Lincoln executive order, April 21, 1861.

106 "All virtue, patriotism": Horatio Seymour Speech in Albany, January 31, 1861.

"We will guarantee them": Horatio Seymour speech, January 7, 1863, quoted in Stewart Mitchell, *Horatio Seymour of New York* (Harvard University Press, Cambridge, Mass., 1938) p. 268.

107 "The action of the administration": Letter from Horatio Seymour to meeting of Democrats at Albany, New York, May 16, 1863.

"Whose position beside that": *Harper's Weekly*, September 19, 1863.

108 In July 1863: *New York Daily News*, July 10, 1863.

Chapter 10: "State Governments Will Be Seized"

113 "Clay was not a practical man": John B. Castleman, *Active Service* (Courier Journal, Louisville, Kentucky, 1917) p. 135.

114 "In passing through the United States": Letter of James Seddon to Thomas Hines, quoted in James D. Horan, *Confederate Agent: A Discovery of History* (Crown, New York City, 1954) p. 72.

115 "Must I shoot a simple-minded soldier boy": Abraham Lincoln, comment made in summer of 1863; quoted in Allen Guelzo, *Abraham Lincoln: Redeemer President* (William B. Eerdman's Publishing Company, Grand Rapids, Michigan, 2003) p. 358.

116 Losing the case before the Supreme Court: David Silver, *Lincoln's Supreme Court* (University of Illinois Press, Urbana, 1957) p. 124.

117 Hines, who had seen men killed: Thomas Hines, personal papers, quoted in Horan, *Confederate Agent*, p. 19.

"State governments of Indiana": Ibid., 92.

117 **"Although intending this"**: Ibid., 93.

119 **"The former will secure"**: Clay to Thompson, August 3, 1864, Clay Papers, quoted in Oscar Kinchen, *Confederate Operations in Canada and the North* . . . (Christopher Publishing House, Quincy, Mass., 1970) p. 61.

Chapter 11: "The People Have Lost All Confidence in Lincoln"

122 **"The people have lost all confidence"**: *The Next Presidential Election*, quoted in David Herbert Donald, *Lincoln* (Simon & Schuster, New York, 1996) p. 481.

126 **In a personal conversation**: Lincoln to Hooker, *Collected Works of Abraham Lincoln* (Rutgers University Press, 1953) vol. 6, pp. 202–03.

"If any of the more prominent": Ben Butler to Winstar, Butler Correspondence, quoted in "Black Flag Warfare . . .", *Pennsylvania Magazine of History and Biography* (July 1991): 301.

127 **"If successful"**: February 26, 1864, John A. Dahlgren Papers, Library of Congress, quoted in "The Dahlgren Papers Revisited," www.history-net.com/the-dahlgren-papers-revisited.htm

128 **The orders and address**: Dahlgren Papers, Ibid., 4.

The *New York Times*: *New York Times*, March 14, 1864.

129 **"Kilpatrick started to make"**: *New York Herald*, March 3, 1864.

"We commend it to the attention": *Richmond Sentinel*, March 5, 1864.

"Truly there is no depth": *Richmond Sentinel*, March 7, 1864.

130 **"Upon them let the execrations"**: *Richmond Daily Dispatch*, March 11, 1864.

131 **"The hopes he appears to entertain"**: *New York Herald*, February 19, 1864.

At one time: *New York Tribune*, February 19, 1864.

"Mr. Lincoln will surely": *New York Times*, March 6, 1864.

One newspaper editor wrote: *Augusta Chronicle & Sentinel*, quoted in John C. Waugh, *Reelecting Lincoln* . . . (Crown, New York, 1997) p. 151.

132 **After the Democrats**: Strong, *Diary*, p. 479.

Chapter 12: "Organize Only in 'the Territory of the Enemy'"

140 **"It is right"**: U.S. Congress, *House Judicial Committee Report*, 39th Congress, 1st sess., vo. 1., no. 104; quoted in Prince, *Burn the Town*, p. 125.

141 **"Those who swam with horses"**: Bennett Young, quoted in Allan Keller, *Morgan's Raid* (Bobbs-Merrill, Indianapolis, Ind., 1961) p. 26.

142 **"Nothing but fire"**: Report of Henry Bellows to Colonel Hoffman, Scott, Official Records . . . , ser. 2, vol. 4, 1862, p. 106.

143 **"You will collect"**: Order of James Seddon to Bennett Young, June 16, 1864, reprinted in L. N. Benjamin, *The St. Albans Raid . . .* (John Lorell, Montreal, Canada, 1865) p. 206.

Curiously, Young's orders: Ibid., 80.

144 **"The towns will burn"**: *St. Albans Daily Messenger*, Oct. 26, 1864, quoted in Prince, *Burn The Towns*, p. 126.

146 **"We're Confederate Soldiers"**: Benjamin, *St. Albans Raid*, p. 28.

Chapter 13: "New York Is Worth Twenty Richmonds"

150 **"He is not truthful"**: Robert Williams, *Horace Greeley: Champion of American Freedom* (New York University Press, New York, 2006) p. 251.

151 **"Having information"**: undated Letter from Robert Martin to Andrew Johnson asking for clemency, National Archives #M1003.

152 **"This Northern spirit"**: John W. Headley, *Confederate Operations in Canada and New York* (The Neale Publishing Company, New York, 1906) pp. 175–76.

154 **"Lake Erie furnishes"**: Ibid., 232–33.

157 **"They chose"**: *Richmond Whig*, October 15, 1864.

Chapter 14: "Set Fire to Cities on Election Day"

162 **Headley matter-of-factly**: Headley, *Confederate Operations . . . New York*, p. 264.

163 **After hearing Hines**: Ibid., 265.

That man was probably: Horan, *Confederate Agent*, p. 68.

165 **When the Irish became:** James McMaster, quoted in James Hennessey, *American Catholics* (Oxford University Press, New York, 1983) p. 148.

166 **The final straw came:** Nat Brandt, *The Man Who Tried to Burn New York* (Syracuse University Press, New York, 1986) p. 32.

168 **The Federals fought us:** Edward A. Jackson, *The Confederate Veteran* (July 1908): 330.

169 **"With great pleasure":** *New York Times*, November 27, 1864.

171 **"Everything about him":** Headley, *Confederate Operations . . . New York*, p. 266.

"Once the city was": Ibid., 267.

"We were also": Ibid., p. 267.

Chapter 15: "Rebel Agents in Canada"

176 **"Against these mediated outrages":** Scott, *Official Records*, no. 91, Series I, vol. 43, p. 486.

177 **"The spirit of revolt":** Headley, *Confederate Operations . . . New York*, p. 269.

179 **The text of the telegram:** David Homer Bates, *Lincoln in the Telegraph Office . . .* (Century Company, New York, 1907) p. 296.

180 **"If it were not":** Scott, *Official Records*, ser. 1, vol. 43, sec. 91, p. 551.

181 **The newspaper assured:** *Official Records*, ibid., 551.

183 ***"This last must not":*** *New York Times*, November 7, 1864.

"But he took the most": *New York Times*, November 9, 1864.

186 **"Give the people":** Headley, *Confederate Operations . . . New York*, p. 271.

Chapter 16: "Something Dead in That Valise"

189 **Even though the planned:** Headley, *Confederate Operations . . . New York*, p. 271.

190 **The newspaper compared:** *New York Times*, November 16, 1864.

The newspaper then: Ibid., November 16, 1864.

191 **Washington Place:** Headley, *Confederate Operations . . . New York*, 272.

194 **The inventor refused:** *San Francisco Chronicle*, February 11, 1862.

195 **"We are now ready":** Headley, *Confederate Operations . . . New York*, p. 272.

Chapter 17: "Do the Greatest Damage to the Business District"

196 **If they could afford it:** A. K. Sandoval-Strausz, *Hotel: An American History* (Yale University Press, New Haven, Conn., 2007) p. 267.

197 **Headley wrote:** Headley, *Confederate Operations . . . New York*, p. 273.

199 **It featured a restaurant:** *King's Handbook of New York City, 1892 . . .* (Barnes & Noble, New York, 2001) p. 210.

"No one talks about anything": Junius Henri Browne, *The Great Metropolis . . .* (American Publishing, Hartford, Conn., 1869).

200 **According to the *New York Times*:** *New York Times*, October 4, 1860.

When the *Times* noted: *New York Times*, October 4, 1860.

201 **Medicinal baths:** Edward Ruggles, *A Picture of New-York in 1846 . . .* (Homans & Ellis, New York) p. 116.

202 **Savvier hotel guests recognized:** Michael and Ariane Batterberry, On the Town in New York: The Landmark History of Eating, Drinking, and Entertainment from the American Revolution to the Food Revolution (Routledge, New York, 1999) p. 62.

"Lord help the poor": Ibid., p. 62.

Still, in the words: Walt Whitman, "I Sit and Look Out", quoted in Ellen W. Kramer, "Contemporary Descriptions of New York City and Its Public Architecture, ca. 1850," *The Journal of the Society of Architectural Historians*, December 1968, p. 274.

Lovejoy's featured 250: Ruggles, *Picture of New York in 1846*, p. 82.

203 **"You must pay something":** Browne, *Great Metropolis*, p. 397.

"Thousands of persons": Ibid., p. 398.

204 **"A man with such a wife":** *New York Times*, March 23, 1902.

205 **In the following decade:** Burrows and Wallace, *Gotham . . .* p. 653.

206 **By 1864, most of the Union navy's:** Edward K. Spann, *Gotham at War . . .* (Roman & Littlefield, Lanham, Md., 2002) p. 40.

Chapter 18: "It Blazed Up Instantly"

207 **That man whose name:** Carman Cumming, *The Devil's Game* (University of Illinois Press, Urbana, 2004) p. 15.

208 **Then, as the agent, he:** Charles Dana, *Recollections of the Civil War* (D. Appleton, 1898) p. 239.

It was found to contain: Ibid., 241.

211 **He carefully opened:** Headley, *Confederate Operations . . . New York*, p. 275.

213 **"Had it not been":** *New York Times*, November 27, 1864.

216 **Headley wrote:** Headley, *Confederate Operations . . . New York*, p. 275.

Kennedy laughed: Ibid., p. 276.

217 **As Headley and Kennedy:** Ibid., p. 277.

Headley speculated: Ibid., p. 277.

Chapter 19: "A Vast and Fiendish Plot"

219 **"He said I did not":** Headley, *Confederate Operations . . . New York*, p. 277.

222 **"In the first place":** *New York Times*, November 28, 1864.

223 **"Will you oblige me":** Ibid.

"Their sole chagrin": *New York Tribune*, November 28, 1864.

224 **"The city of New York":** *New York Herald*, November 27, 1864.

"Rebels of course!": *New York World*, December 8, 1864.

"With the whole night": Ibid.

225 **"This aversion":** Ibid.

"Yet quiet was restored": *New York World*, Nov. 28, 1864.

226 **"Can it be dreamed":** *New York Daily News*, November 26, 1864.

"The fact that": *New York Evening Tribune*, November 26, 1864.

"At a later hour": *New York Sun*, November 26, 1864.

The newspaper editor: *Brooklyn Daily News*, November 26, 1864.

227 **McMaster rejected the idea:** *Freeman's Journal and Catholic Register,* December 3, 1864.

"**There are some**": Ibid.

"**Men, in various ways**": Ibid.

"**Debt is slavery**": *Freeman's Journal,* December 10, 1864.

228 "**We have, in the attempt**": *Harper's Weekly,* December 10, 1864.

"**the inevitable consequence**": Ibid.

"**The numerous fires**": *Richmond Sentinel,* December 9, 1864.

229 "**The tracks to the lion's den all point**": Ibid.

"**They all point to Lincoln**": Ibid.

"**As proof of the efficiency**": *New York Times,* November 27, 1864.

230 "**Here was their grand mistake**": *New York Tribune,* November 28, 1864.

Chapter 20: "If Convicted, They Will Be Executed"

233 "**All such persons**": *New York Times,* November 26, 1864.

"**If anyone fails**": *New York Times,* November 26, 1864.

236 "**Their reliance on**": Headley, *Confederate Operations . . . New York,* p. 294.

Even though Thompson: Letter from Jacob Thompson to Judah Benjamin, ibid., 296.

237 "**All military commanders**": General Orders 97, ibid., 303.

238 **The meaning of the order:** Ibid., 304.

240 **The New Yorkers:** *New York Times,* February 5, 1865.

Chapter 21: "Trust to Luck"

242 **He made his way:** Description of Kennedy's personality and military career comes from Brandt, *Man Who Tried.*

248 **McMaster suggested in court:** Trial transcript of Robert Cobb Kennedy, National Archives, March 1865.

249 "**May God bless you**": Mrs. Hyder A. Kennedy, *History of the Trial and Execution of Robert Cobb Kennedy* (Lafayette, La. 1865) p. 5.

249 "The nation of which you are": Kennedy to Lincoln, quoted from Brandt, *Man Who Tried*, p. 206.

250 "It was not a mere attempt": General Orders 24, reprinted in *New York Times*, March 21, 1864.

He ended the letter with: Kennedy letter to his father.

Chapter 22: "A Terror for Our Citizens"

257 By the 1850s: EH.Net Encyclopedia: Manufactured and Natural Gas Industry (under Natural Gas) at eh.net/encyclopedia.

Chapter 23: "They Sacrificed Everything"

265 "They sacrificed to it": Terry Golway, *So Others Might Live* (Basic Books, New York, 2002) p. 107.

267 The area just north of City Hall: Ibid., 143.

Epilogue: "What Happened to the Principal Characters"

273 Harrington became: Information on Harrington and Ashbrook comes from Brandt, *Man Who Tried*.

Selected Bibliography

Books

Albio, Robert Greenhalgh. *The Rise of New York Port, 1815–1860*. Archon Books, Hamden, Conn., 1961.

Batterberry, Michael and Ariane Batterberry. *On the Town: The Landmark History of Eating, Drinking, and Entertainment from the American Revolution to the Food Revolution*. Routledge, New York, 1999.

Beckert, Sven. *The Monied Metropolis: New York City and the Consolidation of the American Bourgeoisie, 1850–1896*. Harvard University Press, Cambridge, Mass., 2001.

Brandt, Nat. *The Man Who Tried to Burn New York*. Syracuse University Press, Syracuse, N.Y., 1986.

Brown, Dee Alexander. *Morgan's Raiders*. Konecky & Konecky, New York, 1959.

Burrows, Edwin G. and Mike Wallace. *Gotham: A History of New York City to 1989*, Oxford University Press, New York, 2000.

Castleman, John B. *Active Service, Courier Journal Publishing*, Louisville, Ken., 1917.

Crist, Linda Lasswell. *The Papers of Jefferson Davis*. Vols. 10 and 11. Louisiana State University Press, Baton Rouge, 2003 and 2008.

Du Bois, W. E. B. *The Suppression of the African Slave-Trade to the United States of America, 1896*. Reprint Oxford University Press, London, 2007.

Duke, General Basil W. *The Civil War Reminiscences of General Basil W. Duke*. Cooper Square Press, New York City, 1911.

Ellis, Edward Robb. *The Epic of New York City: A Narrative History*. Kodansha International, New York City, 1966.

Foner, Philip S. *Business & Slavery: The New York Merchants and the Irrepressible Conflict*. University of North Carolina Press, Chapel Hill, 1941.

Gayle, Margot and Carol Gayle. *Cast-Iron Architecture in America: The Significance of James Brogardus*. Norton, New York, 1998.

Gellman, David N. *Emancipating New York: The Politics of Slavery and Freedom, 1777–1827*. Louisiana State University Press, Baton Rouge, 2006.

Goodell, William. *Slavery and Anti-Slavery: A History of the Great Struggle in Both Hemispheres with a View of the Slavery Question in the United States*. Self-published, New York, 1853.

Headley, John W. *Confederate Operations in Canada and New York*. The Neale Publishing Company, New York, 1906.

Horan, James D. *Confederate Agent: A Discovery in History*. Crown, New York City, 1954.

Howard, Warren S. *American Slavers and the Federal Law, 1837–1862*. University of California Press, Berkeley, 1963.

Johnson, Adam Rankin. *The Partisan Rangers of the Confederate States Army*. State House Press, Austin, Tex., 1904.

Kinchen, Oscar A. *Confederate Operations Canada and the North: The Story of the Confederate Southern Campaign*. Christopher Publishing House, North Quincy, Mass., 1970.

King, Moses. *King's Handbook of New York City, 1892: An Outline History & Description of the American Metropolis*. Barnes & Noble, New York, 2001.

Lockwood, Charles. *Manhattan Moves Uptown*. Houghton Mifflin, Boston, Mass., 1976.

Mayers, Adam. *Dixie & the Dominion: Canada, the Confederacy, and the War for the Union*. Dundurn Group, Toronto, Canada, 2003.

Melish, Joanne Pope. *Disowning Slavery: Gradual Emancipation and Race in New England, 1780–1860*. Cornell University Press, Ithaca, N.Y., 1998.

Mitchell, Stewart. *Horatio Seymour of New York*. Harvard University Press, Cambridge, Mass., 1938.

Mushkat, Jerome. *Fernando Wood: A Political Biography*. Kent State University Press, Kent, Ohio, 1990.

Prince, Cathryn J. *Burn the Town and Sack the Banks: Confederates Attack Vermont!* Carroll & Graf, New York, 2006.

Ramage, James A. *Rebel Raider: The Life of General John Hunt Morgan*. University Press of Kentucky, Lexington, 1986.

Schecter, Barnet. *The Devil's Own Work: The Civil War Draft Riots and the Fight to Reconstruct America.* Walker, New York, 2005.

Scott, Robert. *The Official Records of the War of the Rebellion.* 128 vols., Government Printing Office, Washington, D.C., 1880.

Starr, Stephen Z. *Colonel Grenfell's Wars: The Life of a Soldier of Fortune.* Louisiana State University Press, Baton Rouge, 1971.

Stern, Philip Van Doren. *Secret Missions of the Civil War.* Bonanza Books, New York, 1959.

Waugh, John C. *Reelecting Lincoln: The Battle for the 1864 Presidency.* Crown, New York, 1997.

Wermiel, Sara E. *Fireproof Building: Technology and Public Safety in the Nineteenth Century American City.* Johns Hopkins University Press, Baltimore, 2000.

Woodman, Harold D. *King Cotton & His Retainers: Financing & Marketing the Cotton Crop of the South, 1800–1925.* University Press of Kentucky, Lexington, 1968.

Yafa, Stephen. *Big Cotton: How a Humble Fiber Created Fortunes, Wrecked Civilizations, and Put America on the Map.* Viking, New York, 2004.

NEWSPAPERS

New York Times

New York Herald

New York Tribune

New York World

New York Evening Tribune

New York Sun

New York Daily News

New York Evening Post

New York Journal of Commerce

Freeman's Journal and Catholic Register

Brooklyn Daily Eagle

Chicago Tribune

Harper's Weekly

Richmond Sentinel

Index